# HOW THE RABBIS
# LIBERATED WOMEN

SOUTH FLORIDA STUDIES IN THE HISTORY OF JUDAISM

Edited by
Jacob Neusner
Bruce D. Chilton, Darrell J. Fasching, William Scott Green,
Sara Mandell, James F. Strange

Number 191
HOW THE RABBIS
LIBERATED WOMEN

by
Jacob Neusner

# HOW THE RABBIS
# LIBERATED WOMEN

by

Jacob Neusner

Scholars Press
Atlanta, Georgia

# HOW THE RABBIS
# LIBERATED WOMEN

by
Jacob Neusner

Publication of this book was made possible by a grant from the Tisch Family Foundation, New York City. The University of South Florida acknowledges with thanks this important support for its scholarly projects.

**Library of Congress Cataloging in Publication Data**
Neusner, Jacob, 1932–
    How the rabbis liberated women / by Jacob Neusner.
       p.   cm. — (South Florida studies in the history of Judaism ; no. 191)
    Contains extensive passages from the Talmud Order Nashim in English translation.
    ISBN 0-7885-0516-5 (cloth : alk. paper)
    1. Women in rabbinical literature.  2. Women in Judaism.
3. Talmud. Nashim—Criticism, interpretation, etc.  I. Talmud. Nashim. English. Selections. II. Title. III. Series.
BM509.W7N48   1998
296.1'20830542—dc21                 98-31613
                                      CIP

Printed in the United States of America
on acid-free paper

# Table Of Contents

# Preface

The rabbis of late antiquity, founders of Judaism as we know it, in the normative law set forth in the Mishnah-Tosefta-Yerushalmi-Bavli liberated Israelite women by according to them what Scripture had denied. That is, the standing and powers of sentient beings, possessed of a role that was, if not entirely equal, then corresponding, to that of men in critical transactions of their existence. They made them active, responsible beings; they legislated to take account of their intentionality. Women were not only chattel, talking cows, animate sofas, as some have maintained. This we see when we focus upon not what individual rabbis said in the aggadah, free-floating, singleton-sayings, but what the collegium of the rabbis did in the halakhah, in systematic, cogent, proportionate, and coherent normative law. The halakhah, as set forth in the Mishnah-Tosefta-Yerushalmi-Bavli, on any principal category-formation tells us the position of the Torah, written as mediated by oral, and the contrast between Scripture and the halakhah repeatedly yields a single pattern. That pattern may be stated very simply: The rabbis liberated women by endowing them with the power of intentionality and the concomitant responsibility for their own actions and condition that Scripture denied them. And that is what I show in these pages.

The policy toward women of the Judaic sages on their own and in dialogue with Scripture emerges only in the contrast between the Written Torah and the Oral Torah on the same turnings in women's lives. Scripture presents matters in its way, the halakhah in its manner, and the latter speaks for the rabbis and defines the law of Judaism. I deal with the category-formations of the halakhah, since the rabbis of formative Judaism bear witness to the ultimate policy and intent of the Torah for women – and that is only when they speak systematically and set forth norms. When we find episodic, not categorical, sayings, and when we encounter anecdotal evidence, we sift only the detritus of a complex corpus of data. But the system speaks through its own structure and establishes its own public policy, and on that, not on bits and pieces of idiosyncratic and schismatic opinion, the system is to be assessed.

What then constitutes my evidence that the rabbis of the halakhah of the Mishnah-Tosefta-Yerushalmi-Bavli claim a place within those that, in their time and in their place and by the standards set in context, liberated women from prior disabilities? I take the three principal turnings in a woman's relationship with a man: betrothal and marriage, his charge of unfaithfulness, and divorce. When we compare Scripture's to the halakhah's provisions for betrothal (no category-formation in Scripture, Qiddushin in the halakhah), the disposition of a charge of unfaithfulness (Numbers 5 and the halakhah of Sotah), and divorce (Deut. 24:1-4 and Gittin), as well as the halakhah's quite original invention of a contract to provide women with substantial material protections in a marriage (Ketubot), my representation of the position of sages as "liberationist" finds its confirmation. In this book I provide a specific, systematic and detailed demonstration of that fact, law by law.

Let me give a single example of the pattern that I discern when I compare Scripture's to the halakhah's treatment of the same category-formation. Scripture takes as fact that a faith may marry off a minor daughter. In his place, the halakhah assumes, the mother or brother who have survived the death of the father may do so as well. The rabbis of the halakhah, by contrast, so define that transaction as simply to nullify it. At Mishnah-tractate Yebamot 13:1 we find the following:

> Those who are betrothed and those who are married exercise the right of refusal. [The right of refusal is exercised] against the husband, and against the levir. It must be exercised in his presence. and not in his presence. in a court and not in a court.

This precis of the regnant opinion yields the following practical result: if a man has entered into not only a betrothal but a consummated marriage with a girl under puberty, when she reaches puberty, she may simply up and walk out of the marriage. She requires no writ of divorce. She may do so even after coitus. She may walk out and declare the relationship null even in the husband's absence and even outside a rabbinical court. The upshot is simple. As soon as she reaches puberty, the girl may nullify the marriage. And, more to the point, the halakhah rules that it is as if she never had been married, so Mishnah-tractate Yebamot 13:4:

> She who exercises the right of refusal against a man – he is permitted to marry her kinswomen, and she is permitted to marry his kinsmen. And he has not invalidated her for marriage into the priesthood. [If] he gave her a writ of divorce, he is prohibited from marrying her kinswomen, and she is prohibited from marrying his kinsmen. And he has invalidated her for marriage into the priesthood. [If] he (1) gave her a writ of divorce and (2) then took

her back, [if] then she (3) exercised the right of refusal against him and (4) married someone else, and (5) was widowed or divorced – she is permitted to go back to him. [If] she (3) exercised the right of refusal and (2) he took her back, [if] he [then] (1) gave her a writ of divorce and she (4) married someone else and (5) was widowed or divorced, she is prohibited from going back to him. This is the general rule: In a case of a writ of divorce following the exercise of the right of refusal, she is prohibited from returning to him. In a case of exercise of the right of refusal after a writ of divorce, she is permitted to go back to him.

All of these provisions yield a single result: this girl (not yet a woman) has never, ever been married to that man. And under what circumstances do we want such a rite to be carried out? It is when the girl has agreed to begin with to enter the marriage. Yebamot 13:2:

Who is the sort of girl who must exercise the right of refusal? Any girl whose mother or brothers have married her off with her knowledge and consent. [If] they married her off without her knowledge and consent, she does not have to exercise the right of refusal [but simply leaves the man].

She is no different from a girl who married herself off without her father's intervention, so Tosefta Yebamot 13:2:

A minor who effected a betrothal in her own behalf, or who married herself off, while her father was yet alive – her betrothal is null, and her act of marriage is null [M. Yeb. 13:2A].

These and comparable provisions effectively nullify child-marriage, and that for a simple reason. They treat any such relationship, prior to puberty, as null: the girl can walk out on the "husband" and reject the "marriage" without any legal consequence whatever, and indeed, with only the most routine action: she has to tell three witnesses she's had it, so Tosefta Yebamot 13:1:

She testified, "I do not care for So-and-so, my husband. I reject the betrothal effected for me by my mother or my brothers." Even if she is sitting in a palanquin and went to the one who betrothed her to him, and said to him, "I do not care for this man, So-and-So, my husband" – there is no statement of refusal more powerful than that [statement].

Now where does the husband find himself? Whatever property transactions have taken place are null. If he had in mind a union of family and heritage, he is disappointed. Through the entire span of time from the betrothal or marriage until the girl reaches puberty, the husband cannot enjoy the security of a long-term relationship. The upshot is, sages have set up conditions that nullify such a transaction between the mother and brothers and the groom. They have defined the outcome in such parlous terms that no rational man is going to want to take the risks built into the relationship. And in that way, the rabbis (not just this rabbi or that rabbi, this school or that school) have done what they could do to abolish a relationship Scripture has ordained. True, the halakhah before us is clear that, if the father has married off the girl, the girl enjoys no right of refusal, since they explicitly assign that right only to the girl married off by those who bear responsibility but no authority. So the rabbis could not and did not legislate in such a way as to contradict the clear requirement of Scripture. But, in the four systematic cases set forth in this book, they could and did legislate – and powerfully so at that! – to endow women with status – defined by intentionality and responsibility – of which Scripture knows nothing; they protected women with a web of juridical rights that Scripture did not weave; and they accorded to women equal rights and responsibilities within a marriage that the Pentateuch did not contemplate. In these ways, they liberated women – in their context, by their lights. In four enormous category-formations of the halakhah, the rabbis defined the public policy of Judaism.

True, by today's standards, the Rabbinic sages cannot be characterized as feminists. And they left an ambiguous legacy. Indeed, a now well-sifted corpus of episodic sayings of these same sages yields the opposite impression. The contemporary polemical, anti-Rabbinic and not infrequently anti-Semitic and anti-Judaic context in which contemporary feminist scholarship has drawn up its indictment of the rabbis as the worst of all oppressors of women has done its work well.[1] If we focus on what sages did in a systematic and normative framework of actual law, as against what individuals said hither and yon, the sages did liberate Israelite women in exactly the way that I claimed in the opening sentence. And that becomes clear, especially, when what their legislation is compared with the Pentateuch's provisions for betrothal, marriage, and divorce. Except for the woman accused of unfaithfulness, Scripture legislates casually (Qiddushin, Gittin) or not at all (Ketubot) in areas upon which sages produce massive and dense legal constructions. So compared to the Written Torah's regulations on the same agenda, those of the halakhah show a one-sided, consistent, and blatant effort to grant women juridical standing. That validates, in the contemporary context, invoking the language of "liberation" – within the framework of the revealed Torah, oral and written. And that liberation consisted in the simple fact that, where the sages could, they did provide for women the

---

[1]Paul Hyman's Belin Lecture at the University of Michigan traces the heroic work of Jewish feminists in identifying and opposing the anti-Semitism and anti-Judaism characteristic of feminist ideology in general.

right to form their own intentionality and the duty to bear full responsibility for their own actions.

Now let me place the modest contribution offered here into the context of principal participants in the contemporary debate, Judith Hauptman, Judith Baskin, and Mayer Gruber.

HAUPTMAN: In today's feminist assessment of Rabbinic Judaism, that judgment of the sages' proto-feminism is not broadly affirmed. But it also is not idiosyncratic to me or even new in detail, except in the mode of demonstration undertaken in this book. The results laid out here support the view best represented in the recent past by Judith Hauptman in her *Rereading the Rabbis: A Woman's Voice* (Boulder, 1998: Westview Press). There she observes, "It is...remarkable that in virtually every major area, the law was moving in the direction of extending to women more rights."[2] Of the four exercises here, all go over ground she ploughed first of all: the reciprocity of the marital transaction (Ketubot, Qiddusin), the recognition of the woman's rights and responsibilities in the provision of a writ of divorce (Gittin), and the "transformation" (her word choice) of the rite of the woman accused of unfaithfulness (Sotah). What I contribute therefore is not a new idea. It is the detailed and systematic comparison of Scripture's and the halakhah's treatment of women at the four key points treated here. In this way I underscore through masses of details the main points Hauptman has already established.

In the shank of this book, I provide ample documentation in support of that proposition. I review Scripture's rules and then survey those of the halakhah, giving the Mishnah in bold face type, the Tosefta in regular type, what is new in Yerushalmi in italics, and one is new in Bavli in lower case caps. So I present the halakhah more or less completely, but differentiate the four sources that supply it. Treating Scripture in comparison with the halakhah of the same topic, I contrast the declarations, on the four topics addressed here, of the Written Torah with those of the documents that record the halakhah of the Oral Torah. Readers may then judge for themselves whether or not my characterization is correct. I see the results as a blatant and systematic exercise of liberation.

That is not to take issue with the accounts of the matter set forth by the principal voices of the study of feminist issues in Rabbinic Judaism, Judith Baskin and Mayer Gruber.. When it comes to feminist scholarship, I rely heavily on both colleagues. Professor Baskin, in "Woman as Other in Rabbinic Literature," and Professor Gruber in "The Status of Women in Ancient Judaism," (both: Jacob Neusner and Alan J.

---

[2]Hauptman, *Rereading the Rabbis*, pp. 117-118; p. 129, n. 34

Avery-Peck, editors, *Judaism in Late Antiquity* [Leiden, 1999: E. J. Brill] Volume III. *Where We Stand. Issues and Debates in Ancient Judaism.* Part iii), review the state of the question in systematic studies.

BASKIN: I do not think Baskin in any way errs or exaggerates when she states the Rabbinic view in simple words: "What unites these [diverse Rabbinic] views is the conviction that 'women are a separate people,' a created human entity essentially different in physical characteristics, innate capacities, and social function from men." Prior work of my own certainly sustains her judgment, and nothing in these pages contradicts it. Baskin in her essay explores "the ways in which this certainty of woman's profound alterity from man in body, in oral and intellectual endowments, in social roles and legal responsibility, and in relationship to the divine, is manifested and justified in Rabbinic literature." She states the facts when she says, "Although wives had distinct personal and property rights, Rabbinic social policy primarily considered a married woman in her relationship to her husband, as she fell under his control, contributed to his comfort and to the bearing and nurturing of his children." Nothing in what I shall show about how, in comparison to Scripture's laws, the sages radically revised the position of women contradicts these judgments. But the results set forth here ought to define a different context in which to interpret the sayings to which Baskin refers, and they are many and, I think, characteristic of the documents. I cannot harmonize episodic sayings of an aggadic or theological character with systematic exercises of normative exposition. Whatever the sages said, whether individually or in consensus, here we see what they actually did when it came to practical law. And if sages said that women are a separate people, they so framed the halakhah as to secure for women the same standing, position, and dignity as marked the position of men: beings possessed of sentience and intentionality, in ways in which animals or slaves or minors, with whom, in one context or another, women are classified, are not.

GRUBER: Gruber showed in "Women in the Cult," that one can point out many specific areas of private and public life with respect to which Rabbinic Judaism extended power to woman.[3] He also points out that there are many specific areas with respect to which Rabbinic Judaism took away from women power they previously held according to the testimony of the Hebrew Scriptures. In a work that runs parallel to the inquiry spelled out here, Gruber examines here three areas – prayer, study of Torah, and divorce – in which over the course of time Rabbinic Judaism disempowered women. At that third point his results and mine part company. That is because I deal solely with Deut. 24:1-4 as

---

[3]Gruber, "Women in the Cult," p. 59, n. 22; pp. 64-65.

understood within the Torah, written as read through the oral part. Then, when I examine the halakhah of Gittin, I see a sustained effort to accord to a woman an active role in the process of divorce. Viewing the language of Deuteronomy not in the framework of the Torah but in its historical *Sitz-im-Leben* yields a different conclusion for Gruber. At the same time he points to examples of the rabbis' yeoman attempt to give women more power than they are given in Hebrew Scripture. The presentation here enriches his portrait. There is one important qualification. Gruber points out:

> The most insidious way in which Rabbinic Judaism disempowered women was in its law of divorce, which it sought to read back into Deut. 24:1-4. In fact, Deut. 24:1-4, as has long been noted, closes an important loophole to what is today often called "swinging" and which in plain language may be called spouse swapping. Since Hebrew and other ancient Near Eastern law prohibited a married woman from having sex with any man other than her husband, the only way that women and men who took seriously the prohibition against adultery, which is called throughout the ancient Near East "the great sin," could engage in swinging was for the wife of A to be legally divorced from A before having sex with B and then to be divorced from B before returning to A at the end of the evening of swinging. Deut. 24 closes this loophole by prohibiting Mrs. A from returning to A after having been the legal wife of B. Deut. 24 mentions in passing that it was the habit of men to write and hand over to their erstwhile wives a bill of divorce. Deut. 24 does not say that only a man can initiate a divorce, nor does it prohibit a woman from initiating a divorce.
>
> In fact, there is significant evidence that in ancient Western Asia from the time of Hammurapi (1792-1750 B.C.E.) onward provision was made for women both 1) to initiate a divorce and 2) to guarantee for themselves in a pre-nuptial agreement their right to initiate a divorce. Moreover, there is significant testimony that in both Second Temple times and in the Tannaitic era Jewish women still had the right to initiate divorce. In fact, as demonstrated by Mordecai Friedman, for a millennium after the dawn of the Rabbinic period, Jewish women throughout the Middle East continued to take advantage of the age-old pre-nuptial guarantee of their rights as persons. Notwithstanding the various precedents for women being able to initiate divorce both in the ancient Near East and among rabbanite Jews, M. Yeb. 14:1 ("A woman may be divorced willingly or unwillingly but a man divorces only willingly") and ultimately all the surviving Judaisms based on the Mishnah granted this right only to men and thereby reduced Jewish women to chattels.

But as I said, our perspective shifts when we read Scripture as sages did and then examine the law as they framed it. Now we see that, even within the premise that the woman cannot initiate a divorce-process, she still participated as an active agent in it. And Scripture's counterpart provision does not contemplate her participation.

When I undertook the comparative study, in connection with a different problem altogether, I did not focus upon the issue addressed here. Specifically, I was not working on the history of the halakhah at all (I had already done so for the Mishnah and Tosefta, which present the bulk of the halakhah for late antiquity, in my *History of Mishnaic Law*), let alone in relationship with Scripture or within its own framework, but only its phenomenology. It was only when I had produced the same result four times over – a result that, despite having read Hauptman's book, still I did not anticipate at all – that I took note of the special interest in regularizing and, within their framework, normalizing the status of women that the halakhic sages clearly had in mind, and, in my opinion, that they realized. Then I determined to single out of the larger study the presentations of Qiddushin, Gittin, Sotah, and Ketubot for a more sharply focused statement. Accordingly, the four chapters of the shank of the book are revised from my *The Halakhah of the Oral Torah: A Religious Commentary*. Atlanta, 1999: Scholars Press for South Florida Studies in the History of Judaism, Volume III Parts 3, 4, and 5; and further from my *Scripture and the Generative Premises of the Halakhah*, in press.

It is always a pleasure to acknowledge thankfully the support for my research provided by my appointments as Distinguished Research Professor of Religious Studies at the University of South Florida and Professor of Religion at Bard College. Correspondence with Professors Baskin and Gruber also proved fruitful, as always. It is a real pleasure to see the coming of age, and the attainment of important achievements, on the part of what was once the younger generation!

JACOB NEUSNER
University of South Florida and Bard College

# 1

## Qiddushin

### I. An Outline of the Halakhah of Qiddushin

The formation of the family of the household begins with the act of betrothal, which, in the context of the halakhah, means we deal with the sanctification of a woman to a particular man. The act of betrothal forms a particular detail of the larger theory of how a man acquires title to, or possession of, persons or property of various classifications. That is the this-worldly side of the halakhah; the transcendent part emerges with the result: the sanctification of the relationship between a particular woman and a particular man, so that she is consecrated to him and to no other.[1] The upshot is, just as a farmer acquired a slave or an ox or real estate, so he effected possession of, gained title to, a woman. But while the slave or ox or field could never be called "consecrated" to that particular farmer, so that the language of sanctification never operates in such transactions, the act of acquisition of a woman also transformed the relationship of the woman not only to that man who acquired her but to all other men.

The woman to begin with is deemed by the Written Torah to form a property belonging to her father, to be transferred to the ownership of her husband. In that regard, the governing analogy for the acquisition of a woman as consecrated wife derives from the rules of the transfer of title to property. But the woman must concur in the transaction, and that separates her from all others subject to the ownership – the free-will – of others. And there is a second difference. The language that is used here, the language of sanctification, derives from the Temple, and, as I said, when we speak of sanctifying or consecrating a woman to a specific man,

---

[1]No one in the formative age deemed the relationship mutual; a particular man was not consecrated to a particular woman, since the halakhah presupposes polygamy.

we are using the language of the altar, which speaks of sanctifying an animal to the altar for a particular purpose.

The unique relationship of the woman to the man finds its counterpart, as I shall explain in my discussion of the religious principles of Qiddushin, in the unique relationship of the animal designated ("consecrated") to the altar by a farmer in expiation of a particular sin. That animal could serve only as a sin-offering, and it could expiate only the particular sin the farmer had in mind to atone. But that intense specificity cannot characterize, e.g., possession of a given slave, who could be rented out to others, or title to a particular piece of real estate, available for share-cropping. A still more striking difference, as we shall see in our survey of the law itself, emerges in every line of the halakhah. The ox, the real estate, and the slave are transferred willy-nilly; no act of will on their part intervenes. But a woman can be consecrated to a particular man only by an act of agreement, her will forming the foundation of the entire transaction. So while without an act of assent a lamb is consecrated by the farmer and so made holy to the altar, only her full and un-coerced agreement will consecrate a woman to a man. The woman is partner in the process of her own sanctification, in a way in which no other classification of persons or property participates in the process of his, her, or its transfer from ownership to ownership. It is in that fundamental principle of the halakhah that the rabbis liberated Israelite women. Now to survey the law, in detail, to validate that judgment.

## I.   Betrothals

### A.   *Rules of Acquisition of Persons and Property*

**M. 1:1 A woman is acquired [as a wife] in three ways, and acquires [freedom for] herself [to be a free agent] in two ways. She is acquired through money, a writ, or sexual intercourse. And she acquires herself through a writ of divorce or through the husband's death. The deceased childless brother's widow is acquired through an act of sexual relations. And acquires [freedom for] herself through a rite of removing the shoe or through the levir's death.**

T. 1:1 A woman is acquired [as a wife] in three ways, and acquires herself to be a free agent in two ways. She is acquired through money, a writ, and sexual intercourse [M. Qid. 1:1A-B]. By money – how so? [If] he gave her money or something worth money, saying to her, "Lo, you are consecrated to me," "Lo, you are betrothed to me," "Lo, you are a wife to me," lo, this one is consecrated. But [if] she gave him money or something worth money and said to him, "Lo, I am betrothed to you," "Lo, I am sanctified to you," "Lo, I am a wife to you," she is not consecrated.

T. 1:2 By a writ [ – how so?] Must one say it is a writ which has a value of a perutah? But even if one wrote it on a sherd and gave it to her, on waste paper and gave it to her, lo, this one is consecrated.

T. 1:3 By sexual intercourse [ – how so?] By any act of sexual relations which is done for the sake of betrothal is she betrothed. But if it is not for the sake of betrothal, she is not betrothed.

T. 1:4 A man should not marry a wife until the daughter of his sister grows up or until he will find a mate suitable for himself, since it is said, "[Do not profane your daughter by making her a harlot lest the land fall into harlotry and the land become full of wickedness" (Lev. 19:29).

B. 1:1 III.51/8B [A WRIT:] A WRIT: HOW SO? IF ONE WROTE ON A PARCHMENT OR ON A POTSHERD, EVEN THOUGH THEY THEMSELVES WERE OF NO INTRINSIC VALUE, "LO, YOUR DAUGHTER IS BETROTHED TO ME," "YOUR DAUGHTER IS ENGAGED TO ME," "YOUR DAUGHTER IS A WIFE FOR ME" – LO, THIS WOMAN IS BETROTHED.

M. 1:2 **A Hebrew slave is acquired through money and a writ. And he acquires himself through the passage of years, by the Jubilee Year, and by deduction from the purchase price [redeeming himself at this outstanding value (Lev. 25:50-51)]. The Hebrew slave girl has an advantage over him. For she acquires herself [in addition] through the appearance of tokens [of puberty]. The slave whose ear is pierced is acquired through an act of piercing the ear (Ex. 21:5). And he acquires himself by the Jubilee and by the death of the master.**

T. 1:5 How does [he redeem himself] by deduction from the purchase price [at his outstanding value] [M. Qid. 1:2B]? [If] he wanted to redeem himself during these years, he reckons the value against the years [left to serve] and pays off his master. And the hand of the slave is on top [in estimating the sum to be paid]. How is usucaption [established in the case of] real estate? [If] he locked, made a fence, broke down a fence in any measure at all, lo, this is usucaption. How is usucaption [established in the case of] slaves? [If] he [the slave] tied on his [the master's] sandal, or loosened his sandal, or carried clothing after him to the bathhouse, lo, this is usucaption.

M. 1:3 **A Canaanite slave is acquired through money, through a writ, or through usucaption. By money paid by himself or by a writ taken on by others, on condition that the money belongs to others.**

B. 1:3 I.5/22B HOW IS A SLAVE ACQUIRED THROUGH AN ACT OF USUCAPTION? IF THE SLAVE FASTENED THE SHOE OF THE MAN OR UNDID IT, OR IF HE CARRIED HIS CLOTHING AFTER HIM TO THE BATHHOUSE, OR IF HE UNDRESSED HIM OR WASHED HIM OR ANOINTED HIM OR SCRAPED HIM OR DRESSED HIM OR PUT ON HIS SHOES OR LIFTED HIM UP, THE MAN ACQUIRES TITLE TO THE SLAVE.'

M. 1:4 **Large cattle are acquired through delivery [of the bit or bridle]. Small cattle are acquired through an act of drawing [the beast by force majeure].**

T. 1:8 What is an act of delivery [M. Qid. 1:4A]? Any act in which he handed over to him the bit or the bridle – lo, this is an act of delivery. Under what circumstances did they rule, Movables are acquired through drawing? In the public domain or in a courtyard which does not belong to either one of them. But if it is the domain of the purchaser, once he has taken upon himself [to pay the agreed upon sum], he has acquired the thing. [And if it is] in the domain of the seller, once he has raised up the object or after he has taken it out from the domain of the owner [it has been acquired]. In the domain of this one in whose hands the bailment is located, an act of acquisition is carried out when he [the owner] will have taken it upon himself [to allow the buyer a portion of the premises to effect an acquisition] or when he [the purchaser] will have rented their place for himself.

**M. 1:5 Property for which there is security is acquired through money, writ, and usucaption. And that for which there is no security is acquired only by an act of drawing [from one place to another]. Property for which there is no security is acquired along with property for which there is security through money, writ, and usucaption. And property for which there is no security imposes the need for an oath on property for which there is security.**

**M. 1:6 Whatever is used as payment for something else – once this one has effected acquisition [thereof] the other has become liable for what is given in exchange. How so? [If] one exchanged an ox for a cow, or an ass for an ox, once this one has effected acquisition, the other has become liable for what is given in exchange. The right of the Most High is effected through money, and the right of ordinary folk through usucaption. One's word of mouth [dedication of an object] to the Most High is equivalent to one's act of delivery to an ordinary person.**

T. 1:9 If one exchanged with another person real estate for other real estate, movables for other movables, real estate for movables, movables for real estate, once this one has made acquisition, the other has become liable for what is given in exchange [M. Qid. 1:6B-C]. The right of the Most High is effected through money [M. Qid. 1:6G] – how so? The Temple-treasurer who paid over coins of the Sanctuary for movables – the Sanctuary has made acquisition wherever [the movables] may be located. But an ordinary person has not made acquisition until he will have drawn [the object]. One's word of mouth [dedication of an object to the Most High is equivalent to one's act of delivery to an ordinary person [M. Qid. I:6H] – how so? "This ox is sanctified," "This house is sanctified" – even if it is located at the end of the world, the Sanctuary has made acquisition wherever it is located. But in the case of an ordinary person, he makes acquisition only when he will effect usucaption.

T. Arakhin 4:4 If a common person performed the act of drawing when the beast was worth a maneh but did not suffice to redeem the beast, paying the money, until the price rose to two hundred zuz, he must pay the two hundred. How come? Scripture says, "And he will pay the money and depart," meaning, if he has given the money, lo, these belong to him, but if not, they do not belong to him. If he performed the act of drawing when it was worth two hundred zuz but did not suffice to redeem it before the price fell to a maneh, he still has to pay two hundred zuz. How come? So that the rights of a common person should not be stronger than those of the sanctuary. If he redeemed it when it was worth two hundred but did not suffice to draw the beast before the price went down to a maneh, he has to pay the two hundred zuz. How come? Scripture says, "And he will pay the money and depart." If he redeems it at a maneh and did not suffice to perform the act of drawing before it went up to two hundred zuz, what he has redeemed is redeemed, and he pays only a maneh.

**M. 1:7 For every commandment concerning the son to which the father is subject – men are liable, and women are exempt. And for every commandment concerning the father to which the son is subject, men and women are equally liable. For every positive commandment dependent upon the time [of year], men are liable, and women are exempt. And for every positive commandment not dependent upon the time, men and women are equally liable. For every negative commandment, whether dependent upon the time or not dependent upon the time, men and women are equally liable, except for not marring the corners of the beard, not rounding the corners of the head (Lev. 19:27), and not becoming unclean because of the dead (Lev. 21:1).**

T. 1:10 What is a positive commandment dependent upon the time [of year, for which men are liable and women are exempt (M. Qid. 1:7C)]? For example, building the Sukkah, taking the lulab, putting tefillin. What is a positive commandment not dependent upon the time [of year (M. Qid. 1:7D)]? For example, restoring lost property to its rightful owner, sending forth the bird, building a parapet, and putting on *sisit*.

T. 1:11 What is a commandment pertaining to the son concerning the father to which men and women are equally liable (M. Qid. 1:7B)]? Giving him food to eat and something to drink and clothing him and covering him and taking him out and bringing him in and washing his face, his hands, and his feet. All the same are men and women. But the husband has sufficient means to do these things for the child, and the wife does not have sufficient means to do them, for others have power over her. What is a commandment pertaining to the father concerning the son [M . Qid. 1:7A]? To circumcise him, to redeem him [if he is kidnapped], and to teach him Torah, and to teach him a trade, and to marry him off to a girl. And there are those who say, "Also: to row him across the river."

**M. 1:8 [The cultic rites of] laying on of hands, waving, drawing near, taking the handful, burning the fat, breaking the neck of a bird, sprinkling, and receiving [the blood] apply to men and not to women, except in the case of a every commandment which is dependent upon the Land applies only in the Land, and which does not depend upon the Land applies both in the Land and outside the Land, except for 'orlah [produce of a fruit tree in the first three years of its growth] and mixed seeds [Lev. 19:23, 19:19], the meal-offering of an accused wife and of a Nazirite girl, which they wave.**

M. 1:10 Whoever does a single commandment – they do well for him and lengthen his days. And he inherits the Land. And whoever does not do a single commandment – they do not do well for him and do not lengthen his days. And he does not inherit the Land. Whoever has learning in Scripture, Mishnah, and right conduct will not quickly sin, since it is said, "And a threefold cord is not quickly broken" (Qoh. 4:12). And whoever does not have learning in Scripture, Mishnah, and right conduct has no share in society.

T. 1:17 Whoever occupies himself with all three of them, with Scripture, Mishnah, and good conduct, concerning such a person it is said, And a threefold cord is not quickly broken (Qoh. 5:12) [cf. M. Qid. 1:10E-G].

B.   *Procedures of Betrothal: Agency, Value, Stipulations*

M. 2:1 A man effects betrothal on his own or through his agent. A woman becomes betrothed on her own or through her agent. A man betroths his daughter when she is a girl on his own or through his agent. He who says to a woman, "Be betrothed to me for this date, be betrothed to me with this," if [either] one of them is of the value of a penny, she is betrothed, and if not, she is not betrothed. [If he said to her,] "By this, and by this, and by this" – if all of them together are worth a penny, she is betrothed, and if not, she is not betrothed. [If] she was eating them one by one, she is not betrothed, unless one of them is worth a penny.

T. 2:1 Just as a man does not effect a betrothal for his son, either on his own or through his agent, so a woman does not effect a betrothal for her daughter, either on her own or through her agent [cf. M. Qid. 2:1C].

T. 2:3 "Be betrothed to me with this and this," and she was eating [the pieces of fruit] one by one [M. Qid. 2:1H-I], if there remained in his possession produce worth a perutah, she is betrothed, and if not, she is not betrothed. "Be betrothed to me with this cup," if the value of the cup and of what is in it is a perutah, she is betrothed, and if not, she is not betrothed. And she has acquired both it and what is in it. "With what is in this cup," if what is in it is worth a perutah, she is betrothed, and if not, she is not betrothed . And she has acquired only what is in it alone.

M. 2:2 "Be betrothed to me for this cup of wine," and it turns out to be honey – "...of honey" – and it turns out to be of wine, "...with this silver denar" – and it turns out to be gold, "...with this gold one" – and it turns out to be silver – "...on condition that I am rich" – and he turns out to be poor, "...on condition that I am poor" – and he turns out to be rich – she is not betrothed.

T. 2:5 "Be betrothed with a sela," and after she took it from his hand, she said, "I was thinking that you were a priest, but you are only a Levite," "...that you were rich, but you are only poor," lo, this woman is betrothed. This is the principle: Once the tokens of betrothal have fallen into her hand, whether he deceived

T. 2:6 "Be betrothed to me with this sela, with this cow, with this cloak," once she has taken the sela, and drawn the cow, and made use of the cloak, lo, this woman is betrothed.

T. 2:7 "Collect this sela for me," and at the moment at which it was given over, he said to her, "Lo, you are betrothed to me," lo, this woman is betrothed. [If this happened] after she has taken it from his hand, [however,] if she agrees, then she is betrothed, but if she does not agree, she is not betrothed . "Here is this sela which I owe you," [if] at the moment of giving it over, he said to her, "Lo, you are betrothed to me," if she concurs, she is betrothed, and if she does not concur, she is not betrothed. [If this happened] after she has taken it from him, even though both of them concur, she is not betrothed. "Be betrothed to me with the sela of mine which is in your hand" – she is not betrothed. What should he do? He should take it from her and then go and give it back to her and say to her, "Lo you are betrothed to me."

T. 2:8 "Be betrothed to me with this sela," [if] after she took if from his hand, she tossed it into the ocean or into the river – she is not betrothed. "Be betrothed to me with this maneh," and she said to him, "Give it to so-and-so" – she is not betrothed. ["Give it to Mr. So-and-so,] who will receive it for me," lo, she is betrothed. [If] he gave her her tokens of betrothal but did not say to her, "Lo, you are betrothed unto me," "Be betrothed to me with this maneh," and it turns out to be a maneh lacking a denar – she is not betrothed. [If] it was a bad denar, let him exchange it for a good one.

T. 3:10 "...with this silver denar," and it turns out to be gold, she is not betrothed [cf M. Qid. 2:2]. What should he do? He should take it back from her and go and give it to her again and say to her, "Lo, you are betrothed to me."

*Y. 2:1 IV:8 "Be betrothed to me with this maneh," and it turns out to lack a denar – she is not betrothed [since she expected a whole maneh]. If there was a counterfeit denar in it, lo, this woman is betrothed, on condition that he exchange the counterfeit for a valid coin. If he was counting out the coins one by one into her hand, she has the right to retract until he completes counting out the entire sum.]*

M. 2:3 **"...On condition that I am a priest," and he turns out to be a Levite, "...on condition that I am a Levite," and he turns out to be a priest, "...a Netin," and he turns out to be a mamzer, "...a mamzer," and he turns out to be a Netin, "...a town dweller," and he turns out to be a villager," and he turns out to be a town dweller, "...on condition that my house is near the bath," and it turns out to be far away, "...far," and it turns out to be near: "...On condition that I have a daughter or a slave girl who is a hairdresser"' and he has none, "...on condition that I have none," and he has one; "...on condition that I have no children," and he has; "...on condition that he has," and he has none – in the case of all of them, even though she says, "In my heart I wanted to become betrothed to him despite that fact," she is not betrothed. And so is the rule if she deceived him.**

T. 2:2 He who says to a woman, "Lo, you are betrothed to me, on condition that I am [called] Joseph," and he turns out to be [called]

Joseph and Simeon, "...on condition that I am a perfumer," and he turns out to be a perfumer and a tanner, "...on condition that I am a town-dweller," and he turns out to be a town-dweller and a villager [M. Qid. 2:3E-F], lo, this woman is betrothed. [If he said, "Lo, you are betrothed to me, on condition that] I am only Joseph," and he turned out to be Joseph and Simeon, "...that I am only a perfumer," and he turned out to be a perfumer and a tanner, "...that I am only a town-dweller," and he turned out to be a town dweller and a villager, she is not betrothed.

T. 2:4 [If a man said to a woman, "Be betrothed to me] on condition that I am poor," and he was poor but got rich, "...on condition that I am rich" and he was rich and became poor, "...on condition that I am a perfumer," and he was a perfumer but became a tanner, "...on condition that I am a tanner," and he was a tanner but became a perfumer, "...on condition that I am a town-dweller," and he was a town dweller but he moved to a village, "...on condition that I am a villager," and he was a villager, but he moved to a town, "...on condition that I have children," and he had children, but then they died, "...on condition that I have no children," and he had no children, and afterward children were born to him – lo, this woman is betrothed. [If he said, however,] that he was only poor, and he was rich and became poor, that he was only rich, and he was poor and became rich, ". . .that I am only a perfumer," and he was a tanner and became a perfumer, "...that I am only a tanner," and he was a perfumer and became a tanner, "...that I am only a town-dweller," and he was a villager and became a town-dweller, "...that I am only a villager," and he was a town-dweller and became a villager, that he had no children, and he had children, but afterward they died, that he had children, and he did not have any, but afterward children were born to him, she is not betrothed. This is the principle: In the case of any condition which is valid at the moment of betrothal, even though it was annulled afterward, lo, this woman is betrothed. And in the case of any condition which is not valid at the moment of betrothal, even though it was validated afterward, lo, this woman is not betrothed.

**M. 2:4 He who says to his messenger, "Go and betroth Miss So-and-so for me, in such-and-such a place," and he went and betrothed her for him in some other place, she is not betrothed. [If he said,] "...lo, she is in such-and-such a place," and he betrothed her in some other place, lo, she is betrothed.**

T. 4:2 He who says to his agent, "Go and betroth for me Miss So-and-so in such-and-such a place," and he went and betrothed her in some other place – she is not betrothed. "...lo, she is in such and such a place," and he went and betrothed her in some other place, lo, this woman is betrothed [M. Qid. 2:4].

**M. 2:5 He who betroths a woman on condition that she is not encumbered by vows, and she turns out to be encumbered by vows – she is not betrothed. [If] he married her without specifying and she turned out to be encumbered by vows, she goes forth without collecting her marriage contract. ...On condition that there are no blemishes on her, and she turns out to**

have blemishes, she is not betrothed. [If] he married her without specifying and she turned out to have blemishes, she goes forth without collecting her marriage contract. All blemishes which invalidate priests [from serving in the Temple] invalidate women. T. 2:9 [If] he was counting out and putting into her hand one by one, she has the power to retract up to the time that he completes [counting out the specified sum]. [If in a dispute about how much was specified for a betrothal,] this one says, "With a maneh," [a hundred zuz] and this one says, "With two hundred zuz," and this one went home and that one went home and afterward they laid claim against one another and effected betrothal, if the man laid claim against the woman let the claims of the woman be carried out. And if the woman laid claim against the man, let the claim of the man be carried out. And so in the case of him who sells an object, and he was counting out [the objects] into the hand of the buyer, he has the power to retract. [If] this one claims, "[You sold it for] a maneh," and that one claims, "[You bought it for] two hundred zuz," and this one went home and that one went home, and afterward they laid claim against one another, if the purchaser laid claim against the seller, let the claim of the seller be done, and if the seller laid claim against the purchaser, let the claim of the purchaser be done.

C. *Impaired Betrothal*

M. 2:6 He who betroths two women with something worth a penny, or one woman with something worth less than a penny, even though he sent along [additional] presents afterward, she is not betrothed, since he sent the presents later on only because of the original act of betrothal [which was null]. And so in the case of a minor who betrothed a woman.

T. 4:4 He who betroths a woman in error, or with something of less than the value of a perutah, and so a minor who effected an act of betrothal – even though he sent along presents afterward, she is not betrothed. For it was on account of the original act of betrothal that he sent the gifts [M. Qid. 2:6].

M. 2:7 He who betroths a woman and her daughter, or a woman and her sister, simultaneously – they are not betrothed.

M. 2:8 He [who was a priest] who betroths a woman with his share [of the priestly gifts], whether they were Most Holy Things or Lesser Holy Things – she is not betrothed.

T. 4:5 He who effects an act of betrothal by means of something which is stolen, or with a bailment, or who grabbed a sela' from her and betrothed her with it – lo, this woman is betrothed. [If] he said to her, "Be betrothed to me with the sela' which is in your hand," she is not betrothed. What should he do? He should take it from her and go and give it back to her, and say to her, "Lo, you are betrothed to me."

T. 4:6 He who betroths a woman with meat of cattle of tithe, even if it is after slaughter – she is not betrothed. [If he does so] with its bones, sinews, horns, hooves, blood, fat, hide, or shearings, lo, this woman is betrothed.

T. 4:7 He who betroths a woman, whether with Most Holy Things or Lesser Holy Things – she is not betrothed [M. Qid. 2:8A-B].

M. 2:9 He who betrothed a woman with (1) orlah fruit, (2) with fruit which was subject to the prohibition against Mixed Seeds in a vineyard, (3) with an ox which was to be stoned, (4) with a heifer the neck of which was to be broken, (5) with birds set aside for the offering of a person afflicted with the skin ailment [Lev. 13-14], (6) with the hair of a Nazir, (7) with the firstborn of an ass, (8) with meat mixed with milk, (9) with unconsecrated animals [meat] which had been slaughtered in the courtyard [of the Temple] – she is not betrothed. [If] he sold them off and betrothed a woman with the money received in exchange for them, she is betrothed.

M. 2:10 He who consecrated a woman with food in the status of heave-offering, tithe, or gifts [to be given to the priest], purification water, purification ash – lo, this woman is betrothed, and even if she is an Israelite.

T. 4:8 He who betroths a woman by means of libation-wine, an idol, a city and its inhabitants which are slated for destruction [for rebellion], hides with a hole cut out at the heart, an asherah and its produce, a high place and what is on it, a statue of Mercury and what is on it, and any sort of object which is subject to a prohibition by reason of deriving from idolatry – in the case of all of them, even though he sold them and betrothed a woman with their proceeds – she is not betrothed [cf. M. Qid. 2:9A-C]. [If he did so] with purification-water and with purification-ash, she is betrothed [cf. M. Qid. 2:10A]. [The Israelite may not benefit from the proceeds, hence the use of the proceeds for the act of betrothal is null.]

M. 3:1 He who says to his fellow, "Go and betroth Miss So-and-so for me," and he went and betrothed her for himself – she is betrothed [to the agent]. And so: He who says to a woman, "Lo, you are betrothed to me after thirty days [have passed]," and someone else came along and betrothed her during the thirty days – she is betrothed to the second party. [If] it is an Israelite girl betrothed to a priest, she may eat heave-offering. [If he said,] "...as of now and after thirty days," and someone else came along and betrothed her during the thirty days, she is betrothed and not betrothed. [If it is either] an Israelite girl betrothed to a priest, or a priest girl betrothed to an Israelite, she should not eat heave-offering.

T. 4:2 And he who says to his fellow, ' ' Go and betroth for me Miss So-and-so, ' ' and he went and betrothed her for himself, she is betrothed [M. Qid. 3:1A-B] to the second man.

T. 4:3 [He who says, "Lo, you are betrothed to me retroactively from now after thirty days," and a second party came along and betrothed her during the thirty days – she is betrothed [M. Qid. 3:1 F-G] to the second party [or: to both of them]. How should they arrange matters? One gives a writ of divorce, and the other marries her. If they were two brothers, she is invalidated from marrying the one or the other

T. 4:4 A creditor and an heir, one of whom went ahead and took over movable goods – lo, this one is prompt and rewarded on that account. He who says to his fellow, "Go and betroth for me Miss So-and-so," [if] he [the fellow] then went and betrothed her for himself – [or if he said to his fellow,] "Go and buy me such-and-such an item," [if] he went and bought it *for* himself, what he has done is done. But he has behaved deceitfully.

D. *Stipulations*

M. 3:2 He who says to a woman, "Behold, you are betrothed to me, on condition that I pay you two hundred zuz" – lo, this woman is betrothed, and he must pay [her what he has promised]. "...On condition that I pay you within the next thirty days," and he paid her during the thirty days, she is betrothed. And if not, she is not betrothed. "...On condition that I have two hundred zuz," lo, this woman is betrothed, and [if] he has that sum. "...On condition that I shall show you two hundred zuz," lo, this woman is betrothed, and [if] he will show her that sum. But if he showed her the money on the table of a money changer, she is not betrothed.

T. 3:1 He who says to a woman, "Lo, you are betrothed to me through the bailment which I have in your hand," [if] she went off and found that it had been stolen or had gotten lost if [of that bailment] there was left in her possession something worth a perutah, she is betrothed, and if not, she is not betrothed. But [if it concerned] a loan, even though there was something worth a perutah left in her possession, she is not betrothed.

T. 3:2 [If he said,] "On condition that I speak in your behalf to the government," if he spoke in her behalf as people generally do it, she is betrothed, and if not, she is not betrothed. "... through the value of my speaking in your behalf to the government," if he spoke in her behalf to the value of a perutah, she is betrothed, and if not, she is not betrothed. "...through the act of labor which I shall do in your behalf," if he worked in her behalf to the value of a perutah, she is betrothed, and if not, she is not betrothed. "...on condition that I shall work with you," "...on condition that I shall labor with you tomorrow," if he did work in her behalf value to the extent of a perutah, she is betrothed, and if not she is not betrothed. "... on condition that I have two hundred zuz," lo, this woman is betrothed [M. Qid. 3:2E], for he may have that sum on the other side of the world. "...on condition that I have two hundred zuz in such-and-such a place, ' if he has the money in that place, she is betrothed, and if not, she is not betrothed.

M. 3:3 "...On condition that I have a kor's space of land," lo, this woman is betrothed, and [if] he has it. "...On condition that I have that land in such-and-such a place," if he has it in that place, she is betrothed, and if not, she is not betrothed. "...On condition that I show you a kor's space of land," lo, this woman is betrothed, and [if] he will show it to her. But if he showed her [land] in a plain [which was not his], she is not betrothed.

T. 3:3 "...on condition that I have [money] in the hand of Mr. so-and- so even though [the other party] said, "He has no money in my hand," she is betrothed. For they might have conspired to defraud her. "...until he will say that he has the money in my hand," if he said, "He has money in my hand," she is betrothed, and if not, she is not betrothed. "...on condition that I show you two hundred zuz, " if he showed her the money on the table [of a money-changer], she is not betrothed. For he stated that he would show her only what in fact belonged to him.

T. 3:4 ".. .on condition that I have a kor of land," lo, this woman is betrothed [M. Qid. 3:3A-B], for he might have such land on the other side of the world. "...on condition that I have it in this place," if he has it in that place she is betrothed, and if not, she is not betrothed. ". . .on condition that I show you a kor of land " if he showed it to her in a plain [of public property], she is not betrothed [M. Qid. 3:3E-G]. For he stated that he would show her only what in fact belonged to him.

**M. 3:5 He who betroths a woman and said, "I was thinking that she is a priest, and lo, she is a Levite," "...a Levite, and lo, she is a priest," "A poor girl, and lo, she is a rich girl," "A rich girl, and lo, she is a poor girl," lo, she is betrothed, for she has not deceived him. He who says to a woman, "Lo, you are betrothed to me after I convert to Judaism," or "after you convert," "...after I am freed" or "after you are freed," "...after your husband died," or "...after your sister dies," "after your levir will have performed the rite of removing the shoe with you" – she is not betrothed. And so he who says to his fellow, "If your wife gives birth to a girl-child, lo, [the baby] is betrothed to me" – she is not betrothed. If the wife of his fellow indeed was pregnant and the foetus was discernible, his statement is confirmed, and if she produced a girl-child, the baby is betrothed.**

T. 4:9 He who says to a woman, "Lo, you are betrothed [to me] after I convert," "...after you convert," "...after I am freed," "...after you are freed," "...after your husband will die," "...after your sister will die," "...after your Levir will perform the rite of halisah with you," even though the condition is met, she is not betrothed [M. Qid. 3:5].

**M. 3:6 He who says to a woman, "Lo, you are betrothed to me, on condition that I speak in your behalf to the government"' or, "That I work for you as a laborer," [if] he spoke in her behalf to the government or worked for her as a laborer, she is betrothed. And if not, she is not betrothed. "...On condition that father will concur," [if] father concurred, she is betrothed. And if not, she is not betrothed. [If] the father died, lo, this woman is betrothed. [If] the son died, they instruct the father to state that he does not concur.**

T. 3:5 "...on condition that So-and-so will concur," even though he said "I do not concur," she is betrothed. For he may concur a while later. "...unless he will say, 'I concur,"' if he says, "I concur," she is betrothed, and if not she is not betrothed.

T. 3:6 "...on condition that father agrees" [M. Qid. 3:6D], even though his father did not agree, she is betrothed. Perhaps he may agree some other time. [If] the father died, lo, this woman is betrothed. [If] the son died – this was a case, and they came and instructed the father to say, "I do not concur" [so that the woman is exempt from the Levirate connection] [M. Qid. 3:6F-G].

E. *Cases of Doubt*

M. 3:7 "I have betrothed my daughter, but I don't know to whom I have betrothed her," and someone came along and said, "I have betrothed her," he is believed. [If] this one said, "I betrothed her," and [at the same time], that one said, "I betrothed her," both of them give her a writ of divorce. But if they wanted, one of them gives her a writ of divorce and one of them consummates the marriage.

T. 4:10 "I betrothed my daughter, but I do not know to whom I betrothed her," and someone came along and said, "I betrothed her" – he is believed [M. Qid. 3:7A-C] to consummate the marriage. [If] after he has consummated the marriage, someone else came along and said, "I betrothed her," he has not got the power to prohibit her [from remaining wed to the husband who got there first].

M. 3:8 [If the father said,] "I have betrothed my daughter," "...I have betrothed her and I have accepted her writ of divorce when she was a minor" – and lo, she is yet a minor – he is believed. "I betrothed her and I accepted her writ of divorce when she was a minor," and lo, she is now an adult – he is not believed. "She was taken captive and I redeemed her," whether she is a minor or whether she is an adult, he is not believed. He who said at the moment of his death, "I have children," is believed. [If he said,] "I have brothers," he is not believed. He who betroths his daughter without specification – the one past girlhood is not taken into account.

T. 4:11 [If a man said], "I betrothed my daughter," the minors are subject to his statement, but the adults are not subject to his statement. "My daughter has been betrothed," – the adults are subject to his statement, but the minors are not subject to his statement. "I received the writ of divorce for my daughters" – the minors are subject to his statement, but the adults are not subject to his statement. "My daughter has been divorced" – the minors are not subject to his statement [cf. M. Qid. 3:8K].

T. 4:12 "She was taken captive and I redeemed her" [M. Qid. 3:8G], or, "She was invalidated by one of those who are invalid" [for marriage with a priest] – he has not got the power to prohibit her [from marrying a priest]. [If he said], "I have betrothed my daughter," and he had ten daughters, all of them are prohibited by reason of doubt [from remarrying without a writ of divorce]. If he said, "The oldest one," only the oldest one is deemed to have been betrothed. If he said, "The youngest," only the youngest is deemed to have been betrothed [cf. M. Qid. 3:9]. And so two brothers who betrothed two sisters – this one does not know which one of them he betrothed, and that one does not know which one of them he betrothed – both of them are prohibited by reason of doubt. But if they were engaged in the betrothal of the older girl to the older man, and the younger girl to the younger man [if] the older one says, "I was betrothed only to the older brother," then the younger sister has been betrothed only to the younger brother.

M. 3:10 He who says to a woman, "I have betrothed you," and she says, "You did not betroth me" – he is prohibited to marry her relatives, but she is permitted to marry his relatives. [If] she says, "You betrothed me," and he says, "I did not betroth you" – he is permitted to marry her relatives, and she is prohibited from marrying his relatives. "I betrothed you," and she says, "You betrothed only my daughter," he is prohibited from marrying the relatives of the older woman, and the older woman is permitted to marry his relatives. He is permitted to marry the relatives of the young girl, and the young girl is permitted to marry his relatives.

T. 4:13 "I have betrothed you, but she says, " You have betrothed only my daughter, " he is prohibited to marry the relatives of the older woman, and the older woman is prohibited to marry his relatives. And he Is permitted to marry the relatives of the younger woman, and the younger woman is permitted to marry his relatives.

M. 3:11 "I have betrothed your daughter," and she says, "You betrothed only me," he is prohibited to marry the relatives of the girl, and the girl is permitted to marry his relatives. He is permitted to marry the relatives of the older woman, but the older woman is prohibited from marrying his relatives."

T. 4:14 "I betrothed your daughter," and she says, " You betrothed only me, " he is prohibited from marrying the relatives of the younger girl, and the younger girl is permitted to marry his relatives. And he is permitted to marry the relatives of the older woman, and the older woman is prohibited from marrying his relatives [M. Qid. 3:10].

## II. Castes for the Purposes of Marriage

### A. *The Status of the Offspring of Impaired Marriages 3:12-13*

M. 3:12 In any situation in which there is a valid betrothal and no commission of a transgression, the offspring follows the status of the male, What is such a situation? It is [in particular] the situation in which a priest girl, a Levite girl, or an Israelite girl was married to a priest, a Levite, or an Israelite. And any situation in which there is a valid betrothal, but there also is the commission of a transgression, the offspring follows the status of the impaired [inferior] party. And what is such a situation? It is a widow married to a high priest, a divorcée or woman who has undergone the rite of removing the shoe married to an ordinary priest, a mamzer girl, or a Netin girl married to an Israelite, an Israelite girl married to a mamzer or a Netin. And in any situation in which a woman has no right to enter betrothal with this man but has the right to enter into betrothal with others, the offspring is a mamzer. What is such a situation? This is a man who had sexual relations with any of those women prohibited to him by the Torah. But any situation in which a woman has no right to enter into betrothal with this man or with any other man – the offspring is in her status. And what is such a situation? It is the offspring of a slave girl or a gentile girl.

T. 4:15 A priest-girl, a Levite-girl, and an Israelite-girl who were married to a proselyte – the offspring is in the status of a proselyte. [And if they married] a freed slave, the offspring is in the status of a freed slave [cf. M. Qid. 3:12].

T. 4:16 A gentile, or a slave who had sexual relations with an Israelite girl, and she produced a son – the offspring is a mamzer.

B. *Castes and Marriage Between Castes*

M. 4:1 Ten castes came up from Babylonia: (1) priests, (2) Levites, (3) Israelites, (4) impaired priests, (5) converts, and (6) freed slaves, (7) mamzers, (8) Netins, (9) "silenced ones" [shetuqi], and (10) foundlings. Priests, Levites, and Israelites are permitted to marry among one another. Levites, Israelites, impaired priests, converts, and freed slaves are permitted to marry among one another. Converts, freed slaves, mamzers, Netins, "silenced ones," and foundlings are permitted to marry among one another.

Y. 4:1 II:5 *He who converts for the sake of love [of a Jew], whether a man because of a woman, or a woman because of a man, and so too those who converted in order to enter Israelite royal service, and so too those who converted out of fear of the lions [that is, the Samaritans], and so too the converts in the time of Mordecai and Esther [who converted out of fear] – they do not accept them.*

M. 4:2 And what are "silenced ones"? Any who knows the identity of his mother but does not know the identity of his father. And foundlings? Any who was discovered in the market and knows neither his father nor his mother.

M. 4:3 All those who are forbidden from entering into the congregation are permitted to marry one another.

M. 4:4 He who marries a priest girl has to investigate her [genealogy] for four [generations, via the] mothers, who are eight: (1) Her mother, and (2) the mother of her mother, and (3) the mother of the father of her mother, and (4) her mother, and (5) the mother of her father, and (6) her mother, and (7) the mother of the father of her father, and (8) her mother. And in the case of a Levite girl and an Israelite girl, they add on to them yet another [generation for genealogical inquiry].

M. 4:5 They do not carry a genealogical inquiry backward from [proof that one's priestly ancestor has served] at the altar, nor from [proof that one's Levitical ancestor has served] on the platform, and from [proof that one's learned ancestor has served] in the Sanhedrin. [It is taken for granted that at the time of the appointment, a full inquiry was undertaken.] And all those whose fathers are known to have held office as public officials or as charity collectors – they marry them into the priesthood, and it is not necessary to conduct an inquiry.

M. 4:6 The daughter of a male of impaired priestly stock is invalid for marriage into the priesthood for all time. An Israelite who married a woman of impaired priestly stock – his daughter is valid for marriage into the priesthood. A man of impaired priestly stock who married an Israelite girl – his daughter is invalid for marriage into the priesthood.

T. 5:3 The daughter of a father of impaired priestly stock is invalid for marrying into the priesthood for all time [M. Qid. 4:6A, D]. A girl of mixed stock is invalid for marriage into the priesthood. [If] she was married to an Israelite, her daughter is valid for marrying into the priesthood. A female convert and a woman of impaired priestly stock are invalid for marriage into the priesthood. [If] she was married to an Israelite, her daughter is valid for marriage into the priesthood. A girl taken captive is invalid for marriage into the priesthood. [If] she was married to an Israelite, her daughter is valid for marriage into the priesthood. A slave-girl is invalid for marriage into the priesthood. [If] she was married to an Israelite, her daughter is valid for marriage into the priesthood. It turns out that Israelites are a [genealogical] purification-pool for priests, and a slave-girl is a purification-pool for all those who are invalid.

B. 4:6-7 III.7/77A [IF A HIGH PRIEST HAD SEXUAL RELATIONS WITH] A WIDOW, A WIDOW, A WIDOW, HE IS LIABLE ON ONLY A SINGLE COUNT; A DIVORCÉE, A DIVORCÉE, A DIVORCÉE, HE IS LIABLE ON ONLY A SINGLE COUNT. [IF A HIGH PRIEST HAD SEXUAL RELATIONS WITH] A WIDOW, A DIVORCÉE, A WOMAN OF IMPAIRED PRIESTLY STOCK, AND A WHORE, IF IT IS IN RESPECT TO THE SAME WOMAN WHO HAS ENTERED THESE VERY CONDITIONS BY ACTIONS TAKEN IN THAT EXACT ORDER, HE IS LIABLE ON EACH COUNT. IF THE SAME WOMAN FIRST OF ALL COMMITTED AN ACT OF FORNICATION, THEN WAS PROFANED FROM PRIESTLY STOCK, THEN WAS DIVORCED, AND THEN WAS WIDOWED, HE IS LIABLE ON ONLY A SINGLE COUNT.

C.  *Cases of Doubt 4:8-11*

M. 4:8 He who says, "This son of mine is a mamzer" is not believed. And even if both parties say concerning the foetus in the mother's womb, "It is a mamzer" – they are not believed.

M. 4:9 He who gave the power to his agent to accept tokens of betrothal for his daughter, but then he himself betrothed her – if his came first, his act of betrothal is valid. And if those of his agent came first, his act of betrothal is valid. And if it is not known [which came first], both parties give a writ of divorce. But if they wanted, one of them gives a writ of divorce, and one consummates the marriage. And so: A woman who gave the power to her agent to accept tokens of betrothal in her behalf, and then she herself went and accepted tokens of betrothal in her own behalf – if hers came first, her act of betrothal is valid. And if those of her agent came first, his act of betrothal is valid. And if it is not known [which of them came first], both parties give a writ of divorce. But if they wanted, one of them gives a writ of divorce and one of them consummates the marriage.

M. 4:10 He who went along with his wife overseas, and he and his wife and children came home, and he said, "The woman who went abroad with me, lo, this is she, and these are her children" –

he does not have to bring proof concerning the woman or the children. [If he said,] "She died, and these are her children," he does bring proof about the children, But he does not bring proof about the woman.

M. 4:11 [If he said], "I married a woman overseas. Lo, this is she, and these are her children" – he brings proof concerning the woman, but he does not have to bring proof concerning the children. "...She died, and these are her children," he has to bring proof concerning the woman and the children.

T. 5:6 He who went, along with his wife, overseas, and he came along with his wife and children, and said, "The woman who went overseas with me, lo, this is she, and these are her children, " does not have to bring proof concerning her or concerning the children. [If he said], "She died, and these are her children, " he brings proof concerning the children, but he does not have to bring proof concerning the woman

T. 5:7 [For] a woman is believed to say, "These are my children." And [he who says], "A woman whom I married overseas, lo this is she and these are her children, " has to bring proof concerning the woman, but does not have to bring proof concerning the children [M. Qid. 4:11].

M. 4:12 A man should not remain alone with two women, but a woman may remain alone with two men. A man may stay alone with his mother or with his daughter. And he sleeps with them with flesh touching. But if they [the son who is with the mother, the daughter with the father] grew up, this one sleeps in her garment, and that one sleeps in his garment.

T. 5:9 A woman remains alone with two men [M. Qid. 4:12A], even if both of them are Samaritans even if both of them are slaves even if one of them is a Samaritan and one a slave except for a minor, for she is shameless about having sexual relations in his presence.

T. 5:10 As to his sister and his sister-in-law and all those women in a prohibited relationship to him which are listed in the Torah – he should not be alone with them [M. Qid. 4:12A] except before two [witnesses]. But she should not be alone even with a hundred gentiles.

M. 4:13 An unmarried man may not teach scribes. Nor may a woman teach scribes.

M. 4:14 Whoever has business with women should not be alone with women. And a man should not teach his son a trade which he has to practice among women.

T. 5:14 Whoever has business with women should not be alone with women [M. Qid. 4:14D] – for example, goldsmiths, carders, [hand-mill] cleaners, pedlars, wool-dressers, barbers, launderers, and mill-stone chisellers.

## II. Analysis: The Problematics of the Topic, Qiddushin

The problematic of the halakhah of Qiddushin, the sanctification of a particular woman for a particular man, emerges in the intersection of the language of acquisition with the language of sanctification. A householder buys a cow, in acquiring it, he does not sanctify it. Unless he means to offer it on the altar in Jerusalem), a person who utilizes the same cow, e.g., milks it or uses it for ploughing, does not offend God. The issue of sanctification does not enter the transaction. But a householder acquires a woman thereby consecrates the woman as his wife. Another person who utilizes the same woman, e.g., has sexual relations with her and produces children by her, enormously outrages God (not to mention the husband). The category, sanctification and its opposite, applies. Yet in both instances the result is, acquiring title to, rights over the cow or the woman. Indeed, slaves, movables, and real estate prove analogous to the betrothal of a woman. The transaction by which a householder acquires a wife, slave, movables or real estate forms the genus, the language and categories and action-symbols proving constant.

But when it comes to the woman, an enormous point of difference renders the woman an active participant in the transfer of title. She has to consent, and when she does, her status as person, not merely as property, changes; and the change is called sanctification. So the opening exposition of the halakhah serves to establish the genus – money, writ, usucaption for the slave, money, writ, act of sexual relations, comparable to usucaption, for the woman. These are compared and contrasted and firmly situated in a single classification: things that are acquired by the householder through a common repertoire of procedures of transfer of title from owner to owner.

The speciation commences in the comparison of the standing before God of the woman's to the man's, the respective obligations being differentiated by reason of the non-negotiable obligation of a woman at specific times to home and family; that takes priority. The introduction of the exposition that stresses how men and women are equally liable, e.g., to all negative commandments and most positive ones, concludes in a remarkable manner the presentation of the modes of acquisition of women, slaves, cattle, and the like. What is remarkable is that no counterpart discussion is accorded to slaves. The difference, which is implicit, is that while women remain possessed of an autonomous will, not being subject to the unmediated will of their husbands, slaves are deemed in the law to have no autonomous will whatsoever. So the halakhic unit that commences with the genus, the acquisition of persons and property, concludes with the distinct species, the woman, with the differentiation of the woman from all other classes of things that are acquired by the householder.

The halakhah of sanctification of a woman to a particular man ("betrothal" in my translation) pursues a fairly standard agendum of issues: agency, value, and stipulations. When it comes to agency, the point to note is that a woman may designate her own agent, just as a man does, for the transaction; a slave cannot do the same. As to value, the issue of joining together discrete items to form the requisite value for the transaction – comparable to the issue of connection – makes an appearance; the language that effects the transaction comes under discussion; and similar standard analytical questions – the impact of stipulations and conditions, met and unmet – are pursued. Stipulations not met nullify the exchange; deception has the same result. The situation prevailing at the critical turning is deemed decisive: In the case of any condition which is valid at the moment of betrothal, even though it was annulled afterward, lo, this woman is betrothed. And in the case of any condition which is not valid at the moment of betrothal, even though it was validated afterward, lo, this woman is not betrothed.

Stipulations must be met, conditions satisfied, instructions carried out. Where the woman has agreed to the transaction without deceit and bears no responsibility for an unmet stipulation or condition, the transaction takes effect; she is betrothed. How cases of doubt are sorted out receives attention. None of these discussions presents surprises, and the rules that govern are in no way particular to the topic at hand. Indeed, out of the halakhic principles at hand one could easily construct a handbook of responsibility in ethical transactions. The premise throughout does not require articulation: the woman must consent to the transaction or it is null. But the fact that the woman can appoint an agent and establish conditions and stipulations as much as the man can bears the implication that the woman is an equal partner in the transaction and must consent to it. (That same point will come before us when we deal with the under-age girl whose father marries her off; when she comes of age, she has the right to refuse the arrangement and simply walk out of the marriage.)

God's stake in the transaction of the sanctification of a woman extends beyond individuals to the castes among which the community of Israel is distributed: priests, Levites, Israelites, and others. A man and a woman belong to a particular classification, and that governs whether or not, to begin with, sanctification is possible, sanctity takes effect in their relationship. The Written Torah defines the classifications of persons who may not intermarry – gentiles do not enter the picture – within the purview of the Torah. A woman's personal status is affected by prior unions, e.g. a marriage to a man to whom the Torah prohibits her, such as a widow to a high priest, a divorcée or equivalent to an ordinary priest, the mamzer (child of parents legally unable ever to marry, such as a brother and a sister, or a married woman and a man other than her husband) to an ordinary Israelite, and so on. These castes are defined in the halakhah, exquisitely summarized at M. 4:1's catalogue of ten castes.

Here we see how the metaphor of the altar overspreads the formation of the household's family unit. The effect of an act of betrothal is qualified by the caste status of the parties to the betrothal. Just as blemished beasts are not susceptible of sanctification for the altar, so persons of blemished genealogy cannot enter into consecrated relationships with those of unblemished family. The family that forms the foundation of the household then compares with the offering on the altar. What the halakhah does is extend to the entire community of Israel the Written Torah's intense interest in the eugenics of the priesthood – thus, once more, the now-familiar pattern, at the critical points, of appealing to the altar for a paradigm of the household.

### III. Interpretation: Religious Principles of Qiddushin

The generative symbol of sanctification linking altar to bed is dual: the priesthood, the animal consecrated for the altar, respectively. If Israel is to form a kingdom of priests and a holy people, and if belonging to the holy people comes about naturally, that is, by birth to a Jewish mother, as the halakhah everywhere takes for granted, then genealogy will take its place beside theology as arbiter of the validity of acts of betrothal. The halakhah of Qiddushin, in particular, defines that principal building block of the social order, the household and the family that constitute its heart and center. It is formed by the householder with women who can be sanctified to the man at hand and who agree to enter into a sacred relationship with him, to maintain the domestic order of the householder and bear and raise children. When that relationship is characterized as holy and the result of an act of sanctification, the intent is not figurative or merely symbolic but material and concrete. Within the walls of the Israelite household through betrothal ("qiddushin") an act of sanctification takes place that bears as weighty consequences as does an act of sanctification of an animal for an offering to God in the Temple; the transaction at hand defines the locus at which Israel attains the sanctity that God proposes to bestow on it.

To state that Israel procreates in accord with rules of sanctification that pertain to the Temple, as much as Israel sustains life in accord with (other) rules of sanctification that radiate outward from the cult, sages could have had no better medium than the halakhah before us. The very categorical structure of the halakhah, its language, its governing considerations – all bear the message of how the life-force of the holy people flows through channels made sacred, table and bed alike forming extensions of the altar's governing principles and (in the present case) the consecration of the offering, on the one side, the priesthood, on the other.

Israel defines itself as holy in two ways: by nature, through birth; and by conviction, through adherence to the Torah. Sanctification by nature, the first of the two media for forming Israel realized in a given household, then, comes about when an Israelite man consecrates an Israelite woman who is available to him – not married or betrothed to someone else (the governing analogy being the consecration of the offering, as we shall note), and not forbidden to him by reason of incest taboos or caste regulations (the governing analogy being the consecration of the priesthood). Then sanctification by nature continues when that union produces offspring. Sanctification by conviction takes place when through those actions specified in connection with, e.g., food-preparation, the Israelite sustains life as life is sustained at the altar.

So Israel both is holy and behaves so as to sanctify itself. How the former? By birth, that is, by nature, Israel is subject to hierarchical classification just as animals are: beasts suitable for the altar compare, first of all to the priesthood, men suitable to serve at the altar, and so on down to ladder. That is one component of the generative metaphor. But, second, let there be no mincing of words, the woman suitable to the man at hand compares with the beast suitable to the altar. The offering consecrated for the altar then supplies the other component of the same governing analogy. She must not exhibit genealogical blemishes, any more than the animal consecrated to the altar may bear physical ones. She must be suitable for marriage to the priest (or Levite, or Israelite, as the case requires), in accord with the Torah's definition of the correct genealogy and status of a woman for marriage into the priesthood. And the rest follows.

But while bed and table come under the rules of sanctification that radiate from the altar, the generative principles that overspread altar and bed differ from those that join altar to table. Since the paramount analogy compares the woman to the offering, what follows? Here the governing principle focuses upon the specificity of the transaction of betrothal that is compared to one with the altar and the particularity of its effects. Now what is at issue is sanctifying a particular woman to a particular man, comparable to sanctifying a given beast to the Lord for a given, particular purpose, e.g., this animal for this classification of offering, and, in the case of a sin-offering, for this specific sin committed inadvertently in particular. That is because in the halakhah to sanctify means to select in a concrete way, for a distinctive purpose, not in a general way or for a generic purpose. Precision of intentionality finds its match in precision of language. The act of selecting a beast for sacrifice on the altar involves setting that beast aside from all others and designating it for the unique purpose of an offering for the sacrifier (the one who benefits, e.g., expiates sin, through the offering) carried out by the priest. The animal must be designated ("consecrated") for an offering; it must be a specific type of offering, e.g., sin-offering; and the particular sin that the sacrifier has in mind must be articulated, there being no such thing as a sin-offering in general. So the act of sanctification finds its definition in the specificity of the selection, designation for a unique purpose, and performance of those rites that effect the selection and designation and carry out the purpose – out of which the transaction of sanctification produces a relationship of sanctity, God to this Israelite among all Israelites.

What follows? The Israelite man is like God, and the Israelite woman is to be sanctified to him in accord with the same principles that govern the consecration of an offering. But that is not the entire statement sages make in the halakhah before us. The counterpart to Hullin's formulaic statement, "abroad, not consecrated, after the Temple was destroyed" – the principles of the law that encompass within the Temple's rules the ordinary food of the Israelite household – is not to be missed. Just as, at critical points, important differences distinguished the Israelite table from the Temple altar ("animals that are consecrated *and not consecrated*, in the Land *and abroad*, whether the Temple is standing *or afterward*"), so built into the law is a critical point of difference between the animal that is consecrated to God for a specific purpose and the woman who is consecrated to a particular Israelite man and no other, also for the specific purpose of building a family, producing a new generation, and forming a solid component of the household of Israel. And that difference lies in the woman's endowment of a valid will, the power of effective intentionality.

The difference between the consecrated offering for the altar and the consecrated woman for the marriage canopy, governing the entire process of sanctification of woman to man, lies in what distinguishes the human being, man or woman, from the beast: the freedom of will, the power of intentionality. The man may declare the woman sanctified, but if she objects, the act is null. If of age, it is by her own act of will that she must accept the tokens of betrothal, directly or through her agent. If not of age, when she comes of age, she may reject an act of betrothal, even consummated, taken by others with control over her in her minority, her father if he is alive, her brothers if he is deceased. Then she simply ups and walks out, not requiring even a writ of divorce. No sanctification has ever taken place, the woman not having confirmed what has happened through the exercise of will of others with temporary jurisdiction over her. So the woman consecrated for her husband is like the beast sanctified for the altar, but with a formidable difference.

Why do I insist that the woman's sanctification vastly differs from the animals and renders the woman a partner with God? Let us broaden the discussion by contrasting the power of the woman to effect an act of intentionality in the transaction of betrothal with the impotence of counterparts in her category, slaves and minors, to effect their will in any way. Along with slaves and minors, women form a classification of Israelites deemed not fully capable of independent will, intentionality, entire responsibility, and action and therefore subject not only to God's will but also to the will of another, the husband or father in the case of the woman, the master in the case of the slave, and the parent in the case of the child, thus M. Ber. 3:3: Women, slaves, and minors are exempt from the recitation of the *Shema* and from the obligation to wear phylacteries, but are obligated to the recitation of the prayer, and to post a *mezuzah* and to recite the blessing over the meal. But they do not form part of the community of holy Israel that is obligated to recite blessings publicly, thus M. Ber. 7:2: Women, slaves or minors who ate together with adult Israelite males – they may not invite others to bless on their account. While comparable to slaves and minors in forming a classification of persons of lesser powers of intentionality than the Israelite man, the Israelite woman in the aspect of betrothal stands far above the others of her class.

How does she differ, even with the power to reject an act of sanctification to a particular man, from man? When Scripture refers to "man," it may cover both man and woman, but special conditions yield the word-choice, so Sifra CXCV:II.1-2: "Every one Hebrew: man of you shall revere his mother and his father, and you shall keep my Sabbaths": I know only that a man is subject to the instruction. How do I know that a woman is also involved? Scripture says, "...shall revere" using the plural. Lo, both genders are covered. If so, why does Scripture refer to "man"? It is because a man controls what he needs, while a woman does not control what she needs, since others have dominion over her. Here we find in explicit language exactly the point just now registered. The householder (and his male equivalents within other social structures) is possessed of an autonomous will, like God's and in contest with God's. The woman's autonomy is limited by her father's, then her husband's will.

In a number of specific contexts, moreover, a man and woman are differentiated not in capacity to effect an act of intentionality but in the functions that they perform or to which they are obligated, e.g., M. Sot. 3:8: What is the difference between a man and a woman? A man goes around with unbound hair and torn garments, but a woman does not go around with unbound hair and torn garments (Lev. 13:44-5). A man imposes a Nazirite vow on his son, and a woman does not impose a Nazirite vow upon her son (M. Naz. 4:6). A man brings the hair offering for the Nazirite vow of his father, and a woman does not bring a hair offering for the Nazirite vow of her father . The man sells his daughter, and the woman does not sell her daughter Ex. 21:6. The man arranges for a betrothal of his daughter, and the woman does not arrange for the betrothal of her daughter (M. Qid. 2:1). A man who incurs the death penalty is stoned naked, but a woman is not stoned naked. A man is hanged after being put to death, and a woman is not hanged (M. San. 6:3-4). A man is sold to make restitution for having stolen something, but a woman is not sold to make restitution for having stolen something (Ex. 22:2).

The matter is further amplified at M. Qid. 1:7-8, which we have already noted: For every commandment concerning the son to which the father is subject-men are liable, and women are exempt. And for every commandment concerning the father to which the son is subject, men and women are equally liable. For every positive commandment dependent upon the time of year, men are liable, and women are exempt. And for every positive commandment not dependent upon the time, men and women are equally liable. For every negative commandment, whether dependent upon the time or not dependent upon the time, men and women are equally liable, except for not marring the comers of the beard, not rounding the corners of the head (Lev. 19:27), and not becoming unclean because of the dead (Lev. 21:1). The cultic rites of laying of hands, waving, drawing near, taking the handful, burning the incense, breaking the neck of a bird, sprinkling, and receiving the blood apply to men and not to women, except in the case of a meal offering of an accused wife and of a Nazirite girl, which they wave. This matter is clarified at T. Qid. 1:10-11: What is a positive commandment dependent upon the time of year, for which men are liable and women are exempt (M. Qid. 1:7C)? For example, building the Sukkah, taking the lulab, putting tefillin. What is a positive commandment not dependent upon the time of year (M. Qid. 1:7D)? For example, restoring lost property to its rightful owner, sending forth the bird, building a parapet, and putting on show-fringes. What is a commandment pertaining to the son concerning the father to which men and women are equally liable (M. Qid. 1:7B)? Giving him food to eat and something to drink and clothing him and covering him and taking him out and bringing him in and washing his face, his hands, and his feet. All the same are men and women. But the husband has sufficient means to do these things for the child, and the wife does not have sufficient means to do them, for others have power over her. So too, a woman is not obligated to study the Torah or to wear tefillin, so Y. Er. 10:1 I.2: He who is liable to study Torah also is liable to wear *tefillin*. women, who are not liable to study Torah, also are not liable to wear *tefillin*.

So women are subject to men, daughters to fathers, then wives to husbands; widows are assumed to return to their fathers' households. But man needs woman to complete his existence. Marriage is the natural condition of man and woman, so b. Yeb. 6:6 II.19-21 Said R. Hanilai, "Any man who has no wife lives without joy, blessing, goodness: Joy: 'and you shall rejoice, you and your house' (Deut. 14:26). Blessing: 'to cause a blessing to rest on your house' (Ezek. 44:30). Goodness: 'it is not good that man should be alone' (Gen. 2:18)." In the West they say: without Torah and without a wall of refuge. without Torah: "Is it that I have no help in me and that sound wisdom is driven entirely out of me" (Job 6:13). without a wall of refuge: "A woman shall form a wall about a man" (Jer. 31:22). Raba bar Ulla said, "Without peace: 'and you shall know that your tent is in peace, and you shall visit your habitation and shall miss nothing' (Job 5:24)." He who loves his wife as he loves himself, he who honors her more than he honors himself, he who raises up his sons and daughters in the right path, and he who marries them off close to the time of their puberty – of such a one, Scripture says, "And you shall know that your tabernacle shall be in peace and you shall visit your habitation and you shall not sin" (Job 5:24).

What we have seen is that from the altar lines of sanctification radiate outward to encompass the table and the bed; these then form a continuous reality, the paired media for the procreation and maintenance of life. But the relationship is not only generic. Particular points of comparison emerge in the very language commonly used for both animals for the altar and women for men. That is, a woman is consecrated to a particular man, just as an animal is consecrated to the altar for the expiation of a particular inadvertent sin that has been carried out by a particular person. A sin-offering consecrated for a particular person and a specific action he has inadvertently performed proves null if it is used for another offering than the designated class, another person, or another sin by the same person. A woman consecrated for a particular man is subject to exactly the same considerations of sanctification (mutatis mutandis).

In both cases the relationship is one of consecration, meaning, differentiation from all secular purposes and designated for a sacred function or task. Just as the Temple altar provides the governing comparison for the formation of the laws about the slaughter of animals for meat for the Israelite table, so the Temple altar provides the pertinent analogy for the transaction that links a selected woman to a given man in a relationship of sanctity. What marks the woman as unique is that, when she is consecrated, she makes a choice of this circumstance, not that, so to effect her sanctification she assents in an act of will responding to the act of will of the counterpart to the sacrifier, the proposed groom.

Then who stands for the Israelite woman, if not Isaac at Horeb?

# 2

## Gittin

### I. An Outline of the Halakhah of Gittin

Designating a woman as "holy" or set apart for a particular man, requires the woman's participation through assent. Unlike a beast sanctified for the altar, a woman enters the relationship of sanctification only when she agrees to do so. The animal does not possess the power of will or intentionality, the woman does, though she surrenders a proportion thereof by agreeing to be betrothed. The consecrated relationship thus involves affirmative intentionality on the part of both parties. That is not so when it comes to the desacralization of the relationship, at which point the woman is no longer consecrated to that particular man but becomes available to any other man of her choice (within the prohibitions of incest). One of two parties – man or God, but not woman – intervenes. In general, the husband acts to desanctify what he has sanctified. His initiative, resulting from his intentionality, is dissolved at his own will. In special cases, Heaven intervenes; the husband dies, leaving the wife free to remarry. In very unusual circumstances, in the halakhah of Yebamot, amplifying Deut. 25:5-10, Heaven intervenes to bring to a conclusion one relationship of consecration but immediately impose another.

Now, in all three transactions equally, what role does the wife possess? None, so far as the Written part of the Torah is concerned. But – as with the woman's ordeal when accused of unfaithfulness – that matter is considerably reshaped in the halakhah of the Oral part of the Torah. Scripture does not contemplate a role for the woman in its account of how the relationship of sanctification to a particular man is secularized, that is, nullified. When Heaven accomplishes the same act of nullification of the existing relationship of sanctification through the husband's death, neither the husband nor the wife participates; when

27

Heaven creates the special circumstance involving levirate connection, no party on earth plays a role.

But even though only the husband may initiate the writ of divorce and have it written and handed over, the Oral Torah provides the wife with important points of participation in the process of ordinary divorce, even when man initiates that process. And the woman's stake in the process correspondingly gains enormous consequence. She has the right to dictate the conditions of delivery. She has the right to be correctly informed, to participate in the transaction as an active player, determining how her half of the matter will be conducted by dictating the circumstances under which she will receive the document. And, above all, because the Oral Torah also imposes the most severe and long-lasting penalties upon a woman whose writ of divorce turns out to be impaired and so invalid, and who on the strength of such a document remarries, the woman must thoughtfully exercise her power within the transaction. So the woman not only is given a role in the process but also a very heavy responsibility in the correct implementation of the transaction. For that reason, she takes anything but a passive role in the matter.

Our special interest focuses upon the way by which the status, or relationship, of sanctification is removed and how the woman reenters secular status of the unattached woman. Here the foci of sages' interest prove consequential, especially when we compare the way in which in the halakhah of Yebamot, Heaven accomplishes the same goal, the desanctification of a woman, with the way in which man does so. For man's part in the matter, everything depends upon a document, which on earth properly done, is ratified in Heaven as an act consequential in the sight of God. A woman enters the relationship of sanctification to a given man through the media specified at tractates Qiddushin and Ketubot. The former identifies as the media of sanctification the willing exchange of money, a writ, or sexual relations with betrothal the intent. The consummation of the union depends, further, on the provision of the marriage-contract, which protects the woman in the event of divorce or the husband's death by providing for alimony. In these transactions, the woman's former status is removed by the provision of a document that nullifies the token of betrothal and the relationship that represents and that brings about the enforcement of the marriage-contract and its provisions. So the document at the end – for which Scripture makes provision – completes the document at the outset, of which Scripture knows nothing, but for which the logic of the transaction, matching beginning to end, surely calls.

Scripture is explicit that at the cessation of the marital bond (for which in Scripture the language of sanctification does not enter) a writ of divorce be handed to the woman. The pertinent verse of Scripture, Deut. 24:1-4, is as follows:

> "When a man takes a wife and marries her, and it happens that she finds no favor in his eyes because he has found some uncleanness in her and he writes her a certificate of divorce, puts it in her hand and sends her out of his house, when she has departed from his house and goes and becomes another man's wife, if the latter husband detests her and writes her a certificate of divorce, puts it in her hand and sends her out of his house, or if the latter husband dies who took her as his wife, then her former husband who divorced her must not take her back to be his wife after she has been defiled; for that is an abomination before the Lord, and you shall not bring sin on the land that the Lord your God is giving you as an inheritance."

Scripture lays emphasis upon the prohibition of a divorced woman, once remarried, to return to the husband who has divorced her. The halakhah of the Oral Torah, by contrast, finds its focus of interest in the subordinated details of the transaction set forth in Scripture.

The wife and the slave are comparable, because by reason of the relationship to the householder, both of them surrender in some measure, partial or entire, their power of intentionality, their unfettered power of free will. But then the contrast has also to be drawn. The slave is never "holy" to the master, and the contrast between the route by which he returns to his prior condition, as a man possessed of free will and no longer subject to the will of another, and the route by which the woman does so, is explicitly drawn. So, as usual, the halakhah contains within itself the results of profound thinking about fundamental questions, and we are fortunate if we may reach only the superficial levels of sages' reflections upon the generative issues of man's this-worldly transactions that bear upon man's relationships with God.

## I.    The Writ of Divorce

### A.    *Transmitting the Writ of Divorce*

**M. 1:1 He who delivers a writ of divorce from overseas must state, "In my presence it was written, and in my presence it was signed." He must state, 'In my presence it was written, and in my presence it was signed,' only in the case of him who delivers a writ of divorce from overseas, and him who takes [one abroad]. And he who delivers [a writ of divorce] from one overseas province to another must state, "In my presence it was written, and in my presence it was signed."**
Y. 1:1 I:3 *He who delivers a writ of divorce from overseas must state, "In my presence it was written by day, and in my presence it was signed by day."*

Y. I:4 *"In my presence it was written especially for her, and in my presence it was signed especially for her."*

M. 1:3 He who delivers a writ of divorce in the Land of Israel does not have to state, "In my presence it was written, and in my presence it was signed." If there are disputants against [the validity of the writ], it is to be confirmed by its signatures. He who delivers a writ of divorce from overseas and cannot say, "In my presence it was written, and in my presence it was signed," if there are witnesses [inscribed] on it – it is to be confirmed by its signatures.

T. 1:1 He who delivers a writ of divorce by boat is equivalent to him who delivers it from abroad [M. Git l:1A]. He has to state, "In my presence it was written, and in my presence it was signed." [He who delivers a writ of divorce] from Transjordan is equivalent to one who delivers a writ of divorce in the Land of Israel, and he does not have to state, "In my presence it was written and in my presence it was sealed" [M. Git. 1:3A]. He who delivers a writ of divorce from overseas lands cannot state, "In my presence it was written, and in my presence it was signed," – if he can confirm it through its signatures, it is valid. And if not, it is invalid [M. Git. 1:3C-E]. One must conclude: They have ruled, He must state, "In my presence it was written, and in my presence it was signed," not to impose a stringent ruling, but to provide for a lenient ruling. He who delivers a writ of divorce from overseas, and it was not written in his presence, and it was not signed in his presence, lo, this one sends it back to its place, and he calls a court in session for that matter, and has it confirmed through its signatures. Then he delivers it again, and states, "I am an agent of a court." In the Land of Israel an agent appoints another agent. At first they would rule, "[He who brings a writ of divorce must testify that in his presence it was written and in his presence it was signed, if he brought it] from one province to another. Then they ruled, From one neighborhood to another.

T. 1:2 A more strict rule applies to [writs of divorce deriving from] overseas than to [writs of divorce deriving from] the Land of Israel, and to [writs of divorce deriving from] the Land of Israel then to [writs of divorce deriving from] overseas. For he who delivers a writ of divorce from overseas must state, "In my presence it was written, and in my presence it was signed." Even though there are disputants [against its validity], it is valid.

T. 1:3 He who brings a writ of divorce from the Land of Israel [and] cannot state, "In my presence it was written, and in my presence it was signed," – if there are witnesses, it is confirmed through its signatures [M. Git. 1:3B-E]. In what way have they ruled, "Let it be confirmed through its signatures?" Witnesses who stated, "This is our handwriting" – it is valid. [If they said], "It is our handwriting, but we do not know either the man or the woman," it is valid. [If they said], "This is not our handwriting," but others give testimony concerning them, that it is their handwriting, or if an example of their handwriting was forthcoming from some other source, it is valid.

M. 1:4 Any sort of writ on which there is a Samaritan witness is invalid, except for writs of divorce for women and writs of emancipation for slaves. All documents which are drawn up in gentile registries, even if their signatures are gentiles, are valid, except for writs of divorce for women and writs of emancipation for slaves.

*Y. 1:4 As regards monetary matters [Samaritans] are suspect, and, [consequently,] as regards their testimony in monetary matters they are deemed invalid [witnesses]. They are not deemed suspect in regard to observing the laws of forbidden connections. And testimony in capital cases is equivalent to testimony in cases involving prohibited connections. [Samaritan testimony is accepted in capital cases.]*

M. 2:1 He who delivers a writ of divorce from overseas and said, "In my presence it was written," but not, "In my presence it was signed," "In my presence it was signed," but not, "In my presence it was written," "In my presence the whole of it was written, but in my presence only part of it was signed," "In my presence part of it was written, but in my presence the whole of it was signed" – it is invalid. [If] one says, "In my presence it was written," and one says, "In my presence it was signed," it is invalid. [If] two say, "In our presence it was written," and one says, "In my presence it was signed," it is invalid. [If] one says, "In my presence it was written," and two say, "In our presence, it was signed," it is valid.

T. 2:1 He who delivers a writ of divorce from overseas and gave it over to the woman, but did not say to her, "In my presence it was written and in my presence it was signed," lo, this one takes it back from her even after three years, and then goes and gives It to her, saying to her, "In my presence it was written, and in my presence it was signed."

T. 2:2 A woman is believed to state, "This is the writ of divorce which you gave to me." [If] it was torn, it is valid. [If] it was ripped up [torn in many places], it is invalid. [If] there is in it a tear made by a court, it is invalid. If one wrote it in this town, he should not sign it in another town. But if he signed it [elsewhere], it is valid. [If] he wrote it in the Land and signed it abroad, he must state, "In my presence it was written, and in my presence it was signed." [If] one wrote it abroad and signed it in the Land of Israel, he does not have to say, "In my presence it was written, and in my presence it was signed."

T. 2:3 If he wrote it with nut shells or pomegranate husks, with congealed blood or congealed milk, on olive leaves or pumpkin leaves, on carob leaves, or on anything which lasts, it is valid [cf. M. Git. 2:3A-G]. [If he wrote it] on leaves of lettuce or onion, on leaves of fenugrec or on vegetables' leaves, on anything which does not last, it is invalid. This is the general principle: [If] he wrote it in anything which lasts on something which does not last, or in something which does not last on something which lasts, it is invalid. [It is not valid] unless he wrote it with something which lasts on something which lasts.

M. 2:6 [If] a minor received [the writ of divorce from the husband,] and then passed the point of maturity, a deaf-mute and he regained the power of speech, a blind man and he regained the power of sight, an idiot and he regained his senses, a gentile and he converted, [it remains] invalid. But [if it was received from the husband] by one of sound senses who then lost the power of speech and then regained his senses, by one who had the power of sight and who was blinded but then recovered the power of sight, by one who was sane and then became insane and regained his sanity, it is valid. This is the governing principle: In any case in which the agent at the outset and at the end was in full command of his senses, it is valid.

M. 2:7 Even women who are not deemed trustworthy to state, "Her husband has died" [M. Yeb. 15:4], are deemed trustworthy to deliver her writ of divorce: her mother-in-law, the daughter of her mother-in-law, her co-wife, her husband's brother's wife, and her husband's daughter. What is the difference between [testifying] when delivering a writ of divorce and [testifying that the husband has] died? For the writing serves as ample evidence [in the case of a writ of divorce]. A woman herself delivers her writ of divorce [from abroad], on condition that she must state, "In my presence it was written, and in my presence it was signed." M. 3:3 He who is bringing a writ of divorce and lost it – [if] he found it on the spot, it is valid. And if not, it is invalid. [If] he found it in a satchel or a bag, if he recognizes it, it is valid. He who is bringing a writ of divorce and left him [the husband] aged or sick hands it over to the woman in the assumption that he [the husband] is [still] alive. An Israelite girl married to a priest, and her husband went overseas, eats heave-offering in the assumption that [her husband] is alive. He who sends his sin-offering from overseas – they offer it up in the assumption that he is alive [cf. M. Tem. 4:1].

T. 2:6 All are believed to deliver a woman's writ of divorce, even her son, even her daughter, and even the five women who are in such a relationship to her that they are not believed to testify that her husband has died are believed to deliver her divorce. her mother-in-law, the daughter of her mother-in-law, her co-wife, her husband's brother's wife, and the daughter of her husband [by another marriage] [M. Git. 2:7A-B].

M. 3:5 He who brings a writ of divorce in the Land of Israel and got sick – lo, this one sends it on by means of someone else. But if he [the husband] had said to him, "Get from her such-and-such an object," he should not send it by means of someone else, for it is not the wish [of the husband] that his bailment should fall into someone else's hands.

T. 2:13 [If the husband said to] bring this writ of divorce to his wife on condition that she give "to my father, or to my brother, two hundred zuz." He [the messenger] has the power to appoint a [messenger]. [If he said,] "...on condition that she give you two hundred zuz," he cannot appoint an agent. For he has relied upon none except this one. [If] he said to him, "Bring this writ of divorce to my wife," he has the power to appoint an agent. [If he said,]

"You bring this writ of divorce to my wife," then he does not have the power to appoint an agent [for the husband] has relied upon no one except this particular man [M. Git. 3:5].

M. 3:6 He who brings a writ of divorce from overseas and got sick appoints a court and sends it [the writ, with someone else]. And he says in their presence, "In my presence it was written, and in my presence it was signed." And the latter does not have to say, "In my presence it was written, and in my presence it was signed." But he merely states, "I am the agent of a court."

B.  *The Writ of Divorce and the Writ of Emancipation of Slaves*

M. 1:4 All the same are writs of divorce for women and writs of emancipation for slaves: They have treated in the same way the one who takes [it] and the one who delivers it. This is one of the ways in which writs of divorce for women and writs of emancipation for slaves are treated as equivalent.

B. 1:3-4 II.1/9A-B: IN THREE ASPECTS WRITS OF DIVORCE FOR WOMEN AND DOCUMENTS OF EMANCIPATION FOR SLAVES ARE EQUIVALENT: IN THE RULE GOVERNING THEIR BEING TAKEN FROM THE LAND OF ISRAEL TO OVERSEAS LOCATIONS OR BRINGING BROUGHT TO THE LAND OF ISRAEL FROM OVERSEAS; IN THE FACT THAT ANY WRIT THAT BEARS THE SIGNATURE OF A SAMARITAN WITNESS IS INVALID EXCEPT FOR WRITS OF DIVORCE FOR WOMEN AND DOCUMENTS OF EMANCIPATION FOR SLAVES; AND ALL DOCUMENTS THAT DERIVE FROM GENTILE ARCHIVES, EVEN THOUGH THE WITNESSES THERETO ARE GENTILES, ARE VALID, EXCEPT FOR WRITS OF DIVORCE FOR WOMEN AND DOCUMENTS OF EMANCIPATION FOR SLAVES.

M. 1:5 Any sort of writ on which there is a Samaritan witness is invalid, except for writs of divorce for women and writs of emancipation for slaves. All documents which are drawn up in gentile registries, even if their signatures are gentiles', are valid, except for writs of divorce for women and writs of emancipation for slaves.

M. 1:6 He who says, "Give this writ of divorce to my wife, and this writ of emancipation to my slave," if he wanted to retract in either case, he may retract for writs of divorce for women but not for writs of emancipation for slaves. For they act to the advantage of another person not in his presence, but they act to his disadvantage only in his presence. For if he wanted not to support his slave, he has the right to make such a decision. [But if he wanted] not to support his wife, he has not got the right [to make such a decision]. He who says, "Give this writ of divorce to my wife and this writ of emancipation to my slave," and who then died – they [to whom he gave the charge] should not give over the documents after his death. [If he said], "Give a maneh to Mr. So-and-so," and then he died, let them give over the money after the man's death.

T. 1:6 He who says, "Give this maneh to So-and-so, which I owe him," "Give this maneh to So-and-so, a bailment which he has in my hands," "Take this maneh to So-and-so, a bailment which he has in my hands," – if he wanted to retract, he may not retract. And he

is responsible to replace it should it be lost, up to that point that he
[to whom it is owing] receives that which belongs to him.

T. 1:7 [He who says], "Take this maneh to So-and-so," "Give this
maneh to So-and-so," – if he wanted to retract, he may retract. [If]
he went and found him dead, let him return the money to the one
who gave it. If he [the one to whom the money is given] should die,
let him hand over the money to the heirs [of the one who originally
gave it].

T. 1:8 [He who said,] "Receive this maneh in behalf of So-and-so,"
"Acquire this gift in behalf of So-and-so," "Receive this writ of gift
for So-and-so," "Acquire this writ of gift for So-and-so," – if he
wanted to retract, he may not retract. [If] he went and found him
dead, let him give it to the heirs. But if after the death of the donee
he made acquisition, he should restore it to the heirs [of the donor],
for they do not acquire an advantage for a deceased person once
death has taken place.

T. 1:9 [If he said], "Carry this maneh to So-and-so," "Take this to
So-and-so," "Let this maneh for So-and-so be in your hand," and he
died, if the heirs [of the sender] wanted to force him [not to deliver
it], they cannot do so. And one need not say, in the case of one who
says, "Acquire possession for him," or who says, "Receive it for
him" [that the rule is the same].

C.  *Preparing a Writ of Divorce*

M. 2:2 [If] it was written by day and signed by day, by night and
signed by night, by night and signed by day [on the next
morning], it is valid. [If it was written] by day and signed by
night, it is invalid.

M. 2:3 With all sorts of things do they write [a writ of divorce]:
with (1) ink, (2) caustic, (3) red dye, (4) gum, (5) copperas, or with
anything which lasts. They do not write [a writ of divorce] with
(1) liquids, or (2) fruit juice, or with anything which does not last.
On anything do they write [a writ of divorce]: (1) on an olive's
leaf, (2) on the horn of a cow, (but he gives the woman the cow)
(3) on the hand of a slave, (but he gives the woman the slave).

T. 2:3 If he wrote it with nut shells or pomegranate husks, with
congealed blood or congealed milk, on olive leaves or pumpkin
leaves, on carob leaves, or on anything which lasts, it is valid [cf. M.
Git. 2:3A-G]. [If he wrote it] on leaves of lettuce or onion, on leaves
of fenugrec or on vegetables' leaves, on anything which does not
last, it is invalid. This is the general principle: [If] he wrote it in
anything which lasts on something which does not last, or in
something which does not last on something which lasts, it is
invalid. [It is not valid] unless he wrote it with something which
lasts on something which lasts.

T. [If] he wrote it for her on the horn of a cow and gave her the cow,
or on the hand of a slave and gave her the slave, she has acquired
possession of these [M. Git. 2:3H-K]. [If] he then said to her, "Lo,
this is your writ of divorce," and the rest of it [the cow, the slave] is
in compensation for the marriage-contract," she has received her
writ of divorce, and she has received her payment of her

marriage-contract. [If he said to her], "Lo, this is your writ of divorce, on condition that you give me back the paper," lo, this one is deemed to have been divorced. "...On condition that the paper is mine," or if he gave her the paper itself [so that the paper was hers to being with], or if she wrote it on her hand, she is not deemed to have been divorced.

T. 2:5 All are valid to receive a woman's writ of divorce [in her behalf], except for a deaf-mute, an idiot, and a minor.

M. 2:4 They do not write [a writ of divorce] on something which is attached to the ground. [If] one wrote it on something attached to the ground, then plucked it up, signed it, and gave it to her, it is valid.

M. 2:5 All are valid for the writing of a writ of divorce, even a deaf-mute, an idiot, or a minor. A woman may write her own writ of divorce, and a man may write his quittance [a receipt for the payment of the marriage contract] , for the confirmation of the writ of divorce is solely through its signatures [of the witnesses]. All are valid for delivering a writ of divorce, except for a deaf-mute, an idiot, and a minor, a blind man, and a gentile.

M. 3:1 Any writ of divorce which is written not for the sake of this particular woman [for whom it is intended] is invalid. How so? [If] one was passing through the market and heard the voice of scribes dictating [to students], "Mr. So-and-so is divorcing Mrs. So-and-so from such-and-such a place," and said, "Why this is my name and the name of my wife" – it is invalid therewith to effect a divorce. Moreover: [If] one wrote a writ of divorce for divorcing his wife therewith and then changed his mind, [and] a fellow townsman found it and said to him, "My name is the same as yours, and my wife's name is the same as your wife's name," it is invalid therewith to effect a divorce. Moreover: [If] one had two wives, and their names were the same, [if] he wrote a writ of divorce to divorce therewith the elder, he shall not divorce the younger with it. Moreover: [If] he said to a scribe, "Write for whichever one I shall decide to divorce," it is invalid therewith to divorce a woman.

T. 2:7 The writ of divorce for a woman which one wrote not for her own name is invalid [cf M. Git. 3:1A], since it says, And he shall write for her (Deut. 24:1] for her in particular. The writ of emancipation of a slave which one wrote not for his own name is invalid, since it says, And not yet ransomed or given her freedom (Lev. 19:20). And below it says, And he shall write to her (Deut. 24:1). Now just as to her stated elsewhere means that it must be for her in particular, so to her stated here must mean that it must be for her in particular. The scroll for a woman accused of adultery which one wrote not for her own name is invalid, since it says, And the priest shall prepare for her this entire Torah (Num. 5:30) – that is all the rites concerning her must be [done] for her sake in particular. [If] the scribe wrote it for her sake, and the witnesses signed it for her sake [in particular], even though they wrote it and signed it and gave it to him and he gave it to her, it is invalid. It is valid only if he [the husband] will say to the scribe, "Write," and to the witnesses, "Sign."

T. 2:8 And not only so, but even if he wrote it in his own hand to the scribe, saying, "Write," and to the witnesses, "Sign," even though they wrote it and signed it and gave it to him and he gave it to her, it is invalid. It is valid only if they hear his [the husband's] voice saying to the scribe, "Write," and to the witnesses, "Sign."

**M. 3:2 He who writes out blank copies of writs of divorce must leave a space for the name of the man, for the name of the woman, and for the date. [If he does so] for bonds of indebtedness, he must leave a space for the lender, the borrower, the sum of money, and the date. [If he does so] for deeds of sale, he must leave a space for the purchaser, the seller, the sum of money, the field, and the date – for good order.**

T. 2:11 A writ of divorce which one lost, and which he found after a while, even though he recognizes its distinguishing traits, is invalid. since distinguishing traits do not apply to writs of divorce. What is the meaning of "after a while"? Sufficient time for someone else to come to that same location. But [if] he handed it over to him in a box, chest, or cupboard, and he locked the door thereof, and then the key was lost even though he found it only after a while it [the writ of divorce] remains valid.

T. 2:12 And three more [cases] did they add [to M. Git. 3:4]: [if] a wild beast was mauling him, or a river was sweeping him away, or a house fell on him, they apply to him the strict rulings applicable to the living and the strict rulings applicable to the dead. An Israelite girl married to a priest, or a priest-girl married to an Israelite does not eat heave-offering [M. Git. 3:4F]. The slave of a priest who fled, and the wife of a priest who rebelled against him [and ran away], lo, these continue to eat heave-offering [in the assumption that the master or husband is yet alive]. A person guilty of manslaughter should not go outside of the frontier of a city of refuge, but should assume that the high priest is yet alive.

**M. 3:7 He who lends money to a priest or to a Levite or to a poor man so that he may set apart [what would be] their [share as heave-offering, tithe, or poor man's tithe, respectively, and sell the heave-offering to another priest or eat the tithe or poor man's tithe, in compensation for this loan] separates the produce in their behalf in the assumption that they are alive. And he does not take account of the possibility that the priest has died, or the Levite, or that the poor man has gotten rich. [If] they died, he has to get permission from [their] heirs [to continue in this way to collect what is owing]. If he lent them this money in the presence of a court, he does not have to get permission from the heirs.**

T. 3:1 He who lends money to a priest and a Levite and a poor man and they died has to get permission from the heirs [of the man to whom he lent the money to continue to collect what is owing to him from heave-offering, tithe, or poorman's tithe] [M. Git. 3:7D].

**M. 3:8 He who put aside produce, so that he may set apart heave-offering and tithes on its account [reckoning that it will serve for these purposes], ...coins, so that he may set apart second tithe on**

its account, he designates produce [as unconsecrated] relying upon them in the assumption that they remain available.

T. 2:9 [If] one borrowed from him a thousand denars with a bond of indebtedness and paid him back, and he now proposes to borrow from him a second time, he should not give him back the first bond of indebtedness, for he weakens the claim of the purchasers.

T. 2:10 [If he] mortgaged a house to him [or] mortgaged a field to him, and he paid him back and proposes to borrow from him a second time – lo, this one should not return him the first bond of mortgage, because he weakens the claim of those who follow him.

T. 3:2 [If] he put aside produce so that he may set apart heave-offering and tithes on its account [reckoning that it will serve for these purposes, coins so that he may set apart second-tithe on its account, he designates produce [as unconsecrated] relying upon them in the assumption that they remain available [M. Git. 3:8A-C]. He does not take account of the possibility that the produce has rotted, that the wine has turned into vinegar, that the coins have gotten rusty. [If] he went and found them rotted, turned into vinegar, or rusted, lo, this one then does take into account that fact. He takes into account the possibility of grain's having rotted during a time sufficient that it rot, for wine, during a time sufficient that it turn into vinegar, for money, during a time sufficient that it rust.

## II. Rules of Agency and Writs of Divorce

M. 4:1 He who sends a writ of divorce to his wife, and overtakes the messenger, or who sent a messenger after him, and said to him, "The writ of divorce which I gave you is null" – lo, this is null. [If] he [the husband] got to his wife first, or [if] he sent a messenger to her, and said to her, "The writ of divorce which I sent to you is null" – lo, this is null. If [this took place] after the writ of divorce reached her possession, he no longer has the power to annul it.

Y. 4:1 I:2 *If one has appointed an agent to bring the writ of divorce, he must hand it over to the wife before two witnesses, and the agent does not count as one of the two. If the agent went to nullify the writ of divorce, he has to do so before two witnesses, and the agent counts as one of the two.*

## III. Rulings Pertinent to the Writ of Divorce Made for Good Order of the World, and Other Rulings in the Same Classification

M. 4:2 At first [the husband] would set up a court in some other place and annul it. Rabban Gamaliel ordained that people should not do so, for the good order of the world. At first he used to change his name and her name, the name of his town and the name of her town [i.e., to give an adopted name]. And Rabban Gamaliel ordained that one should write, "Mr. So-and-so, and whatever alias he has," "Mrs. So-and-so, and whatever alias she has," for the good order of the world.

T. 3:3 [If the husband] got to his wife first, or sent a messenger to her [M. Git. 4:1E-F], [and] said to her, "as to the writ of divorce which I sent you, I don't want you to be divorced with it," lo, this is null [M. Git. 4:1G-H]. At first the husband would set up a court in another place and declare it null [M. Git. 4:2A].

M. 4:3 A widow collects [her marriage contract] from the estate of the orphans only by means of an oath. They held back from imposing the oath on her. Rabban Gamaliel the Elder ordained that she should take any vow the heirs wanted and collect her marriage contract. The witnesses sign the writ of divorce, for the good order of the world. Hillel the Elder ordained the prosbol, for the good order of the world.]

M. 4:7 He who puts his wife away because she has a bad name should not take her back. [If he did so] because of a vow [which she had made], he should not take her back.

T. 3:4 A slave who is taken captive, and they redeemed him as a slave is to be subjugated, and his master is to pay his value. [If he was redeemed,] as a free man, he is not to be subjugated, and his master does not pay his value.

T. 3:5 . What is the sort of vow which requires the examination of a sage? If one said "Qonam be what my wife enjoys of mine, for she has stolen my wallet," "...for she has beaten up my son," [if] he found out that she had not hit him or that she has not stolen it, [he must undergo the examination of a sage for the absolution of his vow]. Under what circumstances? In a case in which he vowed and then divorced her. But if he divorced her and afterward took the vow, he is permitted [to remarry her]. [If] he took a vow to divorce her and changed his mind, he is permitted [to remarry her]. [If] he took a vow to be a Nazirite, or by an offering [Qorban], or by an oath, he is permitted [to remarry her]. On what account did they rule, "He who puts away his wife because of her having a bad name may not remarry her" [M. Git. 4:7A]? For if one puts away his wife because of her having a bad name, and then she is married to someone else and produces a child, and afterward the things said about the first wife turn out to be a joke – if he said, "If I had known that these things were a joke, even if someone had given me a hundred manehs, I should never have divorced her," [then, if he has the power to nullify the divorce and remarry her] the writ of divorce turns out to be invalid, and the offspring [of the second marriage] to be a mamzer. And on what account did they rule, "He who puts away his wife because of a vow may not remarry her" [M. Git. 4:7B]? For, if one puts away his wife because of a vow, and she is married to someone else and she produces a child, . and then the vow should turn out to be null, [if] he said, "If I had known that the vow was null, if someone had given me a hundred manehs, I should never have divorced her," it will turn out that the writ of divorce is invalid, and the offspring a mamzer.

M. 4:8 He who divorces his wife because of sterility may remarry her." [If] she was married to someone else and had children by him, and she then claims payment for her marriage contract – they say to her, "Your silence is better for you than your talking."

M. 4:9 He who sells himself and his children to a gentile – they do not redeem him, but they do redeem the children after their father's death. He who sells his field to a gentile and an Israelite went and purchased it from him – the purchaser brings the fist fruits, on account of the good order of the world.

M. 5:1 As to compensation for damages – they pay out of the highest quality of real estate, and [they pay] a debt out of middling quality of real estate, and [they pay] the marriage contract of a woman out of the poorest quality of real estate.

M. 5:2 They do not exact payment from mortgaged property in a case in which there also is unencumbered property, even if it is of the poorest quality. They exact payment from the property of an estate ["orphans"] only from the poorest quality [real estate].

M. 5:3 They do not exact indemnity for produce consumed ["food eaten by cattle"], or for the improvements made on land, or for the maintenance of a widow or daughters, from mortgaged property – for the good order of the world. He who finds a lost object is not subjected to an oath, for the good order of the world.

M. 5:4 Orphans who boarded with a householder, or for whom their father appointed a guardian – he [who provides for their keep] is liable to separate tithe from their produce. A guardian whom a father of orphans has appointed is to be subjected to an oath. He who imparted uncleanness [to the clean food of someone else], and he who mixed heave-offering into the produce of someone else, and he who mixed another's wine with libation wine – if he did so inadvertently, he is exempt [from punishment]. And if he did so deliberately, he is liable. And priests who deliberately imparted the status of refuse to a sacrifice in the sanctuary are liable.

T. 3:7 At first they ruled, He who causes uncleanness to the clean things of someone else, and he who mixes heave-offering in the produce of someone else – they reverted to rule, Also: he who mixes wine used for idolatrous purposes [in acceptable wine of his fellow] – if he did so inadvertently, he is exempt. If he did so deliberately, he is liable [M. Git. 5:4G-I], for the good order of the world. A. Priests who made a sacrifice refuse [by their improper intention, at the time of slaughtering it, to eat it at the wrong time or in the wrong place], [if they did so] inadvertently, are exempt [M. Git. 5:4J]. [If they did so] deliberately, they are liable, for the good order of the world. A messenger of a court who inflicted a blow by the authority of the court and did bodily harm, [if he did so] inadvertently, he is exempt. [If he did so] deliberately, he is liable, for the good order of the world. An expert physician who prescribed a cure by the authority of a court and did damage, [if he did so] inadvertently, he is exempt. [If he did so] deliberately, he is liable, for the good order of the world.

T. 3:9 He who cuts up the foetus in the womb of the mother did damage – doing so by the authority of the court, [if he did so] inadvertently, he is exempt. [if he did so] deliberately, he is liable, for the good order of the world.

M. 5:5 Testified R. Yohanan b. Gudeggedah concerning (1) a deaf-mute, whose father married her off, that [if she should be divorced], she goes forth with a writ of divorce; and (2) concerning a minor Israelite girl who was married to a priest, that she eats heave-offering, and if she died, her husband inherits her estate; and (3) concerning a stolen beam which one built into his house, that the original owner collects its value – on account of the good order of those who repent; and (4) concerning a stolen sin-offering, that was not publicly known, that it effects atonement – for the good order of the altar.

M. 5:6 The law concerning the usurping occupant did not apply in Judah in the case of those slain in the war. From the time of those slain in the war and thenceforward the law of the usurping occupant did apply. How [does the law apply]? [If] one purchased a property [first] from the usurping occupant and [then] went and [also] purchased it from the householder, his purchase is null. [If he purchased it first] from the householder and [then] went and purchased it from the usurping occupant, his purchase is confirmed. [If] a man purchased it from a man and then purchased it from a woman, his purchase is null. [If] he purchased it from a woman and then purchased it from a man, his purchase is confirmed. This is the first Mishnah. The court after them ruled: He who purchases a property from a usurping occupant pays the owner a fourth of the value. Under what circumstances? When he [the original owner] has not got the means to buy it. But [if] he has got the means to buy it, he takes precedence over all other people. Rabbi called a court into session and they voted that if the property had remained in the hands of the usurping occupant for twelve months, whoever comes first has the right to purchase it. But he pays the owner a quarter of the value.

T. 3:10 The law concerning the usurping occupant does not apply to the Land of Judah, for the sake of securing the settlement of the province [by permitting purchasers freedom from claims against their title to the land bought from a usurper]. ('. Under what circumstances? In the case of those who were slain before the war and in the time of the war [of Bar Kokhba]. But in the case of those who were slain from the war and onward the law of the usurping occupant does apply [M. Git. 5:6B]. As to Galilee, it is always subject to the law of the usurping occupant. He who purchases a field from a usurping occupant and went and purchased it afterward from the householder – his purchase is valid [vs. M. Git. 5:6D-E]. [If he first purchased it] from the householder and then went and purchased it from the usurping occupant, his purchase is null [vs. M. Git. 5:6F]. If the householder made him responsible for it, his purchase is valid. This i., the first Mishnah. L The court which was after them ruled. He who purchased [a property] from a usurping occupant pays to the owner a quarter [M. Git. 5:61-J] – a quarter [of the value, to be paid] in real estate, a quarter in ready money – N and the claim of the owner is uppermost [to decide which he prefers]. /f he has sufficient funds to purchase the field, he takes precedence over anyone else. Rabbi called a court into session, and they voted that, if the field had remained in the possession of the usurping occupant for twelve months, then whoever comes first has the right to purchase it. [Nonetheless the purchaser] pays the owner a quarter of the value [M. Git. 5:6N-O], [either] a quarter in land, [or] a quarter in ready money. And the claim of the owner is uppermost. If [the one from whom the field was seized] has sufficient funds to purchase the field he takes precedence over anyone else.

T. 3:11 Share-croppers, tenant-farmers, and guardians are not subject to the law of the usurping occupant. He who takes over a field in payment of a debt, [or] in payment of a tax-debt payable in installments – they are not subject to the law of the usurping occupant. As to the collection of the tax itself: they wait for the owner [to redeem it] for twelve months.

M. 5:7 A deaf-mute makes signs and receives signs. in the case of movables. And as to little children: Their purchase is valid and their sale is valid in the case of movables.

T. 3:12 As to children. their purchase is valid, and their sale is valid in the case of movables [M. Git. 5:7D-E], but not in the case of real estate.

M. 5:8 And these rules did they state in the interests of peace: A priest reads first, and afterward a Levite, and afterward an Israelite – in the interests of peace. They prepare an meal of commingling for purposes of the Sabbath in the house where it was first placed – in the interests of peace. A well nearest to the stream is filled first – in the interests of peace. Traps for wild beasts, fowl, and fish are subject to the rules against stealing – in the interests of peace. Something found by a deaf-mute, an idiot, and a minor is subject to the rule against stealing – in the interests of peace. A poor man beating the top of an olive tree – what is under it [the tree] is subject to the rule against stealing – in the interests of peace. They do not prevent poor gentiles from collecting produce under the laws of Gleanings, the Forgotten Sheaf, and the Corner of the Field – in the interests of peace.

T. 3:13 A poor man who takes them [olives which he gleans from a tree] in his hand and throws them down one by one – what is under it [the tree] is wholly subject to the prohibition against thievery [cf M. Git. 5:81-K]. A city in which Israelites and gentiles live – the collectors of funds for the support of the poor collect equally from Israelites and from gentiles, for the sake of peace. They provide support for the poor of the gentiles along with the poor of Israel, for the sake of peace.

T. 3:14 They make a lament for, and bury, gentile dead, for the sake of peace. They express condolences to gentile mourners, for the sake of peace.

M. 5:9 A woman lends a sifter, sieve, handmill, or oven to her neighbor who is suspected of transgressing the law of the Seventh Year, but she should not winnow or grind wheat with her. The wife of an associate meticulous about cultic purity at home [haber] lends the wife of an outsider a sifter and sieve. She sifts, winnows, grinds, and sifts wheat with her. But once she has poured water into the flour, she may not come near her, for they do not give assistance to transgressors. And all of these rules they stated only in the interests of peace. They give assistance to

gentiles in the Seventh Year but not Israelites. And they inquire
after their welfare – in the interests of peace.

## IV.   The Slave

M. 4:4 A slave who was taken captive, and they redeemed him – if
as a slave, he is to be kept as a slave; if a freeman, he is not to be
enslaved. A slave who was made over as security for a debt by his
master to others and whom the master [then] freed – legally, the
slave is not liable for anything. But for the good order of the
world, they force his master to free him. And he [the slave] writes
a bond for his purchase price.

*Y. 4:4 I:4 A proselyte who died, whose estate Israelites took over – if there
were slaves in the estate, whether adult or minor, they go forth to freedom.
[They are freed when the owner dies, prior to Israelite entry into the
property.]*

M. 4:5 He who is half-slave and half-free works for his master one
day and for himself one day for the good order of the world, they
force his master to free him. And he [the slave] writes him a bond
covering half his value.

M. 4:6 He who sells his slaves to a gentile, or to someone who
lives abroad – he [the slave] has gone forth a free man. They do
not redeem captives for more than they are worth, for the good
order of the world. And they do not help captives to flee, for the
good order of the world.

M. 4:9 He who sells himself and his children to a gentile – they do
not redeem him, but they do redeem the children after their
father's death. He who sells his field to a gentile and an Israelite
purchased it from him – the purchaser brings the first fruits, on
account of the good order of the world.

## V.   The Wife's Receipt of the Writ of Divorce

M. 6:1 He who says, "Receive this writ of divorce for my wife," or,
"Take this writ of divorce to my wife," if he wanted to retract,
may retract. The woman who said, "Receive my writ of divorce in
my behalf," if he [the husband] wanted to retract, he may not
retract. Therefore if the husband said to him, "I do not want you
to receive it for her, but bring and give it to her," if he wanted to
retract, he may retract.

T. 4:1 [The woman who said to a messenger], "Receive my writ of
divorce in my behalf," and [the messenger said to the husband],
"Your wife said, 'Receive my writ of divorce in my behalf,'" "Bring
[my writ of divorce to me]," and, [the messenger reported to the
husband that she had said,] "Bring it to her," . "Receive it for her,"
and, "Make acquisition of it for her" – . if he wanted to retract, he
may not retract [cf. M. Git. 6:1].

M. 6:2 The woman who said, "Receive my writ of divorce in my
behalf," requires two sets of witnesses: two who say, "In our
presence she made the statement," and two who say, "In our
presence he [the messenger] received and tore it up." Even if the
first set of witnesses are the same as the second set of witnesses,

or there was one of the first set of witnesses and another in the second set of witnesses with one joined with each of them. A betrothed girl – she and her father receive her writ of divorce.

T. 4:2 [If the wife said], "Receive my writ of divorce for me," and "Your wife said, 'Receive my writ of divorce for me,'" "Receive it for me," and, "Your wife said, 'Bring me my writ of divorce...'" "Take it," "Carry it," and, "Give it to her," "Receive it in her behalf," and "Make acquisition of it in her behalf," if he wanted to retract, he may retract. [If she said], "Carry my writ of divorce to me," "Take my writ of divorce to me," "Let my writ of divorce be in your hand for me," it is equivalent to her saying, "Receive my writ of divorce in my behalf." [He who says], "Bring a writ of divorce of your wife," "...a writ of divorce of your daughter," "...a writ of divorce of your sister," and he [to whom it is said] went and gave it to her, it is invalid. [If] they said to him, "Shall we write a writ of divorce for your wife," "Here is a writ of divorce for your wife," "...a writ of divorce for your daughter," "...a writ of divorce for your sister," and he went and delivered it to her, it is valid. Even if the first witnesses are the same as the last ones, or there was one of the first and one of the last even if they are brothers, and a third party joins together with them [M. Git. 6:2E-F]. A minor who knows who to take care of her writ of divorce, lo, this one may be divorced [cf. M. Git. 6:2K]. But she does not [have the power to] appoint a messenger until she produces two pubic hairs.

T. 4:3 What is the sort of minor who knows how to take care of her writ of divorce [M. Git. 6:2K]? This is any girl to whom they give her writ of divorce or some other object and who returns it after a while.

M. 6:3 A minor girl who said, "Receive my writ of divorce for me" – it is not a valid writ of divorce until it reaches her hand. Therefore if the husband wanted to retract, he may retract. for a minor cannot appoint a valid messenger. But if the girl's father said to him, "Go and receive my daughter's writ of divorce in her behalf," if he [the husband] wanted to retract, he may not retract. He who says, "Give this writ of divorce to my wife in such-and-such a place," and he [the messenger] delivered it to her in some other place – it is invalid. [If he said], "Lo, she is in such-and-such a place," and he gave it to her in some other place, it is valid. The woman who said, "Receive my writ of divorce for me in such-and-such a place," and he [the messenger] received it for her in some other place – it is invalid.

T. 4:4 The woman who said, ' 'Receive my writ of divorce for me in such and such a place," and he received it for her in some other place – it is invalid. "Bring me my writ of divorce from such and such a place," and he brought it to her from some other place – it is valid [M. Git. 6:3K-0]. But in the case of all of them she is divorced, unless [the husband said], "I want you to receive it for her only in such-and-such a place."

M. 6:4 [If she said to an agent,] "Bring me writ of divorce," she retains the right to eat food in the status of heave-offering until the writ of divorce reaches her. "Receive my writ of divorce in my behalf," she is prohibited from eating food in the status of heave-offering from that point. "Receive my writ of divorce for me in such-and-such a place" – she continues to have the right to eat food in the status of heave-offering until [the messenger with a writ of divorce] reaches that place.

## VI.  The Husband's Instructions on the Preparation & Delivery of the Writ

### A.   *Instructing Agents to Prepare the Writ*

M. 6:5 He who says, "Write a writ of divorce and give it to my wife," "Divorce her," "Write a letter and give it to her," lo, these [to whom he spoke] should write and give it to her. [If he said,] "Free her," "Feed her," "Do what is customary for her," "Do what is appropriate for her," he has said nothing whatsoever. At first they ruled, "He who goes out in chains and said, 'Write a writ of divorce for my wife' – lo, these should write and deliver it to her." They reverted to rule, "Also: He who is taking leave by sea or going forth in a caravan [may give the same valid instructions]."

B.  6:5AA-I I:1/65B [IF HE SAID,] "SEND HER OUT," "LET HER GO," "DRIVE HER OUT," THEY SHOULD GO AND WRITE IT AND GIVE IT TO HER. IF HE SAID, "RELEASE HER," "PROVIDE FOR HER," "DO WHAT IS CUSTOMARY FOR HER," HE HAS SAID NOTHING.

M. 6:6 He who had been cast into a pit and said, "Whoever hears his [my] voice – let him write a writ of divorce for his [my] wife" – lo, these should write and deliver it to her. A healthy man who said, "Write a writ of divorce for my wife" – his intention was to tease her. There was the case of a healthy man who said, "Write a writ of divorce for my wife," and then went up to the rooftop and fell over and died – if he fell because of his own action, lo, this is a writ of divorce. If the wind pushed him off, it is no writ of divorce.

T. 4:8 A. [If a man] was afraid and shouting from the top of a mountain saying, "Whoever hears my voice – let him write a writ of divorce to my wife," lo, these should write it and hand it over [cf M. Git. 6:5-6]. A healthy man who said, "Write a writ of divorce for my wife, ' ' and who went up to the roof-top and fell down – they write and hand it over to her so long as he is yet breathing.

M. 6:7 [If] he said to two men, "Give a writ of divorce to my wife," or to three, "Write a writ of divorce and give it to my wife," lo, these should write and give it to her. If he said to ten men, "Write a writ of divorce for my wife," one should write it, and two should sign it as witnesses. [If he said], "All of you write it," one of them writes it, and all of them sign it. Therefore if one of them died, lo, this is an invalid writ of divorce.

T. 4:5 He who says, "Banish my wife," – they write and hand over to her a writ of divorce. [If he said], "Lo, this is your writ of divorce," and she said, "Hand it over to so-and-so," – she is not divorced.. [If she added,] "...so that he may receive it in my behalf," lo, she is divorced.

T. 4:6 [If] he said to two, "Give a writ of divorce to my wife," or to three, "Write a writ of divorce and give it to my wife," "Write and give a writ of divorce to my wife," they write and hand it over to her [M. Git. 6:7A-C]. If they do not know how to write it, let them learn how to do so.

T. 4:7 [If] they know the man but do not know the wife, they write and hand it over. [If] they know the wife and do not know the man, they write it but do not hand it over. [If] he said, "Write it," but did not say, "Give it over," even though they know both of them, they write it but do not hand it over.

**M. 7:1 He who was seized by delirium and said, "Write a writ of divorce for my wife," has said nothing whatsoever. [If] he said, "Write a writ of divorce for my wife," and [then] delirium seized him, and then he said, "Do not write it," his second statement is nothing. [If] he lost the power of speech, and they said to him, "Shall we write a writ of divorce for your wife," and he nodded his head, they test him three times. If he said for no, "No," and for yes, "Yes," lo, these should write and deliver the writ of divorce to his wife.**

T. 5:1 [If a man] was crucified or hacked up, and he gave a sign to write a writ of divorce to his wife, they write and hand it over to her, so long as he is breathing [cf. M. Git. 6:6]. [If] he was ill and struck dumb, and they said to him "Shall we write a writ of divorce for your wife," and he nodded his head, they test him three times. If he said for no, "No," and for yes, "Yes" [M . 7:1 D-F], his words are valid. Just as they test him as to a writ of divorce, so they test him as to purchases, gifts, inheritances, and statements of testimony.

**M. 7:2 [If] they said to him, "Shall we write a writ of divorce for your wife?" and he said to them, "Write," [if] they then instructed a scribe and he wrote it, and witnesses and they signed it, even though they wrote it and signed it and delivered it to him, and he handed it over to her, lo, this writ of divorce is null, unless he himself says to the scribe, "Write," and to the witnesses, "Sign."**

B. *The Conditional Writ of Divorce*

**M. 7:3 [If he said], "This is your writ of divorce if I die," "This is your writ of divorce if I die from this ailment," "This is your writ of divorce effective after death," he has said nothing. [If he said, "This is your writ of divorce] effective today if I die," "Effective now if I die," lo, this is a valid writ of divorce. [If he said, "Lo, this is your writ of divorce] effective now and after death," it is a writ of divorce and not a writ of divorce. If he dies, [the widow] performs the rite of removing the shoe but does not enter into levirate marriage. [If he said,] "This is your writ of divorce effective today if I die from this illness," and then he arose and went about in the market, then fell ill and died – they make an estimate of his situation. If he died on account of the first ailment, lo, this is a valid writ of divorce. And if not, it is not a valid writ of divorce.**

T. 5:2 "This is your writ of divorce, effective today, if I die from this illness" [M. Git. 7:3H], "If I die from this illness, lo, this is your writ of divorce effective today," his statement is confirmed [M. Git. 7:3E]. "This is your writ of divorce effective today if I die from this illness," if a house fell on him, or a snake bit him, it is not a writ of divorce. For he did not die of that particular ailment. [If he said, "Lo, this is your writ of divorce], if I do not arise from this ailment," if the house fell on him, or a snake bit him, lo, this is a valid writ of divorce. For in point of fact he did not arise from that illness.

**M. 7:4 She should not afterward continue together with him except in the presence of witnesses, even a slave, even a girl servant, except for her own slave girl, because she is shameless before her slave girl.**

T. 5:4 If they saw that she continued to be with him alone in the dark, or that she slept with him at the foot of the bed, even if he was awake and she was asleep, or he was asleep and she was awake, they do not take account of the possibility that they did some other sort of business, but they do take account solely of the possibility of their having had sexual relations, and they do not take account of the possibility of sexual relations for betrothal.

**M. 7:5 "Lo, this is your writ of divorce on condition that you pay me two hundred zuz," lo, this one is divorced, and she should pay the money. "...on condition that you pay me within thirty days from now," if she paid him during the period of thirty days, she is divorced. And if not, she is not divorced.**

T. 4:9 [If] he said to two men, "Give a writ of divorce to my wife on condition that she wait for me two years [without remarrying]," and then he went and said to two others, "Give a writ of divorce to my wife on condition that she pay me two hundred zuz," the instructions which he gave at the end do not nullify the instructions he gave at the outset. But the choice is hers: If she wanted, she may wait two years, and if she wanted, she may pay off the two hundred zuz [cf: M. Git. 7:5A-B].

T. 4:10 [If] he said to two men, "Give a writ of divorce to my wife on condition that she wait for me two years," and then he went and said to two others, "Give a writ of divorce to my wife on condition that she wait for me three years," the instructions which he gave at the end do nullify the instructions he gave at the outset. And one of the former group and one of the latter group do not join together to deliver her writ of divorce to her. [If he said], "Lo, this is your writ of divorce, on condition that you not have sexual relations with so-and-so," lo, this is a valid writ of divorce, and he does not have to take account of the possibility that she will go and have sexual relations with him. [If he said, "Lo, this is your writ of divorce] on condition that you will marry and have sexual relations with father," or, "with my brother," lo, this one should not remarry, [but if she did remarry], she should not go forth. "...on condition that you have sexual relations with so-and-so," if she had sexual relations with him, lo, this is a valid writ of divorce, and if not, it is not a valid writ of divorce.

T. 5:5 [If the husband said,] "Lo, this is your writ of divorce, on condition that you pay me two hundred zuz'" [M. Git. 7:5A], and he died, if she paid the money, she is not subject to the Levir. And if not, she is subject to the Levir. "Lo this is your writ of divorce, on condition that you pay me two hundred zuz," and the writ of divorce was ripped up or lost – lo, this is a valid writ of divorce. For he who says, "On condition...," is equivalent to one who says "Effective immediately." But she should not remarry before she pays the money. "...when you will pay me two hundred zuz," and the writ of divorce was ripped up or lost, if she had paid over the money, lo, this is a valid writ of divorce. And if not, it is not a valid writ of divorce. [If he said,] "Lo, this is your writ of divorce on condition that you pay me two hundred zuz," and he went and said to her, "Lo, this is your writ of divorce effective immediately," he has said nothing whatsoever. What should he do? Let him take it back from her and go and hand it over to her again and say to her, "Lo, this is your writ of divorce effective immediately."

**M. 7:6 "Lo, this is your writ of divorce on condition that you serve my father" – "...on condition that you give suck to my son" – how long must she give suck to him [for the writ to remain valid]? Two years. If the son died, or the father died, lo, this is a valid writ of divorce. [If he said,] "Lo, this is your writ of divorce on condition that you serve my father for two years," "On condition that you give suck to my son for two years," if the son died, or if the father died, or if the father said, "I don't want her to serve me," [if this is] not because of provocation [on the woman's part], it is not a writ of divorce.**

T. 4:11 "Lo, this is your writ of divorce on condition that you eat pork," and, if she was a non-priest, "On condition that you eat heave-offering," and, if she was a Nazirite-girl, "On condition that you drink wine," if she ate or drank [what he specified] lo, this is a valid writ of divorce . And if not, it is not a valid writ of divorce.

T. 5:6 ' 'Lo, this is your writ of divorce, on condition that you serve father," [M. Git. 7:6A-B], or "...on condition that you give suck to my son," [if] she served him a single hour or gave suck to him a single hour, lo, this is a valid writ of divorce... "...on condition that you give suck to my son."

**M. 7:7 "Lo, this is your writ of divorce, if I do not return within thirty days," and he was going from Judah to Galilee, [if] he reached Antipatris and came home, his condition is null. "Lo, this is your writ of divorce, if I do not return within thirty days," and he was going from Galilee to Judah, [if] he reached Kepar Otenai and came home, his condition is null. "Lo, this is your writ of divorce, if I do not return within thirty days," and he was going overseas, [if] he reached Akko and came home, his condition is null. "Lo, this is your writ of divorce if I remain away from your presence for thirty days," if he was coming and going, coming and going, since he did not continue together with her, lo, this is a writ of divorce.**

T. 4:12 He who says to his wife, "Lo, here is your writ of divorce [effective] one hour before his [my] death," and so, he who says to his servant-girl, "Lo, here is your writ of emancipation [effective] one hour before his [my] death," lo, these women [if married to or owned by a priest] should not eat food in the status of heave-offering, lest the man die an hour later.

T. 4:13 [If] he said to ten men, "Give a writ of divorce to my wife," one of them takes it in behalf of all of them... [If he said,] "All of you take it, one of them hands it over in the presence of all of them. Therefore if one of them died, lo, this is an invalid writ of divorce [M. Git. 7:7G].

T. 5:7 Kepar 'Otenai is in Galilee. Antipatris is in Judah. As to the area between them, they assign it to its more stringent status: she is divorced and not divorced. If he said, "For I am going from Judah to Galilee," if he reached Antipatris and went back, his condition is null. "...I am going from Galilee to Judah," and he reached Kepar 'Otenai and went back, his condition is null. "...I am going overseas," and he reached Akko and came back his condition is null. "...1 am sailing on the Great Sea," and he reached the place at from which the ships sail and went back, his condition is null [cf. M. Git. 7:7].

T. 5:8 "Lo, this is your writ of divorce, if I am apart from your presence for thirty days," [if] he was coming and going, coming and going, since he did not continue with her, lo, this is a writ of divorce [M. Git. 7:7M-P]. But she should not remarry until he is absent for thirty days

**M. 7:8 "Lo, this is your writ of divorce, if I do not come back within twelve months," and he died within twelve months, it is no writ of divorce. "Lo, this is your writ of divorce effective now, if I do not come back here in twelve months," and he died within twelve months, lo, this is a valid writ of divorce.**

T. 5:9 "Lo this is your writ of divorce if I do not come back in twelve months," and he died during the twelve months [M. Git. 7:8A – B] – she should not remarry [without dealing with the levir]. And our rabbis instructed her to remarry. But if the writ of divorce was torn up or lost during the twelvemonth-period, it is not a writ of divorce. [If this happened] after the twelve month period, lo, this is a valid writ of divorce.

T. 5:10 "Lo this is your writ of divorce, on condition that you give me two hundred zuz," and then he went and said to her, "Lo, they are forgiven you," he has said nothing. What should he do? He should take them from her and then go and return them to her, and at that point he should say to her, "Lo, they are forgiven to you."

T. 5:11 "Lo, this is your writ of divorce, on condition that you never again go to your father's house," "On condition that you never again drink wine," – it is not a writ of divorce, for she might go to her father's house or drink wine. "...On condition that you not go to your father's house for thirty days," "On condition that you not drink wine for thirty days," – lo, this is a valid writ of divorce. And one does not take account of the possibility that she might go or might drink. "Lo, this is your writ of divorce on condition that you not climb this tree," and "...on condition that you not go over this wall," if the tree was cut down or the wall torn down, lo, this is a valid writ of divorce. "...on condition that you climb this tree," or, "that you climb over this wall," if the tree was cut down or the wall torn down, lo, this is not a valid writ of divorce.

T. 5:12 "...on condition that you not fly in the air," "...on condition that you not cross over the Great Sea by foot," lo, this is a writ of divorce... "...on condition that you cross the Great Sea by foot," it is not a valid writ of divorce.

M. 7:9 If I do not come back within twelve months, write and hand over a writ of divorce to my wife" – [if] they wrote a writ of divorce during twelve months and handed it over at the end of the twelve months, it is not a valid writ of divorce. "Write and hand over a writ of divorce to my wife, if I do not return within twelve months," [if] they wrote it during the twelve months and handed it over after twelve months, it is not a valid writ of divorce. [If] they wrote a writ of divorce after twelve months and handed it over after twelve months, and then he died, if the writ of divorce came before death, lo, it is a valid writ of divorce. But if the death came before the writ of divorce, it is not a valid writ of divorce. And if the facts are not known, this is the case of which they have said, "She is divorced and not divorced."

T. 7:7 A writ which has no witnesses, but which they gave to her in the presence of witnesses, is valid.

## VII.   The Impaired Writ of Divorce

### A.   *The Writ of Divorce that is Subject to Doubt*

M. 8:1 He who threw a writ of divorce to his wife, and she was in her own house or in her own courtyard – lo, this one is divorced. [If] he threw it to her in his house or in his courtyard, even if it [the writ] is with her in bed, she is not divorced. [If he threw it] into her bosom or into her basket, she is divorced.

M. 8:2 [If] he said to her, "Take this bond of indebtedness," or if she found it behind him and read it, and lo, it is her writ of divorce, it is not a valid writ of divorce – until he says to her, "Here is your writ of divorce." [If] he put it into her hand while she is sleeping, [then] she woke up, read it, and lo, it is her writ of divorce, it is not a valid writ of divorce – until he will say to her, "Here is your writ of divorce." [If] she was standing in public domain and he threw it to her, [if] it is nearer to her, she is divorced. [If] it is nearer to him, she is not divorced. [If] it is exactly halfway, she is divorced and not divorced.

M. 8:3 And so is the rule with regard to betrothals. And so is the rule with regard to a debt. [If] the creditor said to him, "Throw me [what you owe] me [as a debt]," and he threw it to him, [if] it is closer to the lender, the borrower has the advantage. [If] it is closer to the borrower, the borrower is liable. [If] it is exactly in between, both of them divide [the sum, should it be lost]. [If the wife] was standing on the rooftop and he threw it to her, once it has reached the airspace of the roof, lo, this woman is divorced. [If] he is above and she is below and he threw it to her, once it has left the domain of the roof, [even if] it should be blotted out or burned, lo, this woman is divorced.

T. 6:2 A. If she was standing on the roof-top and he threw it to her, once it has reached the airspace of the roof, lo, she is divorced. [If] he is above and she is below, and he threw it to her, once it has gone forth from the domain of the roof, [if it should be] blotted out or burned, lo, she is divorced [M. Git. 8:3G-L]. [If he said to her,] "Lo, this is your writ of divorce," and she took it from his hand and tossed it into the sea or a river, and he then went and said to her, "It really was an invalid writ," "It was blank paper," he has not got the power to prohibit her [from remarrying].

B.   *The Writ of Divorce that is Subject to Flaws or Imperfections*

M. 8:5 **[If] he wrote [the writ of divorce dating it] according to an era which is not applicable, for example, according to the era of the Medes, according to the era of the Greeks, according to the building of the Temple, according to the destruction of the Temple, [if] he was in the east and wrote, "In the west," in the west and wrote, "In the east," she goes forth from this one [whom she married on the strength of the divorce from the former husband] and from that one [the first husband]. And she requires a writ of divorce from this one and from that one. And she has no claim on the payment of her marriage contract, or on the usufruct [of plucking property], or to alimony, or to indemnity [for loss on her plucking property], either against this one or against that one. If she collected [such payment] from this one or from that one, she must return what she has collected. And the offspring from either marriage is a mamzer. And neither one nor the other contracts uncleanness from her [if they are priests, and she should die and require burial]. And neither this one nor the other gains possession of what she may find, or of the fruit of her labor, or is vested with the right to abrogate her vows. [If] she was an Israelite girl, she is invalidated from marrying into the priesthood. [If she was] a Levite girl, [she is invalidated] from eating tithe. [If she was] a priest girl, she is invalidated from eating heave-offering. And the heirs neither of this one nor of that one inherit her marriage contract. And if they died, the brothers of this one and the brothers of that one perform the rite of rite of removing the shoe but do not enter into levirate marriage. [If] he changed his name or her name, the name of his town or the name of her town, she goes forth from this one and from that one. And all these [above] conditions apply to her.**

T. 6:4 [If] he wrote it in accord with the date of a province, in accord with the dating of a hyparchy, or if there were two kings in power, and he wrote the writ of divorce bearing the date of only one of them, it is valid. [If he wrote it in accord] with the date of the father of his [the reigning emperor's] father, it is valid. If he wrote it in accord with the date of the founder of the dynasty [e.g., Arsaces], it is invalid. If they were called by the same name as the founder of the dynasty [e.g., Arsaces IX], it is valid.

T. 6:4 A male convert who changed his [Israelite] name for a gentile name – it is valid. And so you rule in the case of a female convert. Writs of divorce which come from abroad, even though the names written in them are gentile names, are valid, because Israelites overseas use names which are gentile names [cf. M. Git. 8:5R].

T. 6:5 [If] a man has two wives, one in Judah and one in Galilee, and he has two names, one used in Judah and one used in Galilee [if] he divorced his wife in Judah by the name he uses in Galilee, and his wife in Galilee by the name he uses in Judah, it is invalid. If [however] he said, "1, Mr. So and so, from Judah, with the name I use in Galilee, and married to a woman in Galilee," or if he was somewhere else [than Judah or Galilee] and wrote it in the name [used in either one of them], it is valid.

M. 8:6 All those prohibited relationships of which they have said that their co-wives are permitted [to remarry without levirate marriage], [if] these co-wives went and got married and this [woman who is in a prohibited relationship] turns out to be barren – she goes forth from this one and from that one. And all the above conditions apply.

M. 8:7 He who marries his deceased childless brother's widow, and her co-wife went off and married someone else, and this one turned out to be barren – she [the co-wife] goes forth from this one and from that one. And all the above conditions apply.

M. 8:8 [If] the scribe wrote a writ of divorce for the man and a quittance [receipt given to the husband for her marriage contract payment] for the woman, and he erred and gave the writ of divorce to the woman and the quittance to the man, and they then exchanged them for one another, and [if] after a while, lo, the writ of divorce turns up in the hand of the man, and the quittance in the hand of the woman – she goes forth from this one and from that one. And all the above conditions apply. [If] he wrote [a writ of divorce] to divorce his wife and changed his mind, even though he gave it to her on a condition, and the condition was not carried out [so that she is not divorced], he has not invalidated her from marrying into the priesthood.

M. 8:9 He who divorced his wife and spent a night with her in an inn – she requires a second writ of divorce from him. Under what circumstances? When she was divorced following consummation of the marriage. But they concur in the case of one divorced after betrothal alone, that she does not require a second writ of divorce from him. For he is not yet shameless before her. If he married her on the strength of [her having been divorced from a former husband] by a "bald" [defectively witnessed] writ of divorce, she goes forth from this one and from that one. And all the above conditions apply.

Y. 8:9 I:2 *He who divorces his wife – she should not live alongside him either in the same courtyard or in the same locale. If the courtyard belonged to the wife, the man moves out. If it belonged to the husband, the wife moves out. If it belonged to both of them, who moves out because of the other? The woman moves out because of the man. But if they are able to do so, [rather than moving out,] this one makes an opening [in the courtyard] in one direction, and that one makes an opening in the other direction. Under what circumstances? In a case in which they were actually married. But if they were not married, it is not called for. And in the case of a priest girl, even if they were not married, [they may not live side by side].*

C.  *An Invalidating Restriction in a Writ of Divorce*

M. 9:1 He who divorces his wife and said to her, "Lo, you are permitted [to marry] any man except for So-and-so" – sages forbid it. What should he do [in such a circumstance]? He should take it back from her and go and give it to her again, and say to her, "Lo, you are permitted to marry any man." But if he wrote it into the body of the writ, it is invalid.

M. 9:2 [If the husband said,] "Lo, you are permitted to any man, except for my father, and your father, my brother, your brother, a slave, or a gentile," or any man to whom she cannot become betrothed – it is valid. "Lo, you are permitted to any man, except, in the case of a widow, to a high priest, in the case of a divorcée or a woman who has undergone the rite of removing the shoe, to an ordinary priest, a mamzer girl or a netin girl to an Israelite, an Israelite girl to a mamzer or to a netin," or any man to whom she can become betrothed, even though it is in transgression [for her to do so] – it is invalid.

M. 9:3 The text of the writ of divorce [is as follows]: "Lo, you are permitted to any man." The text of a writ of emancipation [is as follows]: "Lo, you are free, lo, you are your own [possession]" [cf. Deut. 21:14].

M. 9:4 There are three writs of divorce which are invalid, but if the wife [subsequently] remarried [on the strength of those documents], the offspring [nonetheless] is valid: [If] he wrote it in his own handwriting, but there are no witnesses on it – if there are witnesses on it, but it is not dated; if it is dated, but there is only a single witness – lo, these are three kinds of invalid writs of divorce, but if the wife [subsequently] remarried, the offspring is valid.

D.  *Confusing Writs of Divorce*

M. 9:5 Two [with identical names] who sent [to their wives, also bearing identical names] two writs of divorce [which were] identical, and which were mixed up – they give both of them to this one and both of them to that one. Therefore if one of them was lost, lo, the second one is null. Five who wrote jointly in one [and the same] bill of divorce [bearing a single date]: "Mr. So-and-so divorces Mrs. Such-and-such," "Mr. So-and-so divorces Mrs. Such-and-such," [..., and so on, five times], and there are witnesses below – all of them are valid. And let it be given over to each one. [If] the formula was written [anew in full] for each of them, and there are witnesses below – that with which the names of the witnesses are read is valid.

B. 9:5 II.2 87A FIVE MEN WHO WROTE JOINTLY IN A WRIT OF DIVORCE, "WE, MR. SO-AND-SO, AND MR. SO-AND-SO, AND MR. SO-AND-SO, AND MR. SO-AND-SO, AND MR. SO-AND-SO, DIVORCE OUR WIVES, MRS. SUCH-AND-SUCH, AND MRS. SUCH-AND-SUCH, AND MRS. SUCH-AND-SUCH, AND MRS. SUCH-AND-SUCH, AND MRS. SUCH-AND-SUCH, WITH MR. SO-

AND-SO DIVORCING MRS. SUCH-AND-SUCH, AND SO FOR THE REST, AND THE WHOLE HAS A SINGLE DATE, WITH WITNESSES SIGNING BELOW, ALL ARE VALID, AND THE DOCUMENT IS HANDED OVER TO EACH ONE. IF THERE IS A SEPARATE DATE FOR EACH ONE, OR SPACE BETWEEN ONE ANOTHER, WITH THE WITNESSES SIGNED AT THE BOTTOM, THE ONE WITH WHICH THE SIGNATURES ATTACHED ARE READ IS VALID.

**M. 9:6 Two writs of divorce which one wrote side by side, and [the signatures of] two witnesses, [written in] Hebrew, run from under this one [on the right] to under that one [on the left], and [the signatures of] two witnesses, [written in] Greek, run from under this one [left] to under that one [right], that with which the first witnesses' [signatures] are read is valid. [If the signatures of] one, [written in Hebrew], and one [written in] Greek, one [written in] Hebrew and one witness [written in Greek] run from under this one to under that one, both of them are invalid.**

T. 7:11 [If] the names of the witnesses were separated from the body of the writ of divorce by a distance of two lines, it is invalid. [If the space between the body of the writ and the signatures of the witnesses is] less than this, it is valid [cf M. Git. 9:6]. A writ of divorce on which five witnesses signed and of which the first three turn out to be invalid – the testimony [of the document] is confirmed by the remainder of the witnesses. A writ of divorce which was written in five languages, and which five witnesses signed in five languages, is invalid. [If] it was torn, it is valid. [If] it was torn with the sort of tear made by a court, it is invalid.

T. 7:12 [If] it was eaten by moths or rotted or was made as full of holes as a sieve, it is valid. [If] it was erased or faded but its impression remains, [if] one can read it, it is valid... If not, it is invalid.

T. 7:13 "I witness it," "I signed it as a witness," if an example of their handwriting is available from some other source, it is valid. And if not, it is invalid.

**M. 9:7 [If] one left over part [of the text of] the writ of divorce and wrote it on the second page, and the witnesses are below, it is valid. [If] the witnesses signed at the top of the page, on the side, or on the backside, in the case of an unfolded writ of divorce, it is invalid. [If] one joined the top of this [writ of divorce] alongside the top of that writ of divorce, and the witnesses are in the middle, both of them are invalid. [If he joined] the bottom of this one with the bottom of that one, with the witnesses in the middle, that with which the names of the witnesses are read [alone] is valid. [If he joined] the head of this one alongside the bottom of that one, with the witnesses in the middle, that with which the witnesses' names are read at the end is valid.**

T. 7:8 A writ of divorce on which there is an erasure or an interlinear insertion, [if this was in] the body of the document, is invalid. [If this is] not in the body of the document, it is valid. If one restores [the erasure] at the bottom, even in the body of the document, it is valid.

T. 7:9 A writ of divorce on which the witnesses signed after an interval sufficient to inquire after one's welfare is invalid. For they have signed only concerning the asking after their welfare. [If] one replied a word or even two words relating to the writ of divorce, it is valid.

T. 7:10 [If] one wrote it on one side of the page, and the witnesses signed on the other side of the page, it is invalid [M. Git. 9:7A-B]. [If] one restored to it some one thing or two things dealing with a writ of divorce, it is valid.

**M. 9:8 A writ of divorce which one wrote in Hebrew with its witnesses' signing in Greek, [or which he wrote in] Greek, with its witnesses' signing in Hebrew, [or which] one witness [signed] in Hebrew and one in Greek, [or which] the scribe wrote which one witness [signed, with the scribe as the second witness] , is valid. [If it was written,] "Mr. So-and-so, a witness," it is valid; "The son of Mr. So-and-so, a witness," it is valid; "Mr. So-and-so, son of Mr. So-and-so," but he did not write, "A witness," it is valid. And thus did the scrupulous in Jerusalem do. [If] he wrote [only] his family name and her family name, it is valid. A writ of divorce imposed by a court – in the case of an Israelite court, it is valid. And in the case of a gentile court, it is invalid. In the case of gentiles, they beat him and say to him, "Do what the Israelites tell you to do," and it is valid.**

**M. 9:9 [If] the word goes around town, "She is betrothed" – lo, she is [deemed] betrothed. "She is divorced" – lo, she is [deemed] divorced, on condition that there should not be some reason to doubt it. And what would be a reason to doubt it? "Mr. So-and-so has divorced his wife conditionally." "He tossed her her tokens of betrothal" – it is a matter of doubt whether it landed nearer to him or nearer to her – lo, these are grounds for doubt.**

**M. 9:10 A man should divorce his wife only because he has found grounds for it in unchastity, even if she spoiled his dish.**

## II. Analysis: The Problematics of the Topic, Gittin

The writ of divorce is compared with the writ of emancipation for a slave, because both represent documents that bring about a radical change in the status of a person. In both instances, the person acquires full freedom of will and intentionality, no longer being subject, wholly (for the slave) or in part (for the wife) to the will of another, the master or the husband, respectively. The point in common is documentary, because the shift is brought about through the preparation of a writ. Heaven has a heavy stake in the wife's writ, but not in the slave's. For while the slave's status shifts in relationship to his worldly master, the wife's changes in the view of Heaven as well. Specifically, she had been in the status of sanctification to a particular man and forbidden to all others. Now she reenters the ordinary condition of availability to any man of her choice; that shift represents an act of secularization.

One main motivation for issuing a writ of divorce involves the law of the levirate connection. Since when a childless man dies, his widow is bound to one of his surviving brothers, betrothed as of the moment of death for subsequent consummation of the marriage, a childless dying man might well provide a writ of divorce for his wife, to sever the connection and avoid the levirate procedure. That accounts for the interest in instructions issued by dying men. But a further consideration should register. Since the husband can issue the writ but the wife cannot, what happens if the husband is lost at sea or disappears? The wife is then unable to remarry. So the conditional writ, specifying a span of time after which, in the husband's absence, the writ takes effect, further accommodates the conditional writ, that is, "Lo, this is your writ...if I do not return..." in a specified span of time; it is then assumed that the husband may have died, and his wife is then free to remarry. She is not chained to him, without the possibility of release. That further explains, in part, why women who may not testify to the death of the husband may assert that he has ordered the writ of divorce to be issued; so too people who may not testify to the wife's affairs in other contexts may deliver the writ of divorce.

The halakhah takes as its principal problem the delivery of the writ of divorce to the wife. The husband may send it through his agents, in which case they must give testimony that they have witnessed the writing and the signing, by witnesses, of the document. That guarantees one of the main requirements of the matter has been met, the document has been prepared for this particular woman, by this particular man. The husband musts know what he is doing; instructions given in delirium are null. He must explicitly instruct the scribe to write. He may, moreover, set conditions for the validity of the document, and these must be met.

One of the principal concerns of the halakhah focuses upon the specificity of the transaction, as attested by the witnesses. Another addresses the issue of a change of heart during the process of delivery. If the writ of divorce has not come into the wife's domain, the husband may retract; once she is in possession, he has no further power over her. That concern extends to attesting the wife's designation of her agents; witnesses must validate the transaction. They must attest that the wife has appointed the agents, and witnesses must attest that the messenger did receive the writ and dispose of it in the proper manner. So it is the moment of delivery of a valid writ that severs the former relationship of sanctification.

The preparation of the writ, including its signing by witnesses, must be completed within a given span of time, whether one night or one day. What is at stake in such a rule? Sages want not only that the writ serve that particular woman, but also that it be a fresh document, not made stale through the passage of time: that woman, those witnesses, on that particular occasion. It must represent a current, effective statement of the husband's will and respond to his attitude toward this particular moment toward this specific woman. Who writes it makes slight difference, by contrast, since the operative conditions are the timely preparation, on the one side, and the correct attestation by valid witnesses, on the other: both marking the particularity of the transaction. The husband may instruct whom it may concern, without knowing the identities of his agents, if circumstances warrant. So the principal concern involves the writ's preparation, in a finite span of time, for that particular woman and no other – even another woman of the same name. Not only so, but the writ is validated by its witnesses, and these make all the difference; the specific identity of the witnesses to the procedure has to be established (even though the husband does not know who they are, as noted).

Contrast the document of emancipation! No such conditions as to time, the particular identity of the recipient, and other considerations important to the preparation of the writ of divorce pertain to the slave's writ of emancipation. The difference is fundamental. The slave was never classified as "holy to his master," the relationship was functional and secular, a business transaction by which the slave in exchange for a fee sold his labor, if also his rights of intentionality, to the master. The slave may work for anyone designated by the master; the husband cannot assign the woman's wifely services to another party. And God has a stake in the relationship of husband and wife that he does not indicate in the relationship of master and slave. Heaven will even take account of the husband's deteriorating attitude toward his wife and supervise the ordeal of the bitter water. The wife is subjected to considerations of a supernatural character, with attention to the timing of the document and its being written specifically for her. What is at issue is not the form but the substance: the name of the man and the woman and the date. And that is no mere formality, as we observed at M. 3:1: the mere coincidence of names does not suffice to meet the requirement of particular preparation. If one wrote a writ of divorce for divorcing his wife therewith and then changed his mind, and a fellow townsman found it and said to him, "My name is the same as yours, and my wife's name is the same as your wife's name," it is invalid therewith to effect a divorce. These and comparable rules show what is meant by the rule of specificity.

Not only must the document be particular to that women, but it must also accommodate her preferences as to its delivery. Since the document must conform to the law or yields no effect and leaves her sanctified to that particular man, she has to make sure it is validly prepared at its critical points. That is why she dictates the conditions of the writ's delivery. While she cannot initiate the procedure – Scripture has accorded her no role in the transaction but the passive one of receiving the document – her will governs where and how the writ will be handed over to her. That is how the halakhah assigns to her a part by allowing her to dictate the conditions under which she receives the document; she may appoint an agent, specify the circumstance of delivery to her agent, and otherwise take an active role in severing the marital bond. Not only so, but the husband must explicitly identify the document as a writ of divorce, and the wife must receive it as such. Thus: If he put it into her hand while she is sleeping, [then] she woke up, read it, and lo, it is her writ of divorce, it is not a valid writ of divorce – until he will say to her, "Here is your writ of divorce." Here again, the transaction requires the wife's full participation, on the one side, and an explicit exchange, understood by both parties, for the marital bond to be severed.

What is at stake in these requirements? They serve to make certain the writ is valid and takes effect, so that all parties to the transaction know that the woman's status has changed irrevocably. But that means, even an imperfection without any bearing on the substance of the transaction, such as mis-dating or mis-identifying the writ (using the wrong date, or mis-identifying the locale of the husband, suffices to invalidate the writ. So too, if the scribe erred and gave the writ of divorce to the woman and the quittance to the man, rather than giving the writ to the man to give to his wife and vice versa, it is a complete disaster. Both cases and comparable ones bring to bear the most severe penalties. Then, if she should remarry on the strength of the impaired writ of divorce, her entire situation is ruined. She has to get a new writ of divorce from the first husband and from the second; she loses her alimony; she loses many of the benefits and guarantees of the marriage-settlement. And the offspring from the marriage fall into the category of those whose parents are legally unable to wed, e.g., the offspring of a married woman by a man other than her husband. Everything is lost by reason of the innocent actions of the wife in remarrying on the strength of an impaired writ, and that means, the wife has an acute interest in, and bears full responsibility for, the validity of the writ. The husband's only unique power is to direct the writing and delivery of the writ; otherwise, the wife bears equal responsibility for the accurate preparation of the document, the valid delivery (hence insistence that she be alert to the transaction), and the fully-correct details inscribed therein.

### III. Interpretation: Religious Principles of Gittin

When a farmer consecrates an animal for a particular cultic purpose, e.g., as a sin-offering, the transaction involves a very specific process. He must identify the particular sin that is to be expiated by the particular animal (or in the case of what is unclear, designate an animal in a way that takes account of his uncertainty as to the sin he has committed). He must then make certain that the officiating priest makes the offering "in the proper name," meaning, it must fall into the category of offering that is required and no other; the act of tossing the blood must be performed with the correct, appropriate, particular intentionality. If the farmer does not utilize the animal he has designated, or consecrated, to the altar for his particular sin, he must undertake the appropriate process of disposing of the still-consecrated beast in a manner appropriate to its status and, more to the point, to the purpose that, by his act of will, he has planned to use the beast. When it comes to the transformation of the woman's status, from secular and available to any appropriate Israelite to sacred to a single, specified individual male, the process of sanctification is equally particular, and the result equivalently decisive.

Then what brings about the deconsecration of the woman takes on heavy significance, since Heaven, as much as man and woman, takes a keen interest in the process. The counterpart to the process of the disposition of the beast sanctified to the altar for a given purpose by a designated sacrifier differs at one fundamental point. The man's act of will in consecrating the beast cannot be nullified by a corresponding act of will to deconsecrate it. Scripture is very clear on that point, when it forbids even an act of substitution of one beast for another (Lev. 27:11). if the man should decide he wishes to offer beast B rather than beast A, beast B is consecrated, but beast A retains its prior status. That is because – so it seems to me – an additional participant in the transaction has had his say and cannot now be dismissed, and that, of course, is Heaven. Once the beast has been consecrated, therefore, it leaves the status of consecration only with Heaven's assent, meaning, by following the procedures that the halakhah deems appropriate, which are discussed in Volume I at the appropriate point.

Heaven has a different relationship to the marriage, and other parties enter in. When the husband determines that he wishes to deconsecrated the wife, he has the power to do so, as we have seen, only in such a manner that the wife is fully informed and takes an active role in the transaction, receiving the writ of divorce – initiated solely on the husband's volition to be sure – on terms that she has the power to dictate. The halakhah states eloquently that she must play a fully conscious role in the transaction when it says she may not be asleep when the writ is handed over to her, and she may not be misinformed as to its character. Thus she must know that the document is a writ of divorce; she must be awake; if she sets conditions for the reception of the document, these must be met. In these fundamental ways, then, she accedes to the process of deconsecration, to the secularization of her status within the Israelite household.

Does Heaven take an equivalent role to its engagement in the disposition of the sanctified beast and if so, where and how does that engagement take effect? The answer is, predictably, that Heaven, not only the husband and wife, concerns itself with the change in the woman's status as holy. Where, in the repertoire of the halakhah, does that concern express itself? It is in the valid preparation of the document itself. That document – properly written, properly witnessed, properly handed over – serves to deconsecrated the woman, as surely as the rites of disposition of the consecrated animal not used for its correct purpose deal with the change in status of that beast. So it is the document that is the medium of effecting, or of annulling, the status of consecration. And what gives the document effect?

The answer is in two parts. First, we know, the witnesses are the key-element in the process; the document is validated by valid witnesses, and lacking valid witnesses, even though it is correctly written and delivered, it has no effect at all. In the end the particular witnesses attest not only to the facts of what is incised in the writing but also to the specificity of the writing: this man, this woman, this document. Then what is to be said about the witnesses to the preparation of the document, for whom do they stand? Given Heaven's stake in the transaction and the witnesses' status as non-participants, we may offer only one answer: the witnesses validate the document and give it effect because they stand as Heaven's surrogates. Israelite males not related to the parties, the witnesses accord cognizance on earth in behalf of Heaven to that change in intentionality and status that the document attests. When the witnesses to the validity of the writ prepared overseas say, "Before us it was written and before us it was signed" (that is, by the witnesses to the document itself), they confirm what is at stake in the entire transaction: Heaven has been informed of the change of intention on the part of the husband, releasing the wife from her status of sanctification to him. So the change in intentionality must be attested on earth in behalf of Heaven. And that which is certified by the witnesses is not only the validity of the writing of the document but the explicit transaction that has brought about the writing: the husband has instructed the scribe to write the writ of divorce, that particular writ of divorce, for his wife, for the named wife and no other woman (even of the same name). When he has done that, pronouncing his intent to nullify the relationship of sanctification that he proffered and the woman accepted, then all else follows.

But Heaven wants something else as well. Not only must the intention be articulated, and explicitly in the transaction at hand and no other. The document itself must give evidence of counterpart specificity. What makes all the difference? The halakhah specifies irregularities of two classes, first, those that do not fundamentally invalidate the transaction, second, those that, as at M. 8:5ff., so completely invalidate the transaction that the original status of sanctification retains effect, despite what the husband has said, despite what the wife has correctly received by way of documentary confirmation of the change of intentionality and therefore status, his and hers, respectively. That represents a most weighty result, with long-term consequences.

What conditions do not nullify the transaction? Confusing the writ of divorce of two couples bearing the same names presents a situation that can be sorted out. If the two writs of divorce are written side by side, so that the signatures have to be assigned to the respective writs, that is a problem that can be solved. The document may be spread over two sheets: If one left over part [of the text of] the writ of divorce and wrote it on the second page, and the witnesses are below, it is valid. On the other hand, we have two explicit situations that produce the catastrophe of a totally invalid exchange, such that the woman remains sanctified to the husband who has indicated the intention of divorcing her. That is to say, in two circumstances the husband's intentionality does not register with Heaven. These are at M. 8:5 and M. 8:8, as follows, to review:

> M. 8:5 If he wrote the writ of divorce dating it according to an era which is not applicable, for example, according to the era of the Medes, according to the era of the Greeks, according to the building of the Temple, according to the destruction of the Temple, [if] he was in the east and wrote, "In the west," in the west and wrote, "In the east," she goes forth from this one [whom she married on the strength of the divorce from the former husband] and from that one [the first husband]. And she requires a writ of divorce from this one and from that one.

> M. 8:8: If the scribe wrote a writ of divorce for the man and a quittance [receipt given to the husband for her marriage contract payment] for the woman, and he erred and gave the writ of divorce to the woman and the quittance to the man, and they then exchanged them for one another, and if after a while, lo, the writ of divorce turns up in the hand of the man, and the quittance in the hand of the woman – she goes forth from this one and from that one.

The two rules produce this question: who has the power to nullify even the effect of the intentionality of the husband? It is the scribe. If he errs in dating the document, or if he errs and writes down the wrong location of the participant, then, whatever the husband's intentionality and whatever the wife's (wrong) impression of what has taken place, the writ is null, and the result is as specified, chaotic. So too if the scribe made a mistake in transmitting the documents that are to be exchanged, the transaction is null.

Then the question presses: why has the scribe so critical a role in the transaction that he can utterly upset the intentionality of the one and the consequent conclusion drawn by the other party, husband and wife, respectively? The reason is clear: the halakhah attributes to the scribe a role in the transaction as critical, in its way, as the role of the husband in commissioning the document and the wife in receiving it. And what is it that the scribe can do to ruin the transaction? He can do two things. First, he can commit the unpardonable sin of not delivering the document to the correct party at the husband's instructions. That is, the husband has told him to deliver the writ of divorce to the wife, but he has given her the quittance instead. The woman has never validly received the writ. The scribe must realize and not thwart the husband's intentionality.

But what about the other matter, mis-dating the document, mis-identifying the parties? Here what has happened is that the writ no longer pertains to those mentioned in it. The scribe has placed the parties in a different period from that in which they live, dating them, by reason of the document, in some other time; or he has placed them in a different locale from the one where they are situated. He has set forth a document for some others than the ones before him, and he has given to those before him a spurious time and place. So the halakhah raises yet again its requirement on the acute localization of the piece of writing: this woman, here and now, her and her alone, this man, here and now, him and him alone. That is to say, the halakhah has underscored the conception, the conviction really, that the moment and act of sanctification are unique, specific, not to be duplicated or replicated in any way or manner. When God oversees this holy relationship, he does not wish it to be confused with any other. That is why, when God is informed of the change of intentionality that has brought about the consecration of the woman to the man, he must be given exact information.

The halakhah before us rests on profound reflection about the character of intentionality and its effects. What the law ascertains encompasses not only the intentionality and will of the husband, not only the conscious, explicit cognizance of the wife, but the facts of the case. Specifically, the halakhah insists that the husband's act of will carries effect only when confirmed by valid action. Intention on its own is null. The full realization of the intention, involving valid provision for all required actions, alone carries effect. Not only so, but a third party, the scribe, intervenes in the realization of the husband's will. That means, facts beyond the husband's control and the wife's power to secure a right to supervise and review matters take over – with truly dreadful and permanent results.

So the wife, having acted on the writ invalidated by the scribe's, not her or her husband's actions or intentionality, emerges as the victim of circumstances quite in contradiction to anybody's will. The upshot is, by the rule of the halakhah, she may not then claim that her intention – in this case, the acquiescence in a successive relationship of consecration – has been thwarted by the actions or errors of a third party and so ought to be honored in the breach. The halakhah rejects that claim. She acted in accord with the rules of intentionality and in good faith – and it makes no difference. And the first husband, with all good will, cannot confirm that he intended to divorce the woman, and her actions fully accord with his initiatory intentionality. The halakhah dismisses that allegation as well. Neither bears material consequence in the validation of what is, by reason of the facts of the case, an invalid transaction.

But the scribe possesses no intentionality in the transaction (other than the will we assume motivates his practice of his profession, that is, professionalism). The very role accorded to the scribe, not to the contracting parties, underscores the position of the halakhah. It is that intentionality not confirmed by the correct deeds in the end does not suffice. The scribe's errors stand athwart the realization of the intentionality of the husband and the participation (where possible) of the wife; but the scribe obviously did not intend to make mistakes. So what stands in judgment of intentionality and its effect are the facts of the case: the objective actions taken by third parties. In a legal system that has made a heavy investment in the priority of intentionality and the power of will, the statement made by the halakhah of Gittin sounds a much-needed note of warning. Good will and proper intentionality do not govern when facts intervene.

What one means to do contradicted by what one has done willy-nilly changes no facts but makes no difference at all. That is because Heaven still insists upon something more than the correct will. It does, in the end, scrutinize actions, and these alone serve not only to confirm, but also to carry out, the will of the principals in any transaction. And, if we refer to the generative myth of the Torah, where to begin with the power of man to form and exercise intentionality is set forth, we find the reason why. The man and the woman enter the excuses that they gave way to the will of another, so their actions should be set aside. But God punishes all the parties to the act of rebellion, the snake, the woman, and the man. Then the lesson at the origin of all things – the power of humanity's will to stand against Heaven's will – finds its complement in its companion: what matters in the end is the deed, not only the intention. That deeply implicates the woman in the transaction and gives her a heavy stake in its proper execution; she is in no way passive, and her intentionality and alertness afford her protection of a fundamental order. The document serves to attest in a tangible manner to the man's intentionality, the correct conditions of receipt of the document to the woman's conscious knowledge of what has happened. Neither can then claim not to have known that the relationship has been severed, and that is why Heaven confirms the act of intentionality embodied in the document. Of all this Scripture knows nothing. The sages liberated Israelite women when they assigned them responsibility for their own condition, so according them the dignity and respect that such an assignment carried in its wake.

# 3

## Sotah

### I. An Outline of the Halakhah of Sotah

The injustice done to the innocent wife, who by the husband's whim is required to undergo the humiliating ordeal of the bitter water, serves as the halakhah's occasion to make its definitive statement that God's justice is perfect: the wicked get their exact punishment, the righteous, their precise reward. For the sages that statement becomes possible only here. For in their view it is not enough to show that sin or crime provokes divine response, that God penalizes evil-doers. Justice in the here and now counts only when the righteous also receive what is coming to them. Scripture's casual remark that the woman found innocent will bear more children provokes elaborate demonstration, out of the established facts of history that Scripture supplies, that both righteous and wicked are subject to God's flawless and exact justice. Then, it goes without saying, sages liberate women from a procedure lacking in all juridical protections and accord to the accused woman the rights that, within their framework, they could to secure justice for her.

The penalty must fit the crime, measure must match measure, and the more exact the result to the cause, the more compelling the proof of immediate and concrete justice as the building block of world order that sages would put forth out of Scripture. That is the point at which justice is transformed from a vague generality – a mere sentiment – to a precise and measurable dimension of the actual social order of morality: how things hold together when subject to tension, at the pressure-points of structure, not merely how they are arrayed in general. Here, in fact, is how God made the world, what is good about the creation that God pronounced good. And to make that point, sages select a rite that reeks of injustice, the case of the wife accused of adultery and the ordeal to which she is subjected. Their presentation of the rite, in the setting of home and family, is framed so as to demonstrate God's perfect justice –

not only in the public life of Israel's social order, but in the here and now of home and family. It is hard to find a less likely candidate for service in demonstrating that proposition than the subject before us. But, for reasons that are now clear, sages identified the topic as the ideal occasion for saying just that.

The ordeal imposed on the woman accused of unfaithfulness, spelled out in the Written Torah, elicits from the sages of the Oral Torah no searching inquiry. The halakhah of the Mishnah narrates the rite, and the Tosefta and two Talmuds fill in some minor details. The tractate expands to cover other rites conducted in Hebrew or in other languages as well. The pertinent verses of Scripture are as follows (Num. 5:1-31):

> The Lord said to Moses, "Command the people of Israel that they put out of the camp every leper and everyone having a discharge and everyone that is unclean through contact with the dead; you shall put out both male and female, putting them outside the camp, that they may not defile their camp, in the midst of which I dwell." And the people of Israel did so and drove them outside the camp as the Lord said to Moses, so the people of Israel did.
>
> And the Lord said to Moses, "Say to the people of Israel, When a man or woman commits any of the sins that men commit by breaking faith with the Lord and that person is guilty, he shall confess his sin that he has committed, and he shall make full restitution for his wrong, adding a fifth to it, and giving it to him to whom he did the wrong. But if the man has no kinsman to whom restitution may be made for the wrong, the restitution for the wrong shall go to the Lord for the priest, in addition to the ram of atonement with which atonement is made for him. And every offering, all the holy things of the people of Israel, which they bring to the priest, shall be his; and every man's holy things shall be his; whatever any man gives to the priest shall be his."
>
> And the Lord said to Moses, "Say to the people of Israel, If any man's wife go astray and act unfaithfully against him, if a man lie with her carnally and it is hidden from the eyes of her husband, and she is undetected though she has defiled herself and there is now witness against her, since she was not taken in the act, and if the spirit of jealousy comes upon him, and he is jealous of his wife who has defiled herself; or if the spirit of jealousy comes upon him and he is jealous of his wife, though she has not defiled herself, then the man shall bring his wife to the priest, and bring the offering required of her, a tenth of an ephah of barley meal; he shall pour no oil upon it and put no frankincense on it, for it is a cereal offering of jealousy, a cereal offering of remembrance, bringing iniquity to remembrance.
>
> "And the priest shall bring her near and set her before the Lord, and the priest shall take holy water in an earthen vessel and take some of the dust that is on the floor of the tabernacle and put it into the water.

""And the priest shall set the woman before the Lord and unbind the hair of the woman's head and place in her hands the cereal offering of remembrance, which is the cereal offering of jealousy. And in his hand the priest shall have the water of bitterness that brings the curse. Then the priest shall make her take an oath, saying, 'If no man has lain with you, and if you have not turned aside to uncleanness, while you were under your husband's authority, be free from this water of bitterness that brings the curse. But if you have gone astray, though you are under your husband's authority, and if you have defiled yourself, and some man other than your husband has lain with you, then (let the woman take the oath of the curse and say to the woman) 'the Lord make you an execration and an oath among your people, when the Lord makes your thigh fall away and your body swell; may this water that brings the curse pass into your bowels and make your body swell and your thigh fall away.' And the woman shall say, 'Amen, Amen.'

"Then the priest shall write these curses in a book and wash them off into the water of bitterness; and he shall make the woman drink the water of bitterness that brings the curse, and the water that brings the curse shall enter into her and cause bitter pain. And the priest shall take the cereal offering of jealousy out of the woman's hand and shall wave the cereal offering before the Lord and bring of the woman's hand and shall wave the cereal offering before the Lord and bring it to the altar; and the priest shall take a handful of the cereal offering as its memorial portion and burn it upon the altar, and afterward shall make the woman drink the water. And when he has made her drink the water, then, if she has defiled herself and has acted unfaithfully against her husband, the water that brings the curse shall enter into her and cause bitter pain, and her body shall swell, and her thigh shall fall away, and the woman shall become an execration among her people. But if the woman has not defiled herself and is clean, then she shall be free and shall conceive children.

"This is the law in cases of jealousy, when a wife, though under her husband's authority, goes astray and defiles herself, or when the spirit of jealousy comes upon a man and he is jealous of his wife; then he shall set the woman before the Lord, and the priest shall execute upon her all this law. The man shall be free from iniquity, but the woman shall bear her iniquity."

The woman accused of unfaithfulness finds her place in the Torah's presentation of those excluded from the camp, the ones who are subject to the uncleanness specified at Lev. 13-15 in particular. Then comes the matter of breaking faith, and, finally, the special case of the accused wife. Scripture speaks both of the wife who has actually committed adultery, and whose husband is made jealous and the woman whose husband expresses jealousy but who is guiltless. As anticipated, Scripture focuses, then, upon the rite at the Temple that accommodates the situation. The halakhah raises its customary questions as well, working its way through its familiar philosophical agendum alongside its theological one.

I.  Invoking the Ordeal

M. 1:1-2 He who expresses jealousy to his wife [concerning her relations with another man (Num. 5:14)] how does he express jealousy to her? [If] he stated to her before two witnesses, "Do not speak with Mr. So-and-so," and she indeed spoke with him, she still is permitted to have sexual relations with her husband and is permitted to eat heave-offering. [If] she went with him to some private place and remained with him for sufficient time to become unclean, she is prohibited from having sexual relations with her husband and [if the husband is a priest,] she is prohibited from eating heave-offering. And if he [her husband] should die, she performs the rite of *halisah* [removing the shoe, which severs her relationship to the childless husband's surviving brother, in line with the law of Deut. 25:5-10] but is not taken into levirate marriage.

T. 1:2 What is the character of the first testimony [M. Sot. 1:2]? This is the testimony concerning her going off alone [with such and such a person]. The second [testimony]? This is testimony concerning her having been made unclean. And how long is the time required for becoming unclean? Sufficient time to have sexual relations. And how much is sufficient time for having sexual relations? Sufficient time for sexual contact.

M. 1:3 And these women [married to priests and accused of unfaithfulness] are prohibited from eating heave-offering: (1) She who says, "I am unclean to you," and (2) she against whom witnesses testified that she is unclean; and (3) she who says, "I shall not drink the bitter water," and (4) she whose husband will not force her to drink it; and (5) she whose husband has sexual relations with her on the way [up to Jerusalem for the rite of drinking the water]. What should he do in respect to her? He brings her to the court in that place [in which they live], and [the judges] hand over to him two disciples of sages, lest he have sexual relations with her on the way.

II.  Narrative of the Ordeal

M. 1:4 They would bring her up to the high court which is in Jerusalem and admonish her as they admonish witnesses in a capital crime. They say to her, "My daughter, much is done by wine, much is done by joking around, much is done by kidding around, much is done by bad friends. For the sake of the great Name which is written in holiness, do it so that it will not be blotted out by water [Num. 5:23]." and they tell her things which neither she nor the family of her father's house should be hearing.

T. 1:6 And just as the court admonishes her to repent [M. Sot. 1:4], so they admonish her not to repent. Therefore they say to her,

"Now my daughter, if it is perfectly clear to you that you are clean, stand your ground and drink. For these waters are only like a dry salve which is put on living flesh and does no harm. If there is a wound, it penetrates and goes through [the skin, and if there is no wound, it has no effect]. Two accused wives are not made to drink simultaneously, so that one not be shameless before the other.

B. 1:4 III.1 7B AND THEY TELL HER THINGS... [M. 1:4C]: HE TELLS HER LESSONS OF NARRATIVE AND EVENTS THAT TOOK PLACE [AND ARE RECORDED] IN THE EARLIER WRITINGS [OF THE PENTATEUCH]. FOR EXAMPLE "WHICH WISE MEN HAVE TOLD AND HAVE NOT HID FROM THEIR FATHERS [BY CONFESSING THEIR SIN]" (JOB 15:18). SPECIFICALLY: JUDAH CONFESSED AND WAS NOT ASHAMED TO DO SO. WHAT WAS HIS DESTINY? HE INHERITED THE WORLD TO COME. REUBEN CONFESSED AND WAS NOT ASHAMED TO DO SO. WHAT WAS HIS DESTINY? HE INHERITED THE WORLD TO COME. WHAT WAS THEIR REWARD? WHAT WAS THEIR REWARD?! RATHER, WHAT WAS THEIR REWARD IN THIS WORLD? "TO THEM ALONE THE LAND WAS GIVEN, AND NO STRANGER PASSED AMONG THEM" (JOB 15:19).

M. 1:5 [Now] if she said, "I am unclean," she gives a quittance for her marriage-contract [which is not paid over to her], and goes forth [with a writ of divorce]. And if she said, "I am clean," they bring her up to the eastern gate, which is at the entrance of Nicanor's Gate. There it is that they force accused wives to drink the bitter water, and they purify women after childbirth and purify lepers. And a priest grabs her clothes – if they tear, they tear, and if they are ripped up, they are ripped up – until he bares her breast. And he tears her hair apart [Num. 5:18].

T. 1:7 Priests cast lots among themselves. Whoever won the lottery, even a high priest, goes out and stands next to the accused wife. And a priest grabs her clothes – if they tear, they tear, and if they are ripped up, they are ripped up – until he bares her breast. And he tears her hair apart

M. 1:6 [If] she was clothed in white clothing, he puts black clothes on her. [If] she had gold jewelry, chains, nose-rings, and finger rings on, they take them away from her to put her to shame. Then he brings a rope made out of twigs and ties it above her breasts. And whoever wants to stare at her comes and stares, except for her boy-slaves and girl-slaves, since in any case she has no shame before them. And all women are allowed to stare at her, since it is said, That all women may be taught not to do after your lewdness (Ezek. 23:48).

M. 1:7 By that same measure by which a man metes out [to others], do they mete out to him: She primped herself for sin, the Omnipresent made her repulsive. She exposed herself for sin, the Omnipresent exposed her. With the thigh she began to sin, and afterward with the belly, therefore the thigh suffers the curse first, and afterward the belly. But the rest of the body does not escape [punishment].

T. 3:2 And so you find that with regard to the accused wife: With the measure with which she measured out, with that measure do they mete out to her. She stood before him so as to be pretty before him, therefore a priest stands her up in front of everybody to display her shame, as it is said, And the priest will set the woman before the Lord (Num. 5:18).

T. 3:3 She wrapped a beautiful scarf for him, therefore a priest takes her cap from her head and puts it under foot. She braided her hair for him, therefore a priest loosens it. She painted her face for him, therefore her face is made to turn yellow. She put blue on her eyes for him, therefore her eyes bulge out.

T. 3:4 She signaled to him with her finger, therefore her fingernails fall out. She showed him her flesh, therefore a priest tears her cloak and shows her shame in public. She tied on a belt for him, therefore a priest brings a rope of twigs and ties it above her breasts, and whoever wants to stare comes and stares at her [M. Sot. 1:6C-D]. She pushed her thigh at him, therefore her thigh falls. She took him on her belly, therefore her belly swells. She fed him goodies, therefore her meal-offering is fit for a cow. She gave him the best wines to drink in elegant goblets, therefore the priest gives her the bitter water to drink in a clay pot.

T. 4:1 I know only with regard to the measure of retribution that by that same measure by which a man metes out, they mete out to him [M. Sot. 1:7A]. How do I know that the same is so with the measure of goodness [M. Sot. 1:9A]? Thus do you say:' The measure of goodness is five hundred times greater than the measure of retribution. With regard to the measure of retribution it is written, Visiting the sin of the fathers on the sons and on the grandsons to the third and fourth generation (Ex. 20:5). And with regard to the measure of goodness it is written, And doing mercy for thousands (Ex. 20:6). You must therefore conclude that the measure of goodness is five hundred times greater than the measure of retribution.

M. 1:8 Samson followed his eyes [where they led him], therefore the Philistines put out his eyes, since it is said, And the Philistines laid hold on him and put out his eyes (Judges 16:21). Absalom was proud of his hair, therefore he was hung by his hair [II Sam. 14:25-26]. And since he had sexual relations with ten concubines of his father, therefore they thrust ten spear heads into his body, since it is said, "And ten young men that carried Jacob's armor surrounded and smote Absalom and killed him" (II Sam. 18:15). And since he stole three hearts – his father's, the court's, and the Israelite's – since it is said, "And Absalom stole the heart of the men of Israel" (II Sam. 15:6) – therefore three darts were thrust into him, since it is said, "And he took three darts in his hand and thrust them through the heart of Absalom" (II Sam. 18:14).

M. 1:9 And so is it on the good side. [The remainder is cited below.]

M. 2:1 He [the husband (Num. 5:15)] would bring her meal-offering in a basket of palm-twigs and lay it into her hands to tire her out. All meal-offerings at the outset and at the end are in a utensil of service. But this one at the outset is in basket of palm-twigs, and [only] at the end is in a utensil of service. All meal-offerings require oil and frankincense, But this one requires neither oil nor frankincense. All meal-offerings derive from wheat. But this one derives from barley. As to the meal-offering of the first sheaf (omer), even though it [too] derives from barley, it would derive from sifted flour. But this one derives from unsifted flour. Just as she acted like a cow, so her offering is food for a cow.

T. 1:9 Priests are permitted to put wine, oil, and honey into the residue of meal-offerings, but they are prohibited from allowing them to leaven.

T. 1:10 All meal-offerings which are specified in the Torah require oil and frankincense, except for the meal-offering of a sinner and the meal-offering of jealousy, since it is said, "He will not pour oil into it, and he will not put frankincense in it" (Num. 5:15).

M. 2:2 He [the husband] would bring a clay bowl and put in it a half-log of water from the laver. And he [the priest] goes into the hekhal and turns to his right. Now there was a place, an amah by an amah, with a marble flagstone, and a ring was attached to it. And when he raised it [the stone], he took the dirt from under it and put it [into the bowl of water], sufficient to be visible on the water, since it says, "And of the dust that is on the floor of the tabernacle the priest shall take and put it into the water" (Num. 5:17).

T. 1:8 Three things must be visible on the water: the dust of the red cow, the dust of the accused wife, and the blood of the bird [used to purify a mesora' (Lev. 14:6)]. The dust of the red cow – sufficient to be visible on the surface of the water. The dust of the accused wife – sufficient to be visible on the surface of the water [M. Sot. 2:2G]. The blood of the bird of a mesora' – sufficient to be visible on the surface of the water. The spit of a deceased childless brother's wife – sufficient to be visible to the sight of the elders.

M. 2:3 He came to write the scroll. From what passage [in Scripture] did he write? From "If no man has lain with thee... but if thou hast gone aside with another instead of thy husband..." (Num. 5:19f.). But he does not write, "And the priest shall cause the woman to swear" (Num. 5:21). And he writes, "The Lord make thee a curse and an oath among thy people... and this water that causeth the curse shall go into thy bowels and make thy belly to swell and thy thigh to fall away." But he does not write, "And the woman shall say, Amen, Amen!"

M. 2:4 He writes (1) neither on a tablet, (2) nor on papyrus, (3) nor on unprepared hide, but only on [parchment] scroll, since it is written, In a book (Num. 5:23). And he writes (1) neither with gum, (2) nor with coppera, (3) nor with anything which makes a lasting impression [on the writing-material], but only with ink, since it is written, And he will blot it out – writing which can be blotted out.

T. 2:1 He would take her scroll and bring it into the ulam. Now there was a gold flagstone set up there by the wall of the hekhal. And it was visible from the ulam. At that point he sees it, and he writes, neither leaving out anything nor adding anything. He goes out and stands by the accused wife. He reads it aloud and explains it and spells out every detail of the pericope. And he says it to her in whatever language she understands, so that she will know for what she is drinking the bitter water and for what incident she is drinking it, on what account she is accused of being unclean, and under what circumstances she is accused of being unclean. And he says to her, "I invoke an oath upon you – And may it come upon you." "And may they come upon you" – this is the curse. "I invoke an oath upon you" – this is an oath.

M. 2:5 To what does she say, Amen, Amen? (1) "Amen to the curse" [Num. 5:21], (2) "Amen to the oath" [Num. 5:19]. (3) "Amen that it was not with this particular man" (4) "Amen that it was with no other man." (5) "Amen that I have not gone aside while betrothed, married, awaiting Levirate marriage, or wholly taken in Levirate marriage." (6) "Amen that I was not made unclean, and if I was made unclean, may it [the bitter water] enter into me."

M. 2:6 All concur that he [the husband] may make no stipulation with her about anything which happened before she was betrothed or after she may be divorced. [If after she was put away], she went aside with some other man and became unclean, and afterward he [the first husband] took her back, he makes no stipulation with her [concerning such an event]. This is the general principle: Concerning any situation in which she may have sexual relations in such wise as not to be prohibited [to her husband], he [the husband] may make no stipulation whatsoever with her.

M. 3:1 He would take her meal-offering from the basket made of twigs and put it into a utensil of service and lay it into her hands. And a priest puts his hand under hers and waves it [the meal-offering].

M. 3:2 He waved it [Num. 5:25] and brought it near the altar. He took a handful [of the meal-offering] and burned it up [on the altar]. And the residue is eaten by the priests. He would give her the water to drink. And [only] afterward he would offer up her meal-offering.

M. 3:3 [If] before the scroll is blotted out, she said, "I am not going to drink the water," her scroll is put away, and her meal-offering is scattered on the ashes. But her scroll is not valid for the water-ordeal of another accused wife. [If] her scroll was blotted out and then she said, "I am not going to drink it," they force her and make her drink it against her will.

T. 2:2 He goes in and writes the scroll, comes out and blots it out. If before the scroll is blotted out, she says, "I am not going to drink it" [M. Sot. 3:3A], or if she said, "I am unclean," or if witnesses came and testified that she is unclean, the water is poured out. And no sanctity adheres to it. And the scroll written for her is hidden under the hekhal, and her meal offering is scattered [M. Sot. 3:3A].

T. 2:3 [If] the scroll is blotted out and she said, "I am unclean," the water is poured out, and her meal-offering is scattered on the ashes. And her scroll is not valid for the water-ordeal of another accused wife [M. Sot. 3:3C, B]. If her scroll is blotted out and then she said, "I am not going to drink it," they force her and make her drink it against her will [M. Sot. 3:3D].

M. 3:4 She hardly sufficed to drink it before her face turns yellow, her eyes bulge out, and her veins swell. And they say, "Take her away! Take her away!" so that the Temple-court will not be made unclean [by her corpse]. [But if nothing happened], if she had merit, she would attribute [her good fortune] to it. There is the possibility that merit suspends the curse for one year, and there is the possibility that merit suspends the curse for two years, and there is the possibility that merit suspends the curse for three years.

M. 3:6 [If] her meal-offering was made unclean before it was sanctified in a utensil, lo, it is in the status of all other such meal-offerings and is to be redeemed. And [if this takes place] after it is sanctified in a utensil, lo, it is in the status of all other such meal-offerings and is to be burned. And these are the ones who meal-offerings are to be burned: (1) the one who says, "I am unclean to you," and (2) the one against whom witnesses come to testify that she is unclean; (3) the one who says, "I am not going to drink the water," and (4) the one whose husband does not want to make her drink it; and (5) the one whose husband has sexual relations with her on the way to Jerusalem [M. 1:3]. (6) And all those who are married to priests – their meal-offerings are burned.

T. 2:4 For every act of sexual relations which her husband had with her, lo, he is liable on her account. If her meal-offering was made unclean before it was sanctified in a utensil, lo, it is in the status of all other such meal-offerings. it is redeemed [M. Sot. 3:6A-B] and eaten. [If] her meal-offering was made unclean] after it was sanctified in a utensil [M. Sot. 3:6C-D], its appearance is allowed to rot, and it goes out to the place of burning.

T. 2:5 [If] the meal-offering was offered, but there was not time to offer up the handful before her husband died, or if she died, the residue is prohibited. [If] the handful was offered, and afterward she died, or the husband died, the residue is permitted. For to begin with it was brought in a case of doubt. Her doubt has been atoned for and gone its way.

T. 2:6 [If] witnesses came against her to testify that she was unclean, one way or the other the meal-offering is prohibited. [If] they turned out to be conspiring witnesses, one way or the other her meal-offering is treated as unconsecrated. In the case of any woman married to a priest, whether she is a priest-girl, or a Levite-girl, or an Israelite-girl, her meal-offering is not eaten, for he has a share in it. But the offering is not wholly consumed in the fire, because she has a share in it. What should he do? The handful is offered by itself, and the residue is offered by itself. A priest stands and makes offerings at the altar, which is not the case of a priest-girl [cf. M. Sot. 3:7].

M. 3:7 An Israelite girl who is married to a priest – her meal-offering is burned. And a priest-girl who is married to an Israelite – her offering is eaten [by the priests]. What is the difference between a priest and a priest-girl? The meal-offering of a priest-girl is eaten, the meal-offering of a priest is not eaten. The priest-girl may be deconsecrated [declassed], but a priest may not be deconsecrated [declassed]. A priest-girl contracts corpse-uncleanness, and a priest does not contract corpse-uncleanness. A priest eats Most Holy Things, but a priest-girl does not eat Most Holy Things.

M. 3:8 What is the difference [along these same lines of comparing and contrasting the male priest and the female priest] between a man and a woman? A man goes around with unbound hair and torn garments, but a woman does not go around with unbound hair and torn garments [Lev. 13:44-5]. A man imposes a Nazirite-vow on his son, and a woman does not impose a Nazirite-vow upon her son [M. Naz. 4:6]. A man brings the hair-offering for the Nazirite-vow of his father, and a woman does not bring a hair-offering for the Nazirite-vow of her father [M. Naz. 4:7]. The man sells his daughter, and the woman does not sell her daughter [Ex. 21:6]. The man arranges for a betrothal of his daughter, and the woman does not arrange for a betrothal of her daughter [M. Qid. 2:1]. A man [who incurs the death-penalty] is stoned naked, but a woman is not stoned naked. A man is hung [after being put to death], and a woman is not hung [M. San. 6:3-4]. A man is sold [to make restitution] for having stolen something, but a woman is not sold to [make restitution] for having stolen something [Ex. 22:2].

T. 2:7 A man has control over his daughter and has power to betroth her through money. a writ, or an act of sexual relations, and he controls what she finds, the produce of her labor, and the abrogation of her tows [M. Ket. 4:4], which is not the case of a woman [cf. M. Sot. 3:8].

T. 2:8 A man is subject to punishment for the transgression of a commandment which has to be performed at a particular time [M. Qid. 1:7], which is not the case with a woman. A man is subject to the transgression of the commandment not to trim the beard and not to remove the beard and [in the case of a priest] not to contract corpse-uncleanness [M. Sot. 3:7F], which is not the case with a woman. A man is subject to the trial as a rebellious son, but a woman is not subject to trial as a rebellious daughter [M. San. 8:1].

T. 2:9 A man wraps himself in a cloak [if he is a mesora'] and he proclaims, ["Unclean, unclean,"], but a woman does not wrap herself in a cloak and so proclaim [cf. M. Sot. 3:8B]. A man may be sold repeatedly, but a woman may not be sold repeatedly. A man is sold as a Hebrew slave, but a woman is not sold as a Hebrew slave. A man is subjected to the ceremony of the awl [having his ear pierced to the door if he refuses to go free], but a woman is not subject to the ceremony of the awl. A man acquires a Hebrew slave, and a woman does not acquire a Hebrew slave.

## III.  Rules of the Ordeal

### A.  *Exemptions and Applicability*

M. 4:1 A betrothed girl and a deceased childless brother's widow awaiting levirate marriage neither undergo the ordeal of drinking the bitter water nor receive a marriage-contract, since it is written, "When a wife, being subject to her husband, goes astray" (Num. 5:29) – excluding the betrothed girl and the deceased childless brother's widow awaiting levirate marriage. A widow married to a high priest, a divorcee and a woman who has undergone the rite of removing the shoe married to an ordinary priest, a mamzer-girl and a Netinah-girl married to an Israelite, an Israelite-girl married to a mamzer or to a Netin neither undergo the ordeal of drinking the bitter water nor receive a marriage-contract.

T. 5:1 He who expresses a warning of jealousy to his betrothed or to his deceased childless brother's widow awaiting Levirate marriage with him [cf. M. Sot. 4:1A] – if after she entered into marriage with him, she went in secret [with the man against whom the prospective husband had warned her not to go], she either undergoes the ordeal of drinking the water or does not receive her marriage-contract.

T. 5:4 A priest-girl, a Levite-girl, and an Israelite-girl, who married a priest, a Levite, or an Israelite, a Netinah-girl married to a Netin, a mamzeret-girl married to a mamzer, the wife of a proselyte, a freed slave, and a barren woman either undergo the ordeal of drinking the bitter water or do not receive a marriage-contract. But he who expresses jealousy to his betrothed or to the deceased childless brother's widow awaiting Levirate marriage with him – [if] before he married her, she went in secret [with the man against whom she was warned], she does not undergo the ordeal of drinking the bitter water and does not collect a marriage contract [M. Sot. 4:1A-C].

Y. 4:1 I:4 *What would be an example of the rule, A betrothed girl and a deceased childless brother's widow awaiting levirate marriage neither undergo the ordeal of drinking the bitter water nor receive a marriage-contract]? [In fact M. 4:1A applies only if the entire ordeal is completed with the woman m the stated status.] [If, however,] the husband expressed jealousy to her when she was still betrothed, consummated the marriage, and she went aside with the named man, then he makes her drink the water by reason of the original expression of jealousy. [So this exemplifies the other side of the rule, the point at which the status specified at M. 4:1A does not exempt the woman from undergoing the ordeal.] [Again:] if he expressed jealousy to her while she was yet awaiting marriage with the levir, then he consummated the marriage, then he requires her to drink the water by reason of the original expression of jealousy. If he expressed jealousy to her while she was yet betrothed, and he married her, and then she went aside, and only thereafter did he have sexual relations, then she goes forth along with collecting her marriage settlement. [This is in line with M. 4:2E: because of his having sexual relations with her, she loses the opportunity to undergo the ordeal, hence collects.] But if not, she goes forth without collecting her marriage settlement. If her husband expressed jealousy to her, then died, and she fell before the levir [for levirate marriage], and he married her, and she went aside with the man originally named by the now-deceased husband, the levir requires her to drink the water by reason of the expression of jealousy of the original husband [the levir's brother]. If her husband did not express jealousy to her, and he died, and she fell before the levir, and he, for his part, expressed jealousy to her about the named man, and he had not consummated the marriage to her before he too died, and then she fell before his brother [yet a further levir], he does not have the right to impose on her the ordeal of the water, for she has fallen to him [as a wife] only because of the relationship to the first brother, [her original husband, who never issued an expression of jealousy to begin with]. But if the levir [the second brother] had expressed jealousy to her and married her and then died, and she then fell before the second levir, and he married her, and she went aside with the named man, he has every right to impose the rite of drinking the water upon her by reason of the expression of jealousy of the second brother.*

M. 4:2 And these do not undergo the ordeal of drinking the bitter water or receive a marriage-contract: She who says, "I am unclean," or against whom witnesses came to testify that she is unclean; and she who says, "I will not drink." [If, however,] her husband said, "I will not make her drink, or [if] her husband had sexual relations with her on the way [to Jerusalem], she receives her marriage-contract and does not undergo the ordeal of drinking the bitter water. [If] their husbands died before they drank the bitter water – do not undergo the ordeal of drinking the bitter water and do not receive the marriage-contract.

M. 4:3 A barren woman and a woman past menopause, and a woman who cannot give birth do not undergo the ordeal of drinking the bitter water and do not receive the marriage-contract. And all other woman either undergo the ordeal of drinking the bitter water or do not collect the marriage-contract.

T. 5:2 A young man who married a barren woman or a woman past menopause, and who has another wife and children – she either undergoes the ordeal of drinking the bitter water or does not receive her marriage-contract [M. Sot. 4:3].

T. 5:3 A. A woman made pregnant by the husband himself or who gives suck to the child of the husband himself either undergoes the ordeal of drinking the bitter water or does not receive payment of her marriage-contract [M. Sot. 4:3A, E].

T. 5:5 A. A young man who married a barren woman or a woman past menopause and who does not have another wife and children – she does not undergo the ordeal of drinking the bitter water and does not collect a marriage-contract [cf. M. Sot. 4:3C-D]. A woman who was pregnant by another husband [who died or divorced [the woman] and a woman who was giving suck to a child by another husband do not undergo the ordeal of drinking the bitter water and do not receive the marriage-contract [M. Sot. 4:3A].

M. 4:4 The wife of a priest drinks the bitter water and [if proved innocent] is permitted [to go back] to her husband. The wife of a eunuch undergoes the ordeal of drinking the bitter water. On account of [men in] all sorts of prohibited relationships [to the woman] are wives subject to warning, except for a minor, and for one who is not human.

T. 5:6 With any sort of man is a woman made unclean, except for a minor and for one who is not human [cf. M. Sot. 4:4C-E].

M. 4:5 And these are the women whom a court subjects to warning [in behalf of the husband]: A woman whose husband became a deaf mute or an imbecile, or was imprisoned – not to impose upon her the ordeal of drinking the water did – they state the rule, but to invalidate her for receiving her marriage-contract.

M. 5:1 Just as the water puts her to the proof, so the water puts him [the lover] to the proof, since it is said, "And it shall come...," "And it shall come..." (Num. 5:22, 5:24). Just as she is prohibited to the husband, so she is prohibited to the lover, since it is said, "And she will be unclean...," "And she will be unclean..." (Num. 5:27, 29).

*Y. 5:1 II:1 Just as she is forbidden to the husband, so she is forbidden to the lover: Just as she is forbidden to the brother of her husband [should he die childless], so she is forbidden to the brother of her lover [under the same circumstances]. [Consequently, her lover's brother cannot marry her.] Just as the water puts her to the test for each act of sexual relations which she has with her husband after she has had sexual relations with her lover, so they put him to the test.*

B. *Testimony and Exemptions from the Ordeal*

M. 6:1 He who expressed jealousy to his wife, but she went aside in secret, even if he heard [that she had done so] from a bird flying by – he puts her away, but pays off her marriage-contract.

M. 6:2 [If] one witness said, "I saw that she was made unclean," she would not undergo the ordeal of drinking the bitter water. And not only so, but even if it was a boy-slave or a girl-slave, lo, these are believed even to invalidate her [from receiving payment of] her marriage-contract. As to her mother-in-law and the daughter of her mother-in-law, her co-wife, and the husband's brother's wife, and the daughter of her husband, lo, these are believed [cf. M. Yeb. 15:4] – not to invalidate her from receiving payment of her marriage-contract, but that she should not undergo the ordeal of drinking the bitter water.

M. 6:3 For logic might dictate as follows: Now, if, in the case of the first kind of testimony [that she has been warned not to get involved with such-and-such a man], which does not impose upon her a permanent prohibition [but only until she has undergone the ordeal of the bitter water], [the accusation] is not sustained by less than two witnesses, in the case of the second kind of testimony [that she has indeed been made unclean], which does impose upon her a permanent prohibition [against remaining wed to her husband], surely [the accusation] should not be sustained by less than two witnesses. But Scripture says, "And there is no witness against her" (Num. 5:13) – [meaning], any sort of testimony which there is against her. On these grounds we may now construct an argument from the lesser to the greater with reference to the first kind of testimony: Now if the second kind of testimony, which imposes upon her a permanent prohibition, lo, is sustained by a single witness, the first kind of testimony, which does not impose upon her a permanent prohibition, surely should be sustained by means of a single witness. But Scripture says, 'Because he has found some unseemly matter in her' (Deut. 24:1), and elsewhere it says, 'At the mouth of two witnesses shall a matter be established" (Deut. 19:15) – just as matter spoken of there requires two witnesses, so matter spoken of here requires two witnesses.

M. 6:4 [If] one witness says, "She was made unclean," and one witness says, "She was not made unclean," [if] one woman says, "She was made unclean," and one woman says, "She was not made unclean," she would undergo the ordeal of drinking the bitter water. [If] one witness says, "She was made unclean," and two witnesses say, "She was not made unclean," she would undergo the ordeal of drinking the bitter water. [If] two say, "She was made unclean," and one says, "She was not made unclean," she would not undergo the ordeal of drinking the bitter water.

T. 5:8 One witness says, "She was made unclean." and one witness says, "She was not made unclean," – a woman says, "She was made unclean," and a woman says, "She was not made unclean" [M. Sot. 6:4] – she either undergoes the ordeal of drinking the water or does not collect her marriage-contract.

## II. Analysis: The Problematics of the Topic, Sotah

The Written Torah appears superficially to have set forth the program of the Oral Torah's halakhah, but in fact, sages have redefined the entire program of the topic. First of all, the halakhah takes the ordeal and encases it in juridical procedures, rules of evidence, guidelines meant to protect the woman from needless exposure to the ordeal to begin with. The halakhah radically revises the entire transaction, when it says, if the husband expresses jealousy by instructing his wife not to speak with a specified person, and the wife spoke with the man, there is no juridical result: she still is permitted to have sexual relations with her husband and is permitted to eat heave-offering. But if she went with him to some private place and remained with him for sufficient time to become unclean, she is prohibited from having sexual relations with her husband and if the husband is a priest, she is prohibited from eating heave-offering.

The halakhah thus conceives of a two-stage process, two kinds of testimony. In the first kind, she is warned not to get involved, but she is not then prohibited to the husband. In the second kind of stage, witnesses attest that she can have committed adultery. Not only so, but the halakhah wants valid evidence if it is to deprive the wife of her marriage-settlement. If a single witness to the act of intercourse is available, that does not suffice. People who ordinarily cannot testify against her do not have the power to deprive her if her property rights in the marriage, e.g., her mother-in-law and the daughter of her mother-in-law, her co-wife, and the husband's brother's wife, and the daughter of her husband. She still collects her settlement. But because of their testimony, she does not undergo the rite; she is divorced in course and the transaction concludes there.

Before the ordeal is invoked, the Oral Torah therefore wants some sort of solid evidence [1] of untoward sexual activity and also [2] of clear action on the part of the wife: at least the possibility, confirmed through a specific case, that adultery has taken place. Scripture leaves everything to the husband's whim, the "spirit of jealousy." So here if the husband gives his statement of jealousy and the wife responds by ignoring the statement, the ordeal does not apply. By her specific action the wife has to indicate the possibility that the husband is right. This is a far cry from Scripture's "spirit of jealousy." For the Written Torah, the ordeal settles all questions. For the Oral Torah, the ordeal takes effect only in carefully defined cases where [1] sufficient evidence exists to invoke the rite, but [2] insufficient evidence to make it unnecessary: well-established doubt, so to speak.

The halakhah of the Oral Torah further introduces the clarification that the marriage must be a valid one; if the marriage violates the law of the Torah, e.g., the marriage of a widow to a high priest, the rite of the ordeal does not apply. The rite does not apply at the stage of betrothal, only of a fully consummated marriage. If the fiancé expressed jealousy to the betrothed or the levir to the deceased childless brother's widow, no rite is inflicted. Sages severely limited the range of applicability of the rite. Not only so, but the marriage may well be severed without the ordeal's being inflicted, if the wife confesses, if there are witnesses to the act, if the wife declines to go through the ordeal, if the husband declines to impose it, or if the husband has sexual relations with her en route to the performance of the ordeal. In such cases the marital bond is called into question, so the wife loses her status as wife of a priest, should the husband be a priest. If in the preliminaries to the ordeal she confesses, she is given a writ of divorce, losing her marriage-settlement. Only if she continues to plead purity is the ordeal imposed. The details of the rite are meant to match the sequence of actions that the unfaithful wife has taken with the paramour, beautifully expounded at M. 1:7 and its accompanying Tosefta-composite, cited in the interpretive section of this account.

The halakhah makes provision for the cancellation of the rite, down to the point at which the scroll is blotted out, with the divine names inscribed therein. At that point, the accused wife can no longer pull out of the ordeal. That moment matches, in effect, the moment of death of the sacrifier, when we have to dispose of the animals that he has sanctified for his offering. But if at that point she confesses, the water is poured out, and she loses her marriage-settlement but otherwise is left alone. So too, if witnesses come, or if she refuses to drink, or if the husband pulls out, the meal offering is burned. If I had to summarize in a single sentence the main thrust of the halakhah of Sotah, it is to create the conditions of perfect, unresolved doubt, so far as the husband is concerned, alongside perfect certainty of innocence, so far as the wife is concerned. Despite the humiliation that awaits, she is willing to place her marriage-settlement on the line, so sure is she that she is innocent. His doubt is well-founded, but remains a matter of doubt, so uncertain is he of her status. Then, and only then, the ordeal intervenes to resolve the exquisitely-balanced scale of her certainty against his doubt.

### III. Interpretation: Religious Principles of Sotah

Justice defines the problematics of the topic, the wife accused of adultery, and the theme of how the righteous are rewarded and the wicked punished through the reliable working of God's justice permeates the Oral Torah's exposition of the topic at hand. And, still more to the point, the sages choose this particular topic – justice in the household, justice for the accused wife – as the centerpiece of its presentation of evidence that, in the end, God does justice for all to see. Sages recapitulate the rite only to recast it into a juridical transaction, one involving procedures that protect the woman's right and secure, so far as possible, her dignity under her husband's accusation. They do not allow the husband lightly to sever the marriage without paying the marriage-settlement, and they do insist on the normal rules of evidence, so far as these pertain.

As the sages re-present the ordeal imposed on the accused wife, they underscore the exact justice that the ordeal executes. The exposition of the topic in the Mishnah and the Tosefta, therefore also in the Talmuds, lays heavy emphasis upon how, measure for measure, the punishment fits the crime – but the reward matches the virtue. What the guilty wife has done, the law punishes appropriately; but also, they point to cases in which acts of merit receive appropriate recognition and reward. In this way sages make the point that, within the walls of the household, rules of justice prevail, with reward for goodness and punishment for evil the standard in the household as much as in public life. Why sages have chosen the halakhah of the accused wife as the venue for their systematic exposition of the divine law of justice is not difficult to explain.

The law of the accused wife renders urgent the question of whether and how justice governs in the household. Scripture, as we note, imposes the ordeal not only upon the adulteress but on the faithful wife. A spirit of jealousy suffices, whether or not the wife warrants the husband's suspicion. Surely the entire procedure reeks of injustice, and the promise of future offspring hardly compensates for the public humiliation that the innocent wife has undergone. It is in that context that, in the very presentation of the halakhah, the Oral Torah systematically lays out the evidence that, here, especially here, justice prevails. And that means not only that the wicked woman is punished, but that the righteous one is rewarded. What for Scripture is tacked on as an afterthought in the Oral Torah becomes a principal focus of exposition.

If we turn from the halakhah to the aggadah, we find precisely the same focus on how God's perfect justice is embodied in the very rite of the accused wife. That underscores sages' own intent in the halakhah, which is to secure to the accused wife the right to absolutely just disposition of her case. In sages' view, which animates every line in the Oral Torah, the will of the one, unique God, made manifest through the Torah, governs, and, further, God's will, for both private life and public activity, is rational. That is to say, within man's understanding of reason, God's will is just. And by "just," sages understood the commonsense meaning: fair, equitable, proportionate, commensurate. In place of fate or impersonal destiny, chance, or simply irrational, inexplicable chaos, God's plan and purpose everywhere come to realization. So the Oral Torah identifies God's will as the active and causative force in the lives of individuals and nations.

But the coherence of the theology hardly presents a surprise. The more urgent question is, how do sages know that God's will is realized in the moral order of justice, involving reward and punishment? Sages turned to Scripture for the pertinent facts; that is where God makes himself manifest. But of the various types of scriptural evidence – explicit commandments, stories, prophetic admonitions – that they had available to show how the moral order prevailed in all being, what type did the prefer? The one bearing the greatest probative weight derived from the exact match between sin and punishment. Here is their starting point; from here all else flows smoothly and in orderly fashion. World order is best embodied when sin is punished, merit rewarded – both; one without the other does not suffice.

That body of evidence, the facts, that Scripture supplied recorded human action and divine reaction, on the one side, and meritorious deed and divine response and reward, on the other. It was comprised by consequential cases, drawn from both private and public life, to underscore sages' insistence upon the match between the personal and the public, all things subject to the same simple rule. That demonstration of not only the principle but the precision of measure for measure, deriving from Scripture's own record of God's actions, takes priority of place in the examination of the rationality of sages' universe. That is because it permeates their system and frames its prevailing modes of explanation and argument. The principle that all being conforms to rules, and that these rules embody principles of justice through exact punishment of particular sin, precise reward of singular acts of virtue defined the starting point of all rational thought and the entire character of sages' theological structure and system. What we see in the topic at hand is of special interest: when sages wish to show the justice of God, they turn to the case before us.

It is here, in particular, that sages identify the sources for their conviction of the order of society, natural and supernatural alike. What captures our interest is not the conviction but the way in which sages set forth that conviction. What they found to overcome the doubt that everyday life surely cast upon their insistence upon the governing of a moral order was the facts of Scripture as they ordered those facts. Now, were we on our own to open Scripture and locate pertinent evidence that God is just and the world he made conforms to rules of equity, we should find Scripture states it in so many words. It is not merely that when God contemplated the world that he had made, he pronounced it good; Scripture leaves no doubt about God's definitive trait of justice, justice understood as man does, in a different context altogether.

That is why, when sages examined the facts of Scripture to establish that principle of rationality and order in conformity to the requirements of justice and equity, what impressed them was not the inevitability but the precision of justice. Scripture portrays the world order as fundamentally just and reasonable, and it does so in countless ways. But Scripture encompasses the complaint of Job and the reflection of Qoheleth. Sages for their part identified those cases that transcended generalities and established the facticity of proportionate justice, treating them as not only exemplary but probative. They set forth their proposition and amassed evidence in support of it. And, to underscore the point that sages demonstrate in the present halakhic category: when God judges and sentences, not only is the judgment fair but the penalty fits the crime with frightening precision. But so too, when God judges and awards a decision of merit, the reward proves equally exact. These two together, the match of sin and penalty, meritorious deed and reward, then are shown to explain the point and purpose of one detail after another, and, all together, they add up to the portrait of a world order that is fundamentally and essentially just – the starting point and foundation of all else.

Here is sages' account of God's justice, which is always commensurate, both for reward and punishment, in consequence of which the present permits us to peer into the future with certainty of what is going to happen, so M. Sot. 1:7ff. What we note is sages' identification of the precision of justice, the exact match of action and reaction, each step in the sin, each step in the response, and, above all, the immediacy of God's presence in the entire transaction. They draw general conclusions from the specifics of the law that Scripture sets forth, and that is where systematic thinking about takes over from exegetical learning about cases, or, in our own categories, philosophy from history, noted earlier:

### Mishnah-tractate Sotah 1:7

A. By that same measure by which a man metes out [to others], do they mete out to him:
B. She primped herself for sin, the Omnipresent made her repulsive.
C. She exposed herself for sin, the Omnipresent exposed her.

We begin with sages' own general observations based on the facts set forth in Scripture. The course of response of the woman accused of adultery to her drinking of the bitter water that is supposed to produce one result for the guilty, another for the innocent, is described in Scripture in this language: "If no man has lain with you...be free from this water of bitterness that brings the curse. But if you have gone astray...then the Lord make you an execration...when the Lord makes your thigh fall away and your body swell; may this water...pass into your bowels and make your body swell and your thigh fall away" (Num. 5:20-22). This is amplified and expanded, extended to the entire rite, where the woman is disheveled; then the order, thigh, belly, shows the perfect precision of the penalty. What Scripture treats as a case, sages transform into a generalization, so making Scripture yield governing rules. The same passage proceeds to further cases, which prove the same point: where the sin begins, there the punishment also commences; but also, where an act of virtue takes its point, there divine reward focuses as well. Merely listing the following names, without spelling out details, for the cognoscenti of Scripture will have made that point: Samson, Absalom, Miriam, Joseph, and Moses. Knowing how Samson and Absalom match, also Miriam, Joseph, and Moses, would then suffice to establish the paired and matched general principles.

Justice requires not only punishment of the sinner or the guilty but reward of the righteous and the good, and so sages find ample, systematic evidence in Scripture for both sides of the equation of justice:

### Mishnah-tractate Sotah 1:9

A. And so is it on the good side:
B. Miriam waited a while for Moses, since it is said, "And his sister stood afar off" (Ex. 2:4), therefore, Israel waited on her seven days in the wilderness, since it is said, "And the people did not travel on until Miriam was brought in again" (Num. 12:15).

## Mishnah-tractate Sotah 1:10

A. Joseph had the merit of burying his father, and none of his brothers was greater than he, since it is said, "And Joseph went up to bury his father...and there went up with him both chariots and horsemen" (Gen. 50:7, 9).

B. We have none so great as Joseph, for only Moses took care of his [bones].

C. Moses had the merit of burying the bones of Joseph, and none in Israel was greater than he, since it is said, "And Moses took the bones of Joseph with him" (Ex. 13:19).

D. We have none so great as Moses, for only the Holy One blessed he Be took care of his [bones], since it is said, "And he buried him in the valley" (Deut. 34:6).

E. And not of Moses alone have they stated [this rule], but of all righteous people, since it is said, "And your righteousness shall go before you. The glory of the Lord shall gather you [in death]" (Isa. 58:8).

Scripture provides the main probative evidence for the anticipation that when God judges, he will match the act of merit with an appropriate reward and the sin with an appropriate punishment. The proposition begins, however, with general observations as to how things are, M. 1:7, and not with specific allusions to proof-texts; the character of the law set forth in Scripture is reflected upon. The accumulated cases yield the generalization.

Sifré to Numbers, a systematic exegesis of the biblical book of Numbers, takes up the Mishnah's proposition concerning Numbers 5:23ff., that, when God punishes, he starts with that with which the transgression commenced, which sages see as a mark of the precision of divine justice:

## Sifré to Numbers XVIII:I.1:

1. A. "And when he has made her drink the water, [then, if she has defiled herself and has acted unfaithfully against her husband, the water that brings the curse shall enter into her and cause bitter pain,] and her body shall swell, and her thigh shall fall away, [and the woman shall become an execration among her people. But if the woman has not defiled herself and is clean, then she shall be free and shall conceive children]" (Num. 5:23-28).

   B. I know only that her body and thigh are affected. How do I know that that is the case for the rest of her limbs?

   C. Scripture states, "...the water that brings the curse shall enter into her."

   D. So I take account of the phrase, "...the water that brings the curse shall enter into her."

   E. Why [if all the limbs are affected equally] then does Scripture specify her body and her thigh in particular?

   F. As to her thigh, the limb with which she began to commit the transgression -- from there the punishment begins.

But the sages represented by Sifré to Numbers, exegetes of Scripture and the Mishnah, like the commentators whom we shall meet in the Tosefta that follows, wish to introduce their own cases in support of the same proposition:

G. Along these same lines:
H. "And he blotted out everything that sprouted from the earth, from man to beast" (Gen. 7:23.
I. From the one who began the transgression [namely Adam, the punishment begins.

Adam sinned first, therefore the flood began with Adam. Now comes a different sort of proportion: the exact match. The Sodomites are smitten with piles:

J. Along these same lines:
K. "..and the men who were at the gate of the house they smote with piles" (Gen. 19:11).
L. From the one who began the transgression the punishment begins.

In the third instance, Pharaoh is in the position of Adam; with him the sin began, with him the punishment starts:

M. Along these same lines:
N. "...and I shall be honored through Pharaoh and through all of his force" (Ex. 14:4).
O. Pharaoh began the transgression, so from him began the punishment.
P. Along these same lines:
Q. "And you will most certainly smite at the edge of the sword the inhabitants of that city" (Deut. 134:15).
R. From the one who began the transgression, the punishment begins.
S. Along these same lines is the present case:
T. the limb with which she began to commit the transgression -- from there the punishment begins.

Here comes a point important to the system: God's mercy vastly exceeds his justice, so the measure of reward is far greater than the measure of punishment – and, if possible, still more prompt:

U. Now does this not yield an argument *a fortiori:*
V. If in the case of the attribution of punishment, which is the lesser, from the limb with which she began to commit the transgression -- from there the punishment begins,
W. in the case of the attribute of bestowing good, which is the greater, how much the more so!

Punishment is rational in yet a more concrete way: it commences with the very thing that has sinned, or with the person who has sinned. So the principles of reason and good order pervade the world. We know that fact because Scripture's account of all that matters has shown it. But the exposition of justice commences with the topic at hand.

The Tosefta contributes further cases illustrating the exact and appropriate character of both divine justice and divine reward. What is important here is what is not made explicit; it concerns a question that the Mishnah does not raise: what about the gentiles? Does the principle of world order of justice apply to them, or are they subject to chaos? The answer given through cases here is that the same rules of justice apply to gentiles, not only Israelites such as are listed in the Mishnah's primary statement of the principle. That point is made through the cases that are selected: Sennacherib, who besieged Jerusalem after destroying Israel comprised by the northern tribes, Nebuchadnezzar, who took and destroyed Jerusalem in the time of Jeremiah. Now the sin is the single most important one, arrogance or hubris, and the penalty is swift and appropriate, the humbling of the proud by an act of humiliation:

### Tosefta tractate Sotah 3:18

A.   Sennacherib took pride before the Omnipresent only through an agent, as it is said, "By your messengers you have mocked the Lord and you have said, "With my many chariots I have gone up the heights of the mountains...I dug wells and drank foreign waters, and I dried up with the sole of my foot all the streams of Egypt" (11 Kings 19:23-24).

B.   So the Omnipresent, blessed be He, exacted punishment from him only through an agent, as it is said, "And that night the messenger of the Lord went forth and slew a hundred and eighty-five thousand in the camp of the Assyrians" ( 2 Kings 19:35).

C.   And all of them were kings, with their crowns bound to their heads.

### Tosefta tractate Sotah 3:19

A.   Nebuchadnezzar said, "The denizens of this earth are not worthy for me to dwell among them. I shall make for myself a little cloud and dwell In it," as it is said, "I will ascend above the heights of the clouds, I will make myself like the Most High" (Isa. 14:14).

B.   Said to him the Omnipresent, blessed be He, "You said in your heart, 'I will ascend to heaven, above the stars of God I will set my throne on high' – I shall bring you down to the depths of the pit" (Isa. 14:13, 15).

C.   What does it say? "But you are brought down to Sheol, to the depths of the pit" (Isa. 14:15).

D.   Were you the one who said, "The denizens of this earth are not worthy for me to dwell among them"?

E.   The king said, "Is not this great Babylon, which I have built by my mighty power as a royal residence and for the glory of my majesty? While the words were still in the king's mouth, there fell a voice from heaven, O King Nebuchadnezzar, to you it is spoken, The kingdom has departed from you, and you shall be driven from among men, and your dwelling shall be with the beasts of the field, and you shall be made to eat grass like an ox" (Dan. 4:29-32).

F.   All this came upon King Nebuchadnezzar at the end of twelve months (Dan. 4:28-29).

As in the Mishnah, so here too, we wish to prove that justice governs not only to penalize sin but also to reward virtue. To this point we have shown the proportionate character of punishment to sin, the exact measure of justice. The first task in this other context is to establish the proportions, now of reward to punishment.

Is reward measured out with the same precision? Not at all, reward many times exceeds punishment. So if the measure of retribution is exactly proportionate to the sin, the measure of reward exceeds the contrary measure by a factor of five hundred. Later on we shall see explicit argument that justice without mercy is incomplete; to have justice, mercy is the required complement. Here we address another aspect of the same matter, that if the measure of punishment precisely matches the measure of sin, when it comes to reward for merit or virtue, matters are not that way:

### Tosefta tractate Sotah 4:1

A.  I know only with regard to the measure of retribution that by that same measure by which a man metes out, they mete out to him [M . Sot. 1:7A]. How do I know that the same is so with the measure of goodness [M. Sot. 1:9A]?

B.  Thus do you say:'

C.  The measure of goodness is five hundred times greater than the measure of retribution.

D.  With regard to the measure of retribution it is written, "Visiting the sin of the fathers on the sons and on the grandsons to the third and fourth generation" (Ex. 20:5).

E.  And with regard to the measure of goodness it is written, "And doing mercy for thousands' (Ex. 20:6).

F.  You must therefore conclude that the measure of goodness is five hundred times greater than the measure of retribution.

Having made that point, we revert to the specifics of cases involving mortals, not God, and here, we wish to show the simple point that reward and punishment meet in the precision of justice.

Before proceeding to the Tosefta's extension of matters in a quite unanticipated direction, let us turn to further amplifications of the basic point concerning the exact character of the punishment for a given sin. The fact is, not only does the sinner lose what he or she wanted, but the sinner also is denied what formerly he or she had possessed, a still more mordant and exact penalty indeed. At T. Sotah 4:16, the statement of the Mishnah, "Just as she is prohibited to her husband, so she is prohibited to her lover" [M. Sot. 5:1], is transformed into a generalization, which is spelled out, and then demonstrated by a list lacking all articulation; the items on the list serve to make the point. The illustrative case – the snake and Eve – is given at T. 4:17-18. The list then follows at T. 4:19.

## Tosefta Sotah 4:16

A. Just as she is prohibited to her husband, so she is prohibited to her lover:

B. You turn out to rule in the case of an accused wife who set her eyes on someone who was not available to her:

C. What she wanted is not given to her, and what she had in hand is taken away from her.

## Tosefta Sotah 4:17

The poetry of justice is not lost: what the sinner wanted he does not get, and what he had he loses:

A. And so you find in the case of the snake of olden times, who was smarter than all the cattle and wild beasts of the field, as it is said, 'Now the serpent was smarter than any other wild creature that the Lord God had made'" (Gen. 3:1 ).

B. He wanted to slay Adam and to marry Eve.

C. The Omnipresent said to him, "I said that you should be king over all beasts and wild animals. Now that you did not want things that way, 'You are more cursed than all the beasts and wild animals of the field' (Gen. 3:14).

D. "I said that you should walk straight-up like man. Now that you did not want things that way, 'Upon your belly you shall go' (Gen. 3:14).

E. "I said that you should eat human food and drink human drink. Now: 'And dust you shall eat all the days of your life' (Gen. 3:14).

## Tosefta Sotah 4:18

A. "You wanted to kill Adam and marry Eve? 'And 1 will put enmity between you and the woman' (Gen. 3:15)."

B. You turn out to rule, What he wanted was not given to him, and what he had in hand was taken away from him.

Sages' mode of thought through classification and hierarchization to uncover patterns does not require the spelling out of the consequences of the pattern through endless cases. On the contrary, sages are perfectly happy to list the other examples of the same rule, knowing that we can reconstruct the details if we know the facts of Scripture that have been shown to follow a common paradigm:

## Tosefta Sotah 4:19

A. And so you find in the case of Cain, Korah, Balaam, Doeg, Ahitophel, Gahazi, Absalom, Adonijah, Uzziah, and Haman, all of whom set their eyes on what they did not have coming to them.

B. What they wanted was not given to them, and what they had in hand was taken away from them.

Were we given only T. 4:19A, a construction lacking all explanation, we should have been able to reach T. 4:19B! Here is a fine example of how a pattern signals its own details, and how knowing the native categories allows us to elaborate the pattern with little further data. But whether we should have identified as the generative message, What he wanted was not given to him, and what he had in hand was taken away from him, is not equivalently clear, and I am inclined to think that without the fully-exposed example, we could not have done what the compositor has instructed us to do: fill out the *et cetera*. What a passage of this kind underscores is sages' confidence that those who would study their writings saw the paradigm within the case and possessed minds capable of generalization and objective demonstration.

As to Tosefta Sotah 4:1, which we considered above, sages both distinguish the realm of the Torah from the realm of idolatry, Israel from the gentiles, but also treat the two realms as subject to one and the same rule justice. But then what difference does the Torah make for holy Israel, the Torah's sector of humanity? As the Tosefta's passage that we first met just now proceeds, discussion shades over into a response to this very question. The point concerning reward and punishment is made not at random but through the close reading of Scripture's record concerning not only the line of Noah – the Generation of the Flood, the men of Sodom and Gomorrah, the Egyptians – but also the founder of God's line on earth, Abraham. Abraham here, often head of the line with Isaac and Jacob, is deemed the archetype for Israel, his extended family. What he did affects his heirs. His actions form models for the right conduct of his heirs. What happened to him will be recapitulated in the lives and fate of his heirs.

So from retributive justice and the gentiles, the discourse shifts to distributive reward, shared by the founder and his heirs later on. Reward also is governed by exact justice, the precision of the deed matched by the precision of the response:

### Tosefta tractate Sotah 4:1

G. And so you find in the case of Abraham that by that same measure by which a man metes out, they mete out to him.

H. He ran before the ministering angels three times, as it is said, "When he saw them, he ran to meet them" (Gen. 18:2), "And Abraham hastened to the tent" (Gen. 18:6), "And Abraham ran to the herd" (Gen. 18:7).

I. So did the Omnipresent, blessed be He, run before his children three times, as it is said, 'The Lord came from Sinai, and dawned from Seir upon us; he shone forth from Mount Paran" (Deut. 33:2).

Justice extends beyond the limits of a single life, when the life is Abraham's. Now justice requires that Abraham's heirs participate in the heritage of virtue that he has bequeathed. Point by point, God remembers Abraham's generous actions in favor of Abraham's children into the long future, an intimation of a doctrine involving a heritage of grace that will play a considerable role in the theological system. Here, point by point, what Abraham does brings benefit to his heirs:

### Tosefta tractate Sotah 4:2

A. Of Abraham it is said, "He bowed himself to the earth" (Gen. 18:2).
B. So will the Omnipresent, blessed be He, respond graciously to his children in time to come, "Kings will be your foster-fathers, and their queens your nursing mothers. With their faces to the ground they shall bow down to you and lick the dust of your feet" (Isa. 49:23).
C. Of Abraham it is said, 'Let a little water be brought" (Gen. 18:4).
D. So did the Omnipresent, blessed be He, respond graciously and give to his children a well in the wilderness, which gushed through the whole camp of Israel, as it is said, "The well which the princes dug, which the nobles of the people delved (Num. 21:18) teaching that it went over the whole south and watered the entire desert, which looks down upon the desert" (Num. 2 1 :20).
E. Of Abraham it is said, 'And rest yourselves under the tree" (Gen. 18:4).
F. So the Omnipresent gave his children seven glorious clouds in the wilderness, one on their right, one on their left, one before them, one behind them, one above their heads, and one as the Presence among them.

The same theme is expounded in a systematic way through the entire account; it is worth dealing with the complete statement:

### Tosefta tractate Sotah 4:3

A. Of Abraham it is said, "While I fetch a morsel of bread that you may refresh yourselves" (Gen. 18:5).
B. So did the Omnipresent, blessed be He, give them manna in the wilderness, as it is said, "The people went about and gathered it...and made cakes of it, and the taste of it was like the taste of cakes baked with oil" (Num. 11:8).

### Tosefta tractate Sotah 4:4

A. Of Abraham it is said, "And Abraham ran to the herd and took a calf, tender and good" (Gen. 18:7).
B. So the Omnipresent, blessed be He, rained down quail from the sea for his children, as it is said, "And there went forth a wind from the Lord, and it brought quails from the sea, and let them fall beside the camp" (Num. 11:31).

### Tosefta tractate Sotah 4:5

A. Of Abraham what does it say? 'And Abraham stood over them" (Gen. I 8:8).
B. So the Omnipresent, blessed be He, watched over his children in Egypt, as it is said, "And the Lord passed over the door" (Ex. 12:23).

### Tosefta tractate Sotah 4:6

A. Of Abraham what does it say? 'And Abraham went with them to set them on their way" (Gen. 18:16).

B. So the Omnipresent, blessed be He, accompanied his children for forty years, as it is said, "These forty years the Lord your God has been with you" (Deut. 2:7).

The evidence is of the same character as that adduced in the Mishnah: cases of Scripture. But the power of the Tosefta's treatment of Abraham must be felt: finding an exact counterpart in Israel's later history to each gesture of the progenitor, Abraham, shows the match between the deeds of the patriarchs and the destiny of their family later on. Justice now is given dimensions we should not have anticipated, involving not only the individual but the individual's family, meaning, the entire community of holy Israel. Once more, we note, a systematic effort focuses upon details. Justice is not a generalized expectation but a very particular fact, bread/manna, calf/quail, and so on. There is where sages find the kind of detailed evidence that corresponds to the sort suitable in natural history.

The focus now shifts shift from how justice applies to the actions of named individuals – Samson, Absalom, Sennacherib and Nebuchadnezzar – to the future history of Israel, the entire sector of humanity formed by those whom God has chosen and to whom he will give eternal life. It is a jarring initiative. The kinds of instances of justice that are given until that point concern sin and punishment, or the reward of individuals for their own actions. And these cases surely conform to the context: justice as the principle that governs what happens to individuals in an orderly world. But now we find ample evidence of the fundamental position in sages' system, the generative character in their consideration of all issues that, as the first principle of world order, that justice governs.

For sages not only accept the burden of proving, against all experience, that goodness goes to the good and evil to the wicked. They have also alleged, and here propose to instantiate, that the holy people Israel itself, its history, its destiny, conform to the principle of justice. And if claim that justice governs in the lives and actions of private persons conflicts with experience, the condition of Israel, conquered and scattered, surely calls into question any allegation that Israel's story embodies that same orderly and reasonable principle. Before us sages take one step forward in their consideration of that very difficult question, how to explain the prosperity of the idolators, the gentiles, and the humiliation of those who serve the one true God, Israel. That step consists only in matching what Abraham does with what happens to his family later on.

If sages had to state the logic that imposes order and proportion upon all relationships – the social counterpart to the laws of gravity – they would point to justice: what accords with justice is logical, and what does not is irrational. Ample evidence derives from Scripture's enormous corpus of facts to sustain in sages view that the moral order, based on justice, governs the affairs of men and nations. But justice begins in the adjudication of the affairs of men and women in the Israelite household and from there radiates outward, to the social order of Israel, and thence, the world order of the nations. It is from the halakhah before us that sages commence their exposition of God's perfect justice, in rewarding the innocent and punishing the guilty, because only there could they state their deepest conviction concerning justice: all things start in the Israelite household, the smallest whole social unit of creation. That is why the law of the accused wife forms the ideal occasion, within the halakhic system, to underscore the requirements of justice.

# 4

## Ketubot

### I. An Outline of the Halakhah of Ketubot

Lacking any foundations in Scripture, the Ketubah, which provides for support for the wife by the husband and alimony in the event of divorce or the husband's death, liberates women from the uncertainty of life after the husband's death, on the one side, or divorce without alimony, on the other. This promises also restoration to the wife's family and patrimony of lands, goods and capital brought by the wife into the marriage and reserved for her male children by that husband. The point that, in my view, marks the woman's liberation from Scripture's formulation of her situation is simple. Here are spelled out not only the wife's obligations, but, concommitantly and equally, the husband's – and vice versa. Scripture does not pay attention to what the husband owes to the marriage, and takes for granted the wife's obligation. So the rabbis here take a substantial step toward the redefinition of the woman's rights within their encompassing system.

That then underscores the basic question facing the halakhah – as distinct from the generative premise, which we reach only at the end. It is how to spell out the reciprocal and corresponding rights and obligations of all parties to the marriage as it unfolds. The marriage-contract defines the locus for working out those rights and obligations; each party has an interest in the orderly formation of the social and economic fact of the marriage – and in its fair and orderly dissolution as well. Here the dissolution involves collecting the marriage-settlement from the husband's estate; as noted, elsewhere we deal with other aspects of the dissolution of the marriage (which may involve the dissolution of the household as well). That document and the arrangements it represents have no foundations in Scripture and constitute a contribution of the Oral part of the Torah alone.

Contributing no system but only anecdotal facts, Scripture figures only episodically, especially in two matters. First comes the fine for rape, which is paid to the father, so Deut. 22:28-29:

> "If a man meets a virgin who is not betrothed and seizes her and lies with her and they are found, then the man who lay with her shall give to the father of the young woman fifty shekels of silver and she shall be his wife, because he has violated her; he may not put her away all his days."

Next comes Ex. 22:15-16:

> "If a man seduces a virgin who is not betrothed and lies with her, he shall give the marriage present for her and make her his wife. If her father utterly refuses to give her to him, he shall pay money equivalent to the marriage-present for virgins."

Another aspect of the halakhah to which Scripture contributes concerns conflicting claims as to the virginity of the bride, so Deut. 22:13-21:

> "If any man takes a wife and goes in to her and then spurns her and charges her with shameful conduct and brings an evil name upon her, saying, 'I took this woman and when I came near her, I did not find in her the tokens of virginity,' then the father of the young woman and her mother shall take and bring out the tokens of her virginity to the elders of the city in the gate; and the father of the young woman shall say to the elders, 'I gave my daughter to this man to wife, and he spurns her, and lo, he has made shameful charges against her, saying, I did not find in your daughter the tokens of virginity. And yet these are the tokens of my daughter's virginity.' And they shall spread the garment before the elders of the city. Then the elders of that city shall take the man and whip him, and they shall fine him a hundred shekels of silver and give them to the father of the young woman, because he has brought an evil name upon a virgin of Israel; and she shall be his wife; he may not put her away all his days. But if the thing is true, that the tokens of virginity were not found in the young woman, then they shall bring out the young woman to the door of her father's house, and the men of her city shall stone her to death with stones, because she has wrought folly in Israel, by playing the harlot in her father's house; so you shall purge the evil from the midst of you."

But Scripture does not contribute the requirement of a marriage-agreement that provides for the woman's support in the event of divorce of death of the husband.

The topic of marriage-contracts takes as its generative problem reciprocal and corresponding rights and obligations of all parties to the marriage, at each point in the unfolding of the marriage. These parties are the girl, the boy, and the girl's family (father). The marriage-contract then defines the locus for the negotiation of the rights and obligations of each. All parties have an interest in the orderly formation of the social and economic fact of the marriage – the foundation, after all, of the household – and in its orderly dissolution as well. In the present context, that means, collecting the settlement from the husband's estate. Ketubot deals with the beginning, middle, and end of the marriage through human action, Yebamot, which does not figure in this study, through supernatural action (death of the husband without children and disposition of the marital bond between the widow and the deceased's surviving brother).

I.   **Foundation of the Household: The Material Rights of the Parties to the Marital Union [1] The Wife**

A.   *'The Marriage Contract of the Virgin*

M. 1:1 A virgin is married on Wednesday, and a widow on Thursday. For twice weekly are the courts in session in the towns, on Monday and on Thursday. So if he [the husband] had a complaint as to virginity, he goes early to court.

T. 1:1 On what account did they rule, A virgin is married on Wednesday [M. Ket. 1:1A]? So that if he had a complaint against her virginity, he goes to court early /on the next morning, when it is in session]. If so, she should [just as well] be married after the Sabbath [on Sunday ]. But because the husband does his preparations [for the wedding feast] through the [three] weekdays, they arranged that he should marry her on Wednesday. From the time of the danger [Bar Kokhba's War] and thereafter, they began the custom of marrying her on Tuesday, and sages did not stop them. [If] he wanted to marry her on Monday, they do not listen to him. But if it is on account of constraint [a death in the family], it is permitted. On what account do they keep the husband apart from the bride on the night of the Sabbath for the first act of sexual relations? Because he makes a bruise. On what account did they rule, A widow is married on Thursday [M. Ket. 1:1A]?. For if he should marry her on any day of the week, he may leave her and go back to work. So they arranged that he should marry her on Thursday, so that he should remain away from work for three successive days, Thursday, the eve of the Sabbath [Friday], and the Sabbath – three days away from work.. He turns out to take pleasure with her for three days running.

B. 1:1 I.11/4A Lo, IF HIS BREAD WAS BAKED, MEAT SLAUGHTERED, WINE MIXED, AND WATER POURED ON THE MEAT, BUT THEN THE FATHER OF THE GROOM OR THE MOTHER OF THE BRIDE DROPPED DEAD, THEY PUT THE DECEASED INTO A ROOM AND THEN BRING THE GROOM AND BRIDE INTO THE MARRIAGE CANOPY, WHERE THE GROOM HAS SEXUAL RELATIONS WITH THE BRIDE IN FULFILLMENT OF THE RELIGIOUS DUTY, BUT THEN [THE BURIAL OF THE DECEASED TAKES PLACE, AND, OF COURSE, THE GROOM FOR THE MOURNING PERIOD] SEPARATES HIMSELF FROM HER. THE SEVEN DAYS OF BANQUETING ARE OBSERVED, THEN THE SEVEN DAYS OF MOURNING, AND DURING ALL THOSE DAYS, HE SLEEPS AMONG THE MEN, AND SHE AMONG THE WOMEN. AND SO, IF HIS WIFE HAD HER PERIOD, HE

SLEEPS AMONG THE MEN AND SHE AMONG THE WOMEN. BUT THEY DO
NOT WITHHOLD ANY FORM OF ORNAMENT FROM THE BRIDE FOR ALL
THIRTY DAYS. ONE WAY OR THE OTHER, HE SHOULD NOT HAVE HIS FIRST
ACT OF SEXUAL RELATIONS ON A FRIDAY OR SATURDAY NIGHT.

M. 1:2 A virgin – her marriage contract is two hundred [zuz]. And
a widow, a maneh [one hundred zuz]. A virgin-widow, divorcée,
and one who has severed the levirate connection through a rite of
removing the shoe at the stage of betrothal – their marriage
contract is two hundred [zuz]. And they are subject to the claim
against their virginity. A convert, a woman taken captive, and a
slave girl who were redeemed or who converted or who were
freed at an age of less than three years and one day – their
marriage contract is two hundred [zuz]. And they are subject to
the claim against their virginity.

M. 1:3 An adult male who had sexual relations with a minor
female, and a minor male who had sexual relations with an adult
female – their marriage contract is two hundred zuz. The girl
injured by a blow – her marriage contract is a maneh.

T. 1:2 An adult male who had sexual relations with a minor female,
and a minor male who had sexual relations with an adult female,
and a girl injured by a blow [so that her signs of virginity are
destroyed] – their marriage-contract [for a marriage] to another is
two hundred [zuz [M. Ket. 1:3A-D].

M. 1:4 A virgin, a widow, a divorcée, or one who has severed the
levirate connection through a rite of removing the shoe – at the
stage of consummation of the marriage – their marriage contract is
a maneh. And they are not subject to a claim against their
virginity. A convert, a girl taken captive, or a slave girl who were
redeemed, or who converted, or who were freed at an age older
than three years and one day – their marriage contract is a maneh.
And they are not subject to a claim against their virginity.

T. 1:3 A man of sound senses who married a deaf-mute girl or an
idiot – their marriage-contract is two hundred zuz, for he wants to
gain a hold on their possessions. A deaf-mute or an idiot who
married a woman of sound senses, even though the deaf-mute went
and became sound in his senses, or the idiot regained his mind –
they [these women of sound senses] do not receive a marriage-
contract. [If after being healed] they went to confirm the marriage,
they pay a maneh as the marriage-contract. A gentile or a slave who
had sexual relations with an Israelite girl even though the gentile
went and converted, the slave went and was freed, they [the
women] do not have a marriage-contract. [If they [the convert, the
freed slave] wanted to confirm the marriage, they pay a maneh as
the marriage-contract. An Israelite who had sexual relations with a
slave-girl or with a gentile woman, even though the slave-girl went
and was freed, or the gentile-girl went and converted – they [the
women] do not have a marriage contract. [If] he wanted to confirm
the marriage, he gives a maneh as the marriage contract. An adult
woman and a barren woman – their marriage contract is two
hundred zuz. [If she was married in the assumption that she is
suitable and turned out to be barren, she has no marriage-contract.

[If] he wanted to confirm the marriage, he gives a maneh as the marriage-contract. He who has sexual relations with a deaf-mute girl or with an idiot or with a mature woman or with a girl wounded by a blow – they are not subject to a claim of virginity. In the case of a blind woman or a barren woman, they are subject to a claim of virginity.

B. *Conflicting Claims for the Marriage-Contract of a Virgin*

**M. 1:5 He who lives ["eats"] with his father-in-law in Judah, not with witnesses, cannot lodge a claim against the girl's virginity, for he has been alone with her. All the same are the widow of an Israelite and the widow of a priest – their marriage contract is a maneh [a hundred zuz]. The priests' court would collect four hundred zuz for a virgin.**

**M. 2:1 The woman who was widowed or divorced – she says, "You married me as a virgin" – and he says, "Not so, but I married you as a widow" – if there are witnesses that [when she got married], she went forth to music, with her hair flowing loose, her marriage contract is two hundred [zuz].**

T. 1:4 [If] he married her in the assumption that she was suitable and she turned out to have had prior sexual relations, even though she was in private [with him], [or] there are witnesses that she was not alone with him for sufficient time to have sexual relations, the second has no claim of virginity against her. Therefore the marriage-contract on his account is only maneh.

T. 1:5 He who accuses [his bride of having had sexual relations with another man before marriage], and his witnesses against her turn out to be conspirators – he is scourged and pays four hundred zuz [to the accused woman]. And the conspiratorial witnesses are taken out for stoning. [If] she was an orphan, he is scourged, and her marriage-contract remains valid, and he pays her four hundred zuz [in addition to it]. And the conspiratorial witnesses are taken out for stoning. [If] he did not tell the witnesses to bear witness, but they came along on their own and testified against the girl [and they turned out to be conspirators] – he [the husband] is not scourged and does not pay her four hundred zuz. But the conspiratorial witnesses are taken out for stoning. [If] she committed fornication when she was a girl, and after she had matured, he accused her [of having done so], he is not scourged and does not pay four hundred zuz. And she or the conspiratorial witnesses against her are then taken out for stoning.

T. 2:1 Witnesses who said," We testify about So-and-so, that he is the son of a divorcee, or the son of a woman who has performed the rite of halisah, of a Samaritan, of a Netin, or a Mamzer" – [if] before their testimony was cross-examined in court, they said, "We were joking," lo, they are believed. If after their testimony was cross-examined in court, they said, "We are joking," they are not believed. This is the general principle of the matter: Witnesses who testified to declare someone unclean or clean, to bring someone near or to put someone afar, to prohibit or to permit, to exempt or to render liable – [if] before their testimony was cross-examined in

court, they said, "We are joking," lo, these are believed. [If] after
their testimony was cross-examined in court, they said, "We are
joking," they are not believed.

T. 2:1 Greater is the power of a writ [document] than the power of
witnesses, and [greater is the power of] witnesses than the power of
a writ. Greater is the power of a writ, for a writ [of divorce]
removes a woman from the domain of her husband, which is not
the case with witnesses. Greater is the power of witnesses, for
witnesses who said, "So-and-so has died," – his wife may remarry.
But if it was written in a writ, "So-and-so has died," his wife may
not remarry. If they said, "What is written in this document we in
fact had heard but forgot," his wife may remarry. A man may write
down his testimony in a document and give testimony on the
strength of that document and continue even a hundred years after
[the date of the document]. Greater is the power of a document than
the power of money, and greater is the power of money than the
power of a document. For a document allows one to collect from
indentured [mortgaged] property, which is not the case with
money. Greater is the power of money, for money serves for the
redemption of things which have been given as Valuations and as
herem [to the sanctuary], things which have been sanctified, and
second tithe, which is not the case with a document. Greater is the
power of a document and of money than the power of possession,
and greater is the power of possession than the power of a
document and money. Greater is the power of a document and
money, for a document or money serve to acquire a Hebrew slave,
which is not the case with [mere] possession. Greater is the power
of possession, for if one sold a man ten fields, as soon as he takes
possession of one of them, he has acquired ownership of all of
them. But if he gave him only the price of one of them, or wrote him
a document only for one of them, he has acquired ownership of that
field alone.

C.  *The Rules of Evidence in Connection with the Validation of the Marriage-
    Contract*

**M. 2:2 In the case of him who says to his fellow, "This field
belonged to your father, and I bought it from him," he is
believed. For the mouth that prohibited is the mouth that
permitted. And if there are [other] witnesses that it had belonged
to his father, and he claims, "I bought it from him," he is not
believed.**

**M. 2:3 The witnesses who said, "This is our handwriting, but we
were forced [to sign]," "...we were minors," "...we were invalid
[as relatives] for testimony" – lo, these are believed, [and the writ
is invalid]. But if there are witnesses that it is their handwriting,
or if their handwriting was available from some other source,
they are not believed.**

**M. 2:4 This one says, "This is my handwriting, and this is the
handwriting of my fellow," and this one says, "This is my
handwriting, and this is the handwriting of my fellow" – lo, these
are believed. This one says, "This is my handwriting" and this**

one says, "This is my handwriting – they do not have to add another to them. But: A man is believed to say, "This is my handwriting."

M. 2:5 The woman who said, "I was married, and I am divorced," is believed. For the testimony that imposed a prohibition is the testimony that remitted the prohibition. But if there are witnesses that she was married, and she says, "I am divorced," she is not believed. [If] she said, "I was taken captive, but I am pure," she is believed. For the testimony that imposed a prohibition is the testimony that remitted the prohibition. But if there are witnesses to the fact that she was taken captive, and she says, "I am pure," she is not believed. But if the witnesses appeared [to testify that she was taken captive] only after she had remarried, lo, this one should not go forth.

B. 2:5 I:5/22A IF TWO WITNESSES SAY THE HUSBAND HAS DIED, AND TWO SAY HE HAS NOT DIED, TWO SAY THE WIFE HAS BEEN DIVORCED, AND TWO SAY SHE HAS NOT BEEN DIVORCED, LO, THIS WOMAN MAY NOT REMARRY, AND IF SHE HAS REMARRIED, SHE ALSO DOES NOT HAVE TO LEAVE HER SECOND HUSBAND.

B. 2:5 I:8 22B IF TWO WITNESSES SAY SHE WAS BETROTHED AND TWO SAY SHE WAS NOT BETROTHED, SHE SHOULD NOT MARRY, AND IF SHE HAS MARRIED, SHE SHALL NOT GO FORTH. IF TWO SAY SHE WAS DIVORCED AND TWO SAY SHE WAS NOT DIVORCED, SHE SHALL NOT MARRY, AND IF SHE HAS MARRIED, SHE WILL GO FORTH.

M. 2:6 Two women who were taken captive – this one says, "I was taken captive, but I am pure," and that one says, "I was taken captive, but I am pure" – they are not believed. And when they give evidence about one another, lo, they are believed.

M. 2:7 And so two men – this one says, "I am a priest," and that one says, "I am a priest" – they are not believed. But when they give evidence about one another, lo, they are believed.

T. 2:2 The two hundred zuz owing to a virgin, the maneh owing to a widow, the compensation for damages and half-damages, double payment, and four- and five-times payment – all of them, even though they are not written in a document, do people collect from indentured property. The woman who said, "I am married," and then went and said, "I am not married" is believed. For the mouth which prohibited is the mouth which permitted [M. Ket. 2:5A-B]. [If] she said, "I was taken captive, but I am pure, and I have witnesses that I am pure," they do not say, "Let us wait until the witnesses come and render her permitted." But they permit her [to return to her husband] forthwith [M. Ket. 2:5E-F]. If once she has been permitted, witnesses come and say, "She was taken captive," lo, this one should not remarry. [If they say,] "She was taken captive and was contaminated," even though she has children, she should go forth [M. Ket. 2:5I]. One witness says, "She was taken captive and has been contaminated," and one witness says, "She was taken captive but is pure" – One woman says, "She was taken captive and is contaminated," and one woman says, "She was taken captive but is pure" – lo, this one should not remarry. But if she remarried, she should not go forth. Two women who were taken captive [M. Ket. 2:6H] – This one says, "I am unclean, but my girlfriend is clean," – she is believed. [If] she says, "I am clean, and my girlfriend is unclean," she is not believed. "I and my girlfriend are unclean" – she is believed concerning herself, but she is not believed concerning her girlfriend. "I and my girlfriend are clean" – she is believed concerning her girlfriend but she is not believed concerning herself [M. Ket. 2:6E]. And so too with two men [M. Ket. 2:7A]: This one says, "My friend is a priest," and this one says, "My friend is a priest," – they give them [heave-offering] [M. Ket. 2:7E]. But as to confirming that they are priests [for genealogical purposes], they are not believed until there will be three of them, so that there will be two giving testimony about this one, and two giving testimony about that one.

T. 2:3 They raise to he priesthood [people thought to be] Levites or Israelites on the strength of the testimony of a single witness [M. Ket. 2:8C]. But they lower someone from the priesthood only on the evidence of two witnesses. How does one cast doubt about the matter? If they said, "How does Mr. So-and-so jump up into the priesthood, who never raised his hands to give the priestly blessing in his entire life, who never took his share [of heave-offering] in his entire life" – this is not a suitable casting of doubt. [If they said], "He is the son of a divorcee or of a woman who has performed the rite of halisah, of a Samaritan, a Netin, or a mamzer," lo, this constitutes casting doubt about the matter.

T. 3:1 There are two presumptive grounds for a person's being deemed to be in the priesthood in the Land of Israel: Raising up hands [in the priestly benediction], and sharing heave-offering at the threshing floor. And in Syria: Up to the point at which the agents announcing the new moon reach, the raising of hands in the priestly benediction [constitutes adequate grounds], but not sharing heave-offering at the threshing floor. Babylonia is in the same status as Syria.

M. 2:9 **The woman who was taken prisoner by gentiles – [if it was] for an offense concerning property, she is permitted [to return] to her husband. [If it was for] a capital offense, she is prohibited to her husband. A city which was overcome by siege – all the priest girls found therein are invalid [to return to their husbands]. But if they have witnesses, even a man slave or a girl slave, lo, they are believed. But a person is not believed to testify in his own behalf.**

T. 3:2 All are believed to give testimony about her, even her son, even her daughter – except for her and her husband, for a man does not give testimony in his own behalf.

M. 2:10 **And these are believed to give testimony when they reach maturity about what they saw when they were minors: A man is believed to say, (1) "This is the handwriting of Father," and (2) "This is the handwriting of Rabbi," and (3) "This is the handwriting of my brother" (4) "I remember about Mrs. So-and-so that she went forth to music with her hair flowing loose [when she was married]" [M. 2:1] (5) "I remember that Mr. So-and-so would go forth from school to immerse to eat food in the status of** priestly rations," (6) "That he would take a share [of food in the status of priestly rations] with us at the threshing floor" (7) "This place is a grave area" (8) "Up to here did we walk on the Sabbath." But a man is not believed to say, (9) "Mr. So-and-so had a right of way in this place," (10) "So-and-so had the right of halting and holding a lamentation in this place."

T. 3:3 A man is believed to say, "Father told me this family is unclean," "That family is clean," "We ate at the cutting off [ceremony marking the marriage of a man or woman to someone beneath his or her genealogical rank] of Mrs. So-and-so," "and that his teacher said to So-and-so, 'Go and immerse [to be clean for] your heave-offering,'" "We used to bring heave-offerings and tithes to So-and-so." They are believed so far as allowing the giving of heave-offerings and tithes to So-and-so, but not to confirm him in the priesthood [for genealogical purposes]. Or [if he said], "Others brought him [heave-offering and tithes]" – they are not believed. But if he was a gentile and converted, a slave and was freed, lo, these are not believed. They are not believed to say, "I remember about So-and-so that he owes Mrs. So-and-so a maneh" – and "Such-and-such a road crosses such-and-such a field" – for this [right of way] is equivalent to property. Under what circumstances? When they gave testimony on the spot [about their own hometown]. But if they went forth and came back, they are not believed, for they may have stated matters only because of enticement or fear.

T. 3:4 All the same are men, women, slaves, and minors: they are believed to say, "This place is unclean," and "This place is clean" [M. Ket. 2:10E].

B. 2:10 IX.4/28B WHAT IS THE CUTTING-OFF CEREMONY? IF ONE OF THE BROTHERS MARRIED A WOMAN THAT WAS NOT APPROPRIATE IN GENEALOGY TO HIM, THE MEMBERS OF THE FAMILY COME AND BRING A JUG FULL OF PRODUCE, AND THEY BREAK IT IN THE MIDDLE OF THE STREET, AND THEY SAY, "OUR BRETHREN, HOUSE OF ISRAEL, GIVE EAR! OUR BROTHER, MR. SO-AND-SO, HAS MARRIED A WOMAN WHO IS NOT GENEALOGICALLY FIT FOR HIM, AND WE ARE AFRAID THAT HIS OFFSPRING WILL GET MIXED UP WITH OUR OFFSPRING. COME AND TAKE FOR YOU A TOKEN FOR FUTURE GENERATIONS, THAT HIS OFFSPRING IS NOT TO MIX UP WITH OUR OFFSPRING," AND THIS IS THE CUTTING-OFF CEREMONY CONCERNING WHICH A CHILD IS BELIEVED WHEN HE GIVES TESTIMONY.

## II. The Formation of the Marriage: The Material Rights of the Parties to the Marital Union [2] The Father and the Husband

A. *The Fine that Is Paid to the Father for Rape or Seduction (Deut. 21:22)*

M. 3:1 These are the girls [invalid for marriage to an Israelite] who [nonetheless] receive a fine [from the man who seduces them]: He who has sexual relations with (1) a mamzer girl, (2) a netin girl, or (3) a Samaritan girl; he who has sexual relations with (4) a convert girl, and with (5) a girl taken captive, and (6) a slave girl who were redeemed, who converted, or who were freed [respectively] when they were at an age of less than three years and one day [and who remain in the status of virgins]; he who has sexual relations with (7) his sister, and with (8) the sister of his father, and with (9) the sister of his mother, and with (10) his wife's sister, and with (11) the wife of his brother, and with (12) the wife of the brother of his father, and with (13) the menstruating woman – they receive a fine [from the man who seduces them]. Even though [sexual relations with] them are subject to extirpation, one does not incur through having sexual relations with them the death penalty at the hands of an earthly court.

B. 3:1 III.19/35B-36A THOSE WHO STAND IN A CONSANGUINEOUS RELATIONSHIP WITH THE LOVER, AND THOSE FORBIDDEN TO HIM AT THE SECOND REMOVE, HAVE NO CLAIM ON PAYMENT OF A FINE IN THE CASE OF RAPE OR TO AN INDEMNITY IN THE CASE OF SEDUCTION. A GIRL WHO EXERCISES THE RIGHT OF REFUSAL HAS NO CLAIM ON PAYMENT OF A FINE IN THE CASE OF RAPE OR TO AN INDEMNITY IN THE CASE OF SEDUCTION. A BARREN WOMAN HAS NO CLAIM ON PAYMENT OF A FINE IN THE CASE OF RAPE OR TO AN INDEMNITY IN THE CASE OF SEDUCTION. SHE WHO IS SENT OFF ON ACCOUNT OF A BAD REPUTATION HAS NO CLAIM ON PAYMENT OF A FINE IN THE CASE OF RAPE OR TO AN INDEMNITY IN THE CASE OF SEDUCTION.

M. 3:2 And these do not receive a fine [from the man who seduces them]: he who has sexual relations with (1) a convert, (2) a girl taken captive, or (3) a slave girl, who was redeemed, or who converted, or who was freed, when any of these was at an age of more than three years and one day – he who has sexual relations with (4) his daughter, (5) his daughter's daughter, (6) with the daughter of his son, (7) with the daughter of his wife, (8) with the daughter of her son, (9) with the daughter of her daughter – they do not receive a fine [from the man who seduces them], for he incurs the death penalty. For the death penalty inflicted upon him is at the hands of an earthly court, and whoever incurs the death penalty [at the hands of an earthly court] does not pay out a financial penalty [in addition], since it says, "If no damage befall he shall surely be fined" (Ex. 21:22).

T. 3:5 He who has sexual relations with a deaf-mute, or with an idiot, or with a mature woman, or with a woman injured by a blow [and so without a hymen] – they do not receive a penalty. For a blind girl and a barren girl they receive a penalty.

M. 3:4 The one who seduces a girl pays on three counts, and the one who rapes a girl pays on four: the one who seduces a girl pays for (1) the shame, (2) the damage, and (3) a fine, and the one who rapes a girl adds to these, for he in addition pays for (4) the pain [which he has inflicted]. What is the difference between the one who rapes a girl and the one who seduces her? (1) The one who rapes a girl pays for the pain, and the one who seduces her does not pay for the pain. (2) The one who rapes a girl pays the financial penalties forthwith, but the one who seduces her pays the penalties when he puts her away. (3) The one who rapes the girl [forever after] drinks out of his earthen pot, but the one who seduces her, if he wanted to put her away, does put her away.

T. 3:6 All the same are the one who rapes and the one who seduces [both of them pay fifty sheqels as a fine]. What is the difference between him who rapes and him who seduces? The one who rapes pays compensation for pain, and the one who seduces does not pay compensation for pain [M. Ket. 3:4E-F]. Even though they said, The one who rapes pays the penalty immediately [M. Ket. 3:4G], but if he should put her away, he pays nothing [in addition]. Even though they said, The one who seduces, if he should divorce her, pays a penalty [M. Ket. 3:4H], but the compensation for her shame and her injury he pays forthwith. What is the difference between paying forthwith and paying later on? As to paying forthwith, if the girl dies, her father inherits [her estate, inclusive of the fines]. But if he pays later on, if she should die, her husband inherits [her estate].

T. 3:7 All the same are the one who rapes and the one who spreads a bad story about a girl, who divorced [the woman they have raped or maligned, respectively]: they force him to bring her back. [If] they are priests, they incur forty stripes. All the same are the one who rapes and the one who seduces – either she or her father is able to dissent [from the required marriage], since it says, And if refusing, her father shall refuse [Ex. 22:16], and it further says, And she shall be a wife to him (Deut. 22:29) – with her consent. Him do you force, but you do not force the levir.

M. 3:5 How does he "drink from his earthen pot"? Even if she is lame, even if she is blind, and even if she is afflicted with boils, [he must remain married to her]. [If] a matter of unchastity turned out to pertain to her, or if she is not appropriate to enter into the Israelite congregation, he is not permitted to confirm her as his wife, [but, if he has married her, he must divorce her,] since it is said, "And she will be a wife to him" (Deut. 22:29) – a wife appropriate for him.

M. 3:7 What is the [mode of assessing compensation for] shame? All [is assessed] in accord with the status of the one who shames and the one who is shamed. [How is the compensation for] damage [assessed]? They regard her as if she is a slave girl for sale: How much was she worth [before the sexual incident], and how much is she worth now. The fine? It is the same for every person [fifty selas, Deut. 22:29]. And any [fine] which is subject to a fixed amount decreed by the Torah is equivalent for every person.

M. 3:8 In any situation in which there is a right of sale, there is no fine. And in any situation in which there is a fine, there is no right of sale. A minor girl is subject to sale and does not receive a fine. A girl receives a fine and is not subject to sale. A mature woman is not subject to sale and [does] not [receive] a fine.

M. 3:9 He who says, "I seduced Mr. So-and-so's daughter," pays the penalties of shame and damage on the basis of his own testimony. But he does not pay a fine. He who says, "I stole and I slaughtered and sold [an animal belonging to So-and-so]," pays back the principal on the basis of his own testimony, but he does not pay double damages or four- or fivefold damages. [If he says], "My ox killed So-and-so," or "the ox of So-and-so," lo, this one pays on the basis of his own testimony. [If he says], "My ox killed So-and-so's slave," he does not pay on the basis of his own evidence. This is the general principle: Whoever pays compensation greater than the damage he has actually done does not pay said damages on the basis of his own testimony [alone, and he cannot be assessed for such damages].

M. 4:1 A girl [twelve to twelve-and-a-half years of age] who was seduced – [the financial penalties] for her shame, damage, and fine belong to her father, and the [compensation for] pain in the case of a girl who was seized [(Deut. 22:28) and raped, also belongs to the father]. [If] she won in court before her father died, lo, they [the funds] belong to the father. [If] the father [then] died, lo, they belong to the brothers. [If] she did not suffice to win her case in court before the father died, lo, they are hers. [If] she won her case in court before she matured [at the age of twelve years and six months], lo, they belong to the father. [If] the father died, lo, they belong to the brothers. [If] she did not suffice to win her case in court before the father died, lo, they are hers. [As to] the fruit of her labor and the things which she finds, even though she did not collect [her wages] – [if] the father died, lo, they belong to the brothers.

B.　*The Father*

M. 4:2 He who betrothed his daughter, and he [the husband] divorced her, [and] he [the father] betrothed her [to someone else], and she was widowed – her marriage contract [in both instances] belongs to him [the father]. [If] he [the father] married her off, [however], and he [the husband] divorced her, he [the father] married her off, and she was widowed – her marriage contract belongs to her.

M. 4:3 The convert whose daughter converted with her, and she [the daughter) committed an act of fornication [when she was a betrothed girl] – lo, this one is put to death through strangling. She is not subject to the rule, "At the door of her father's house" (Deut. 22:21), nor to "a hundred selas" [Deut. 22:19, in the case of one who slandered her]. [If] her conception was not in a state of sanctity but her parturition was in a state of sanctity, lo, this one is put to death with stoning. She is not subject to the rule, "At the door of her father's house," nor to a hundred selas. [If] her conception and parturition were in a state of sanctity, lo, she is equivalent to an Israelite girl for every purpose. [If] she has a father but no "door of her father's house" [her father has no house], [or if ] she has a "door of her father's house" but no father, lo, this one is put to death with stoning. "At the door of her father's house" is stated only as a duty [in addition to stoning].

C.　*The Father and the Husband*

M. 4:4 The father retains control of his daughter [younger than twelve and a half] as to effecting any of the tokens of betrothal:

money, document, or sexual intercourse. And he retains control of what she finds, of the fruit of her labor, and of abrogating her vows. And he receives her writ of divorce [from a betrothal]. But he does not dispose of the return [on property received by the girl from her mother] during her lifetime. [When] she is married, the husband exceeds the father, for he disposes of the return [on property received by the girl from her mother] during her lifetime. But he is liable to maintain her, and to ransom her, and to bury her.

T. 4:1 Greater is the power of the husband than that of the father, and [greater is] the power of the father than that of the husband. Greater is the power of the husband, for the husband disposes of the fruit of her labor during her lifetime, which is not so for the father [M. Ket. 4:4D].

T. 4:2 Greater is the power of the father, for the husband is liable to maintain her, to redeem he if she is taken captive], and to bury her [M. Ket. 4:4F], and, in a place in which it is customary to say a lamentation, to arrange for a lamentation for her, which is not incumbent on the father.

T. 4:3 Greater is the power of a wife than the power of the sister-in-law [the deceased, childless brother's wife], and [greater is the power of] the sister-in-law than of the wife. Greater is the power of the wife, for the wife eats heave-offering as soon as she enters the marriage canopy, even if she has not yet had sexual relations with the husband, which is not the case for the sister-in-law. Greater is the power of the sister-in-law, for he who has sexual relations with his sister-in-law [deceased, childless brother's widow], whether inadvertently or intentionally, whether under constraint or willingly, even if she is in her father's house, has acquired her as his wife, which is not the case with a wife.

*Y. 4:4 I:7 Under no circumstances is the husband flogged, nor is he required to pay a hundred selas, unless [the contrary] witnesses are stoned to death [by being proved to be perjurers]. [Merely contradicting their testimony does not suffice.]*

B. 4:4/VIII.1/47A IF THE FATHER WROTE A DEED FOR THE DAUGHTER ASSIGNING PRODUCE, CLOTHES, OR OTHER MOVABLES THAT SHE MAY TAKE WITH HER FROM HER FATHER'S HOUSE TO HER HUSBAND'S, AND SHE DIED [WHILE BETROTHED, NOT BRINGING THESE THINGS WITH HER TO THE HUSBAND'S HOUSEHOLD] – THE HUSBAND HAS NOT ACQUIRED THE TITLE OF THESE THINGS.

M. 4:5 Under all circumstances is she in the domain of the father, until she enters the domain of the husband through marriage. [If] the father handed her over to the agents of the husband, lo, she [from that point on] is in the domain of the husband. [If] the father went along with the agents of the husband, or [if] the agents of the father went along with the agents of the husband, lo, she is in the domain of the father. [If] the agents of the father handed her over to the agents of the husband, lo, she is in the domain of the husband.

T. 4:4 [If the father went along with her agents or with the agents of the husband. or if the agents of the father went along with the agents of the husband [M. Ket. 4:5C], ('. if she had a courtyard along the way and went in and spent the night in it or if [the husband] entered the marriage-canopy not for the purpose of consummating the marriage, and she died, even though her marriage-contract is with her husband, her father inherits it. Ci. If the father gave her over to the agents of the husband, or the agents of the father gave her over to the agents of the husband [M. Ket. 4:5B-D], or if she had a courtyard on the way and went in there and spent the nigh in it, or if she entered the marriage-canopy for the purpose of consummating the marriage, and she died, even though her marriage-contract is with her father, her husband inherits it. Under what circumstances? In the case of her marriage-contract. But as to heave-offering, she does not eat heave-offering until she enters the marriage-canopy [M. Ket. 5:3].

M. 4:6 The father [while alive] is not liable for the maintenance of his daughter.

D.  *The Husband*

M. 4:7 [If] he did not write a marriage contract for her, the virgin [nonetheless] collects two hundred [zuz in the event of divorce or widowhood], and the widow, a maneh, for this is [in all events] an unstated condition imposed by the court. [If] he assigned to her in writing a field worth a maneh instead of two hundred zuz, and did not write for her, *"All property which I have is surety for your marriage contract,"* he is nonetheless liable, for this is [in all events] an unstated condition imposed by the court.

M. 4:8 [If] he did not write for her, *"If you are taken captive, I shall redeem you and bring you back to my side as my wife,"* or, in the case of a priest girl, *"I shall bring you back to your town,"* he is nonetheless liable [to do so], for this is [in all events] an unstated condition imposed by the court.

B. 4:8 III.2/52A IF THE WOMAN WAS TAKEN CAPTIVE DURING THE LIFETIME OF HER HUSBAND, BUT THEN HE DIED, AND HER HUSBAND KNEW ABOUT HER SITUATION, HIS HEIRS HAVE TO RANSOM HER, BUT IF HER HUSBAND DID NOT KNOW ABOUT HER SITUATION, HIS HEIRS ARE NOT REQUIRED TO RANSOM HER.

B. 4:8 III 4/52A IF SHE WAS TAKEN CAPTIVE, AND THEY DEMANDED FROM HER HUSBAND TEN TIMES HER VALUE, HE STILL HAS TO RANSOM HER, AT LEAST ONCE. SUBSEQUENTLY, HOWEVER, HE MAY RANSOM HER IF HE WANTED, BUT HE DOES NOT HAVE TO DO SO IF HE DOESN'T WANT TO.

M. 4:9 [If] she was taken captive, he is liable to redeem her. And if he said, "Lo, here is her writ of divorce and [the funds owing on] her marriage contract, let her redeem herself," he has no right to do so. [If] she fell ill, he is liable to heal her. [If] he said, "Lo, here is her writ of divorce and [the funds owing

T. 4:5 [I f] she was taken captive, he is not liable to redeem her. Under what circumstances? In the case of a girl taken captive by a government official. If she was taken captive by a thug, he redeems her. If [then] he wants to confirm the marriage, he confirms it. If not, he puts her away and pays her a maneh as her marriage-contract [M. Ket. 4:8C] [If] she was taken captive after her husband's death, the levirs are not liable to redeem her. And not only so, but even if she is taken captive while her husband was alive, and afterward her husband died, the levirs are not liable to redeem her. [If] she was maintained by his property and required medical attention, lo, that is equivalent to any other aspect of her support [M. Ket. 4:9D-E]. If there were years of famine, [if] he then said to her, "Take your writ of divorce and your marriage-contract, go and feed yourself," he has that right.

M. 4:10 [If] he did not write for her, *"Male children which you will have with me will inherit the proceeds of your marriage contract, in addition to their share with their other brothers,"* he nonetheless is liable [to pay over the proceeds of the marriage contract to the woman's sons], for this is [in all events] an unstated condition imposed by the court.

T. 4:6 [If] he did not write for her in her marriage-contract, "Male children which you will have from me will inherit the proceeds of your marriage-contract in addition to their share with their older brothers," he is liable For this is in all events an unstated condition imposed by the court on all marriage-contracts [M. Ket. 4:10]. All provinces wrote their marriage-contracts as did the Jerusalemites [M. Ket. 4:12D].

T. 4:7 A man marries a woman on condition of not having to maintain her and of not having to support her. And not only so, but he may make an agreement with her that she maintain and support him and teach him Torah.

M. 4:11 [If he did not write for her,] *"Female children which you will have from me will dwell in my house and derive support from my property until they will be married to husbands,"* h e nonetheless is liable [to support her daughters] , for this is [in all events] an unstated condition imposed by the court.

M. 4:12 [If he did not write for her,] *"You will dwell in my house and derive support from my property so long as you are a widow in my house,"* [his estate] nonetheless is liable [to support his widow], for this is [in all events] an unstated condition imposed by the court. So did the Jerusalemites write into a marriage contract. The Galileans wrote the marriage contract as did the Jerusalemites. The Judeans wrote into the marriage contract, "Until such time as the heirs will choose to pay off your marriage contract." Therefore if the heirs wanted, they pay off her marriage contract and let her go.

M. 5:1 Even though they have said, "A virgin collects two hundred zuz and a widow a maneh" [M. 4:7A], if [the husband] wanted to increase that sum, even by a hundred maneh, he may add to it. [If] she was widowed or divorced, whether at the stage of betrothal or at the stage of consummated marriage, she collects the full amount.

T. 4:14 A. The father of the groom who has made a pledge for the marriage contract of his daughter-in-law, if there are available possessions belonging to the son, they collect the marriage-contract from the property of the son. And if not, they collect from the property of the father. [If] the father wrote over a house or a field as a surety for the marriage-contract of his daughter-in-law, one way or the other, they collect from them. He who went abroad, and whom they told, "Your son has died," [and] who went and wrote over all his property as a gift, and afterward who was informed that his son was alive – his deed of gift is valid.

T. 4:15 If he was sick in bed, and they said to him, "To whom will your property go," and he said to them, "I had imagined that I should have a son. Now that I do not have a son, my property goes to So-and-so," and afterward he was informed that he had a son – he has not said anything [to annul the gift]. If he was sick in bed, and they said to him, "To whom will your property go'?" and he said to them, "I had imagined that my wife would be pregnant, but now that she is not pregnant, my property goes to So-and-so," and afterward he was informed that his wife was pregnant – he has said nothing.

4:16 A proselyte who died, and whose property Israelites took over [assuming he had no Israelite heirs], and afterward it became known that he had had sons, or that his wife was pregnant – they all are liable to restore [to his legitimate heirs the property they took over]. [If] they returned it all, and the sons died, or his wife miscarried, he who took possession in the second go-around has acquired possession, but he who had taken possession in the first go-round has not acquired possession.

T. 4:17 The daughters, whether they were married before they reached full maturity, or whether they reached full maturity before they were married, lose their right to sustenance, but do not lose their right to dowry. What do they do? They hire husbands for themselves who collect their dowry for them.

Y 5:1 I:2 *Just as the husband agrees to pay [a sum over and above the minimum amount of the marriage settlement], so the father agrees to a dowry [and thereby is obligated]. But the husband assigns ownership through a bond, while the father assigns ownership [of what he promises to give] only verbally. And that is on condition [that the matter subject to the pledge is] something which is acquired through a verbal declaration.*

## III. The Duration of the Marriage. The Reciprocal Responsibilities and Rights of the Husband and Wife

### A. The Wife's Duties to the Husband

M. 5:2 They give a virgin twelve months to provide for herself from the time that the husband has demanded her. And just as they give [a time of preparation] to the woman, so they give a time of preparation to a man to provide for himself. And to a widow they give thirty days. [If the time came and he did not marry her,] she in any event is supported. And she eats heave-offering [if he is a priest, and she is not].

T. 5:1 Reaching maturity is equivalent to a demand [on the part of the prospective husband that the betrothed prepare herself for marriage] [M. Ket. 5:2A]. [And] they give her twelve months in which to prepare for marriage. If she was a minor, either she or her father can dissent.

M. 5:3 The levir [who is a priest] cannot feed heave-offering [to the sister-in-law [his deceased childless brother's wife] who is widowed at the stage of betrothal and is awaiting consummation of the levirate marriage (M. Yeb. 7:4)]. If she had waited six months for the husband [M. 5:2A], and six months awaited the levir, [or] even if all of them were waiting for the husband but only one day was spent waiting for the levir, or all of them were awaiting the levir, except one day awaiting the husband, she does not eat heave-offering. This is the first Mishnah. The succeeding court ruled: "The woman does not eat heave-offering until she enters the marriage canopy."

T. 5:2 What is the law as to providing food for the sister-in-law awaiting levirate marriage? So long as the husband is obligated [having supported her in his lifetime], the levirs are obligated. If] the husband is not obligated, the levirs are not obligated. Who controls the fruit of her labor? If she is supported by them, lo, they belong to them, and if not, lo they remain her own possession. What she inherits and what she finds, one way or the other, lo, they belong to her.

B. 5:2-3 I.4/57B HE WHO BETROTHS A VIRGIN, WHETHER THE HUSBAND NOW DEMANDS HER TO COMPLETE THE MARRIAGE AND SHE OBJECTS, OR SHE DEMANDS AND THE HUSBAND OBJECTS – THEY ASSIGN HER TWELVE MONTHS FROM THE MOMENT OF THE DEMAND, BUT NOT FROM THE MOMENT OF THE BETROTHAL. IF SHE REACHED PUBERTY, LO, IT IS AS THOUGH SHE WERE DEMANDED. HOW SO? IF SHE REACHED PUBERTY BY ONLY A SINGLE DAY AND THEN WAS BETROTHED, THEY GIVE HER TWELVE MONTHS, AND TO A BETROTHED GIRL, THIRTY DAYS.

M. 5:4 He who sanctifies to the Temple the fruits of his wife's labor [her wages], lo, this woman [continues to] work and eat [maintain herself].

M. 5:5 These are the kinds of labor which a woman performs for her husband: she (1) grinds flour, (2) bakes bread, (3) does laundry, (4) prepares meals, (5) gives suck to her child, (6) makes the bed, (7) works in wool. [If] she brought with her a single slave girl, she does not (1) grind, (2) bake bread, or (3) do laundry. [If she brought] two, she does not (4) prepare meals and does not (5) feed her child. [If she brought] three, she does not (6) make the bed for him and does not (7) work in wool. If she brought four, she sits on a throne.

T. 5:3 He who sanctifies to the Temple the fruit of his wife's labor [M. Ket. 5:4A] – lo, this one provides food for her from it [the fruit of her labor]. But the remainder is sanctified.

T. 5:4 The kinds of work which a woman does for her husband – seven basic categories of labor did they enumerate. And the rest did not require enumeration [M. Ket. 5:5A-B]. If she brought slaves to him, whether on his account or on her account, she does not spin or bake or do laundry [M. Ket. 5:5C]. He may not force her to work for his son, daughter, his brothers, or her brothers, or to feed his cattle.

In a place in which it is not customary to do any one of these [listed at M. Ket. 5:5B], he cannot force her to do them.

B.  *The Husband's Obligations to the Wife*

**M. 5:6 He who takes a vow not to have sexual relations with his wife may allow this situation to continue] for one week. Disciples go forth for Torah study without [the wife's] consent for thirty days. Workers go out for one week.**

T. 5:6 Workers [must engage in sexual relations] twice a week. If they were employed in another town, then they must have sexual relations at least once a week. Ass-drivers must have sexual relations once in two weeks, camel drivers once in thirty days, sailors once in six months [M. Ket. 5:6F].

**M. 5:7 She who rebels against her husband [declining to perform wifely services (M. 5:5)] – they deduct from her marriage contract seven denars a week. How long does one continue to deduct? Until her entire marriage contract [has been voided]. And so is the rule for the man who rebels against his wife [declining to do the husband's duties (M. 5:4)] – they add three denars a week to her marriage contract.**

T. 5:7 She who rebels against her husband, etc. [M. Ket. 5:7A] – this is the first Mishnah. Our rabbis ordained that a court should warn her four or five consecutive weeks, twice a week. [If she persists] any longer than that, even if her marriage-contract is a hundred maneh, she has lost the whole thing. All the same is the betrothed girl and the woman awaiting levirate marriage, and even a menstruating woman, or a sick woman.

**M. 5:8 He who maintains his wife by a third party may not provide for her less than two qabs of wheat or four qabs of barley [per week]. And one pays over to her a half-qab of pulse, a half-log of oil, and a qab of dried figs or a maneh of fig cake. And if he does not have it, he provides instead fruit of some other type. And he gives her a bed, a cover, and a mat. And he annually gives her a cap for her head, and a girdle for her loins, and shoes from one festival season to the next, and clothing worth fifty zuz from one year to the next. And they do not give her either new ones in the sunny season or old ones in the rainy season. But they provide for her clothing fifty zuz in the rainy season, and she clothes herself with the remnants in the sunny season. And the rags remain hers.**

T. 5:8 He who supports his wife by means of a third party [M. Ket. 5:8A] – all of them are measured out by Italian measure. Even a menstruating woman, and even a sick woman, and even a sister-in-law awaiting levirate marriage [receive the support specified at M. Ket. 5:8]. He gives her a cup, a plate, a bowl, an oil cruse, a lamp, and a wick. She has no claim for wine, for the wives of the poor do not drink wine. She has no claim for a pillow, for the wives of the poor do not sleep on pillows.

**M. 5:9 He gives her in addition a silver maah [a sixth of a denar] for her needs [per week]. And she eats with him on the night of the Sabbath. And if he does not give her a silver maah for her**

needs, the fruit of her labor belongs to her. And how much work does she do for him? The weight of five selas of warp must she spin for him [M. 5:5B7] in Judea (which is ten selas weight in Galilee), or the weight of ten selas of woof in Judah (which are twenty selas in Galilee). And if she was nursing a child, they take off [the required weight of wool which she must spin as] the fruit of her labor, and they provide more food for her. Under what circumstances? In the case of the most poverty-stricken man in Israel. But in the case of a weightier person, all follows the extent of his capacity [to support his wife].

T. 5:9 The excess of food [beyond her needs] goes back to him. The excess of worn out clothing belongs to her. If he gets rich she goes up with him, but if he becomes poor, she does not go down with him.

M. 6:1 What a wife finds and the fruit of her labor go to her husband [M. 4:4]. And as to what comes to her as an inheritance, he has use of the return while she is alive. [Payments made for] shaming her or injuring her are hers.

C. *The Dowry*

M. 6:2 He who agrees to pay over money [as a dowry] to his son-in-law, and his son-in-law dies can claim, 'To your brother was I willing to give [money], but to you [the levir] I am not willing to give money.

M. 6:3 [If a woman] agreed to bring into [the marriage for] him a thousand denars [ten manehs], he [the husband] agrees [to pay over in her marriage contract] fifteen manehs over against this. And over against the goods [which she agreed to bring in] estimated [to be at a given value], he agrees [to restore, as a condition of her marriage contract] a fifth less. [That is, if] the estimated value [to be inscribed in the marriage contract] is a maneh, and the actual value is [specified at] a maneh, he has [value] only for one maneh [and not a fifth more in value]. [If] the estimated value [to be inscribed in the marriage contract] is a maneh [but not specified at a maneh, as at D], she must give over thirty-one selas and a denar [= 125 denars in value of goods]. And [if the value to be written into the marriage contract is to be] four hundred, she must give over five hundred. What the husband agrees [to have inscribed in the marriage contract] he agrees to, less a fifth [than the appraised value].

T. 6:5 [If] she agreed to bring in to him two selas, they are treated as equivalent to six denars [M. Ket. 6:4A]. What the husband agrees to have inscribed in the marriage-contract he agrees to, less a fifth [M. Ket. 6:3G], except with regard to the two hundred zuz to be paid to the virgin, and the maneh to be paid to the widow [which are paid in full]. [If] she agreed to bring in to him gold, lo, gold is equivalent to utensils [and diminished from the estimated value]. [If] she stipulated to bring into him golden denars lo, the gold is then treated as equivalent to ready money [M. Ket. 6:3A-B. 6:4A]. [If] she brought in to him [things of value], whether estimated in value or ready money, and he contemplated divorcing her, [right after the marriage, before the capital and goods have been utilized], she may not say to him, "Give me the estimated value [of what I brought in to you]." And he may not say to her, "Take your money." But she takes everything which he has written over to her in her marriage-contract.

M. 6:4 [If] she agreed to bring in to him ready money, a silver sela is treated as six denars [instead of four]. The husband takes upon himself [responsibility to give] ten denars for pocket money ["for her basket"] in exchange for each and every maneh [which she brings in].

T. 6:6 [If she agreed to bring in to him ready money, selas are treated as equivalent to six denars [M. Ket. 6:4A]. A bridegroom takes upon himself to provide ten denars per maneh for money for cosmetics. [If] she went to a place in which they were not accustomed to diminish the value of the estimate, or to increase the value over that of the ready money, they do not vary from the customs of the place. [If] she agreed to bring in to him five hundred denars of estimated value [of goods], and he wrote over to her a thousand denars in her marriage-contract, if she made her stipulation, she takes what he wrote over to her. And if not, he takes off three denars for each and every sela [written into the contract]. If she agreed to bring into him five hundred denars in ready money [and he wrote over to her a thousand denars in her marriage-contract, if she made her stipulation, she takes what he wrote over to her. And if not, he takes off six denars for each and every sela [written into the contract]. If she brought into him a thousand denars in her marriage-contract, and he wrote over to her a field worth twelve manehs, if she made her stipulation, she takes what he wrote over to her. And if not, he should not pay less to a virgin than two hundred zuz and to a widow a maneh.

M. 6:5 He who marries off his daughter without specified conditions should not assign to her less than fifty zuz. [If] he agreed to bring her in naked, the husband may not say, "When I shall bring her into my house, I shall cover her with a garment belonging to me." But he clothes her while she is still in her father's house. And so: He who marries off an orphan girl should not assign to her less than fifty zuz. If there is sufficient money in the fund, they provide her with a dowry according to the honor due her.

M. 6:6 An orphan girl [lacking a father], whose mother or brothers married her off [even] with her consent, for whom they wrote over as her portion a hundred zuz or fifty zuz, can, when she grows up, exact from them what should rightly have been given to her.

T. 6:7 He who married off his daughter and agreed with his son-in-law that she should stand naked and he, [the son-in-law] should clothe her, they do not say, "Let her stand naked and have him clothe her." But he covers her in a manner fitting to her. And so they who marry off an orphan girl should not provide for her less than fifty zuz. And if there is sufficient money in the fund, they provide her with a dowry according to the honor due her [M. Ket. 6:5D-E].

T. 6:8 An orphan girl whose mother or brothers married her off for whom they wrote over a hundred zuz or fifty zuz – [M. Ket. 6:6A-B] even though the husband wrote for them, "I have no judgment or claim with her," she can, when she grows up, exact from them what should rightly have been given to her [M. Ket. 6:6C]. A man makes an agreement in behalf of his daughter, but a woman does not make an agreement in behalf of her daughter. An orphan boy or an orphan girl who seek to be supported – they support the orphan girl first, then they support the orphan boy, for the orphan boy can go begging in any event, but the orphan girl cannot go begging in any event. An orphan boy and an orphan girl who seek to marry – they marry off the orphan girl first, and then they marry off the orphan boy, for the shame of a girl is greater than that of a boy. An orphan boy who seeks to marry – they rent a house for him, then they lay out a bed, and afterward they marry off a girl to him. since it is said, [But you shall open your hand to him] and lend him sufficient for his need, whatever it may be (Deut. 15:8) – even a slave, even a horse. For him – this refers to a wife, since it says elsewhere, I shall make for him a helpmate (Gen. 2:18) – Just as for him in the other context refers to a wife, so for him in this context refers to a wife.

T. 6:10 He who says, "Give over a sheqel from my property to my children for their maintenance for a week," but they are supposed to take a sela – they give over to them a sela. But if he said, "Give them only a sheqel," they give them only a sheqel. If he said, "If they die, let others inherit me," whether he said, "Give," and whether he did not say, "Give," they give them over to them only a sheqel. As to food for the widow and the daughters, whether he said, "Give," or said, "Do not give," they give to them a sela.

D. *The Marital Rights and Duties of the Wife*

M. 7:1 He who prohibits his wife by vow from deriving benefit from him for a period of thirty days, appoints an agent to provide for her. [If the effects of the vow are not nullified] for a longer period, he puts her away and pays off her marriage contract.

M. 7:2 He who prohibits his wife by vow from tasting any single kind of produce whatsoever must put her away and pay off her marriage contract.

T. 7:2 A. [If] he prohibited her by vow from tasting any type [of produce whatsoever, M. Ket. 7:2A], whether it is foul or delectable food, even if she for her part had never tasted that sort of produce once in her entire life, he must put her away and pay off her marriage-contract.

M. 7:3 He who prohibits his wife by a vow from adorning herself with any single sort of jewelry must put her away and pay off her marriage contract.

M. 7:4 He who prohibits his wife by a vow from going home to her father's house – when he [father] is with her in [the same] town, [if it is] for a month, he may persist in the marriage. [If it is] for two, he must put her away and pay off her marriage contract. And when he is in another town, [if the vow is in effect] for one festival season he may persist in the marriage. [But if the vow remains in force] for three, he must put her away and pay off her marriage contract.

T. 7:3 [If] he prohibited her by vow from adorning herself with any sort of adornment [M. Ket. 7:4A], even if she is a young girl, and he prohibited her by vow from putting on the clothes of an old lady, even if she is an old lady, and he prohibited her by vow from putting on the clothes of a young girl, he must put her away and pay off her marriage-contract.

M. 7:5 He who prohibits his wife by a vow from going to a house of mourning or to a house of celebration must put her away and pay off her marriage contract, because he locks the door before her. But if he claimed that he took such a vow because of some other thing, he is permitted to impose such a vow. [If he took a vow,] saying to her, (1) "On condition that you say to So-and-so what you said to me," or (2) "what I said to you," or (3) "that you draw water and pour it out onto the ash heap," he must put her away and pay off her marriage contract.

T. 7:4 [If] he prohibited her by vow from lending a sieve or a strainer, millstones or oven [to her girlfriend], he must put her away and pay off her marriage-contract, because he gives her a bad name among her neighboring women. And so she who prohibited him by vow from lending a sieve or a strainer, millstones or oven, must go forth without payment of her marriage-contract, because she gives him a bad name in his neighborhood.

T. 7:5 [If] he prohibited her by vow from going to a house of mourning or to a house of celebration, he must put her away and pay off her marriage-contract, because sometime later she will be laid out [for burial] and not a single human being will come to pay respects to her.

T. 7:6 [If] he required her by vow to give a taste of what she was cooking to everybody [who came by], or that she draw water and pour it out onto the ash-heap [M. Ket 7:5D], or that she tell everybody about things which are between him and her [M. Ket. 7:5D], he must put her away and pay off her marriage-contract, because he has not behaved with her in accord with the law of Moses and of Israel.

M. 7:6 And those women go forth without the payment of the marriage contract at all: She who transgresses against the law of Moses and Jewish law. And what is the law of Moses [which she has transgressed]? [If] (1) she feeds him food which has not been tithed, or (2) has sexual relations with him while she is menstruating, or [if] (3) she does not cut off her dough-offering, or [if] (4) she vows and does not carry out her vow. And what is the Jewish law? If (1) she goes out with her hair flowing loose, or (2) she spins in the marketplace, or (3) she talks with just anybody.

T. 7:6 And so she who goes out with her hair flowing loose [M. Ket. 7:6D], who goes out with her clothes in a mess, who acts without shame in the presence of her boy-slaves and girl-slaves and her neighbors, who goes out and spins wool in the marketplace [M. Ket. 7:6], who washes and bathes in the public bath with just anyone, goes forth without payment of her marriage-contract, for she has not behaved with him [her husband] in accord with the law of Moses and Israel [M. Ket. 7:6].

T. 7:7 What is a loudmouth? Anyone who, when she talks in her own house – her neighbors can hear her voice [M. Ket. 7:6P]. All these women who have transgressed the law must have fair warning, but [if they persist after fair warning], then they go forth without receiving payment of their marriage-contract. [If] one did not give them fair warning, he must put her away but pay off her marriage-contract – and one need not say it is two hundred to a virgin and a maneh to a widow. But as to more than this: Even if her marriage-contract is in the sum of a hundred manehs, she has lost the whole thing. She takes merely the old rags which are laid out before her [and leaves].

**M. 7:7 He who betrothed a woman on condition that there are no encumbering vows upon her, and it turns out that there are encumbering vows upon her – she is not betrothed. [If] he married her without [further] specification and encumbering vows turned out to be upon her, she must go forth without payment of her marriage contract. [If he betrothed her] on condition that she had no blemishes on her, and blemishes turned up on her, she is not betrothed. [If] he married her without [further] specification and blemishes turned up on her, she must go forth without payment of her marriage contract. All those blemishes which invalidate priests also invalidate women.**

T. 7:8 He who betroths a woman on condition that there are no encumbering vows upon her. and it turns out that there are encumbering vows upon her – she is not betrothed [M. Ket. 7:7A-B =M. Qid. 2:5]. [If] she went to a sage and he released her vow, lo, this woman is betrothed. If he married her without further specification and encumbering vows turned out to be upon her, she must go forth without payment of her marriage contract [M. Ket. 7:7C]. [If] she went to a sage and he released her vow, lo this one confirms the marriage. [If he betrothed her] on condition that she had no blemishes on her, and blemishes turned up on her, she is not betrothed [M. Ket. 7:7D]. [If] she went to a physician and he healed her, lo, this woman is betrothed. If he married her without further specification and blemishes turned up on her, she must go forth without payment of her marriage-contract [M. Ket. 7:7E]. Even though she went to a physician and he healed her, she goes out without receiving payment of her marriage contract. Of what sort of vows did they speak? For example, [if] she vowed not to eat meat, not to drink wine, or not to wear stylish clothing.

T. 7:9 All those blemishes which invalidate priests invalidate women [M. Ket. 7:7F]. In addition to them in the case of the woman are bad breath, a sweaty body odor, and a mole that has no hair on it.

T. 7:10 He who says to his fellow, "Betroth this daughter of yours to me on condition that there are no blemishes on her," [if] he [the father] said to him, "This daughter of mine is sick, is an idiot, is epileptic, is demented" – [if] there was some other sort of blemish on her, and he concealed it among these blemishes [which he did specify], lo, this is a purchase made in error [and null] [M. Ket. 7:7]. [If, however, he said], "There are these blemishes, and there is yet another [unspecified] blemish among them," this is by no means a purchase made in error.

**M. 7:9 A man who suffered blemishes – they do not force him to put her away.**

**M. 7:10 And these are the ones whom they force to put her away: (1) he who is afflicted with boils, or (2) who has a polypus, or (3) who collects [dog shit], or (4) a coppersmith, or (5) a tanner – whether these [blemishes] were present before they were married or whether after they were married they made their appearance.**

T. 7:11 Who is one who collects [M. Ket 7: 10A3]? This is a tanner. And some say, "This is one who collects dog-excrement." A coppersmith [M. Ket. 7:10A4] – this is a metal-pourer. Under what circumstances did they rule, He must put her away [M. Ket. 7:10A] and pay off her marriage-contract? When he wants, but she does not want, [or] she wants, but he does not want [to continue the marriage]. But if both want [to continue the marriage], they do continue the marriage. One who is afflicted with boils – even though both of them want [to continue the marriage], they may not continue the marriage [M. Ket. 7:10D-E].

E.   *Property Rights of the Wife*

**M. 8:1 The woman to whom property came before she was betrothed sells or gives away [the property], and the transaction is valid. [If] they [goods or property] came to her after she was betrothed, she may not sell them. If she sold or gave away [goods or property], the transaction is valid.**

**M. 8:3 [If] ready cash fell to her, land should be purchased with it. And he [the husband] has the usufruct thereof. [If there fell to her] produce plucked up from the ground, [likewise] land should be purchased with its [proceeds]. And he has the usufruct thereof. And as to produce attached to the ground [which the wife inherits] [The value of the produce] attached to the ground belongs to him. [The value of that which is] plucked up from the ground is hers. And land is purchased with the [proceeds of the latter]. And he has the usufruct thereof.**

T. 8:3 He who enters into an expropriated estate and heard a report that they [assumed to have died and left the estate] are returning – if he went ahead and plucked up produce from the ground in any measure at all, lo, this one is rewarded for his promptness. What is meant by the expropriated estate? Any whose father or brothers or one of those who leave him an inheritance went overseas and he heard that they had died, and he entered into his inheritance. What is an abandoned estate? It is any estate, the death of the owner of which has not been reported, but into which one nonetheless one has entered for purpose of inheritance.

T. 8:4 The robber or the thief who grabbed from this one and gave to the other – what he has grabbed, he has grabbed, and what he has given he has given. The thief who grabbed from this one and gave to that one – what he has grabbed he has grabbed, and what he has given he has given. The Jordan River which took from this one and gave to that one – what it has taken, it has taken, and what it has given it has given. If the river swept away wood, stones, and beams from this one and deposited them on the property of that one, if the owner has despaired of recovering his property, lo, these belong to him [on whose property they have been swept up]. And if the owner pursued [his property, as it flowed down the river], or if he was in some other place [and did not know about the flood], lo, this remains in the possession of the owner.

T. 8:6 He who acquires a field from his fellow as a sharecropper, and it is an irrigated field or an orchard, if there is produce attached to the ground,

they make an estimate of its value.

T. 8:7 He who acquires a field from his fellow as a sharecropper and the year of release came, if there is produce attached to the ground, they make an estimate of its value. He who acquires a field from his fellow as a sharecropper, and the time came for him to quit the land [and make a final reckoning], if there is produce there attached to the ground, they make an estimate of its value. And in the case of all of them, they make an estimate as in the case of a sharecropper.

T. 8:9 A. He who takes over ruins belonging to someone else and rebuilt it without permission, [if] when he leaves them, he says, "Give me my wood and stones," they do not accept his claim.

T. 8:10 He who takes over ruins belonging to someone else and rebuilt them without permission, they estimate its value. But his hand is on the bottom. [If he did so] with permission, they estimate its value, and his hand is now on top. How is it that his hand is on the bottom? If the increase in value is greater than the outlay for the restoration, he [who retrieves his property] pays him his expenses. But if the expenses are greater than the increase in value, he pays him only the increase in value.

M. 8:5 [If] old slave men or slave women fell to her [possession], they are to be sold. And land should be purchased with their [proceeds]. And he [the husband] has the usufruct thereof. [If] old olive trees or grapevines fell to her [possession], they are to be sold [for their value as] wood. And land should be purchased with their [proceeds]. And he has the usufruct thereof. He who lays out the expenses for [the upkeep of] the property of his wife – [whether] he laid out a great deal of money and received little usufruct, [or whether he laid out] a small amount of money and received much – what he has laid out, he has laid out, and the usufruct which he has enjoyed, he has enjoyed. [But] if he laid out [money for the upkeep of the estate] and did not enjoy the usufruct [at all, there being no return], he should take an oath [to verify] the amount which he has laid out [as expenses]. And that should he collect [in recompense, from her by deduction from her marriage contract].

M. 8:6 A woman awaiting levirate marriage with her deceased childless husband's brother to whom property came sells or gives away her property, and the transaction is valid. [If] she died, how should they dispose of her marriage contract and of the property which comes into the marriage with her and goes out of the marriage with her [= plucking property]? The property remains in the hands of its presumptive owners: the [value of the] marriage contract in the possession of the heirs of the husband, and the property which goes in and comes out with her in the possession of the heirs of the father.

M. 8:7 [If] the brother [the deceased husband] left ready cash, land should be purchased with it. And he [the levir] has the usufruct thereof. [If he left] produce plucked up from the ground, [it should be sold] and land should be purchased with the [proceeds]. And he has the usufruct thereof. [If he left] produce yet attached to the ground – produce attached to the ground belongs to him. Produce plucked up from the ground – whoever gets it first keeps it. [If] he got it first, he keeps it. [If] she got it first, land should be purchased with their [proceeds]. And he has the usufruct thereof." [If] he consummated the marriage with her, lo, she is deemed to be his wife for every purpose, except that her marriage contract is a lien on the estate of her first husband.

M. 8:8 [The levir] may not say to her, "There is [the repayment for] your marriage contract, lying on the table." But all of his property is subject to lien for the payment of her marriage contract. And so a man may not say to his wife, "There is [the repayment for] your marriage contract, lying on the table." But all of his property is subject to lien for the payment of her marriage contract. [If] he divorced her, she has a claim only on her marriage contract. [If] he remarried her, lo, she is equivalent to all women. And she has a claim only on her marriage contract alone.

T. 9:1 He who died and left his wife awaiting marriage with her deceased childless husband's brother, even if he left an estate worth a hundred manehs and the charge of her marriage-contract is only a maneh, the heirs cannot sell [his estate], for all of his property is encumbered for the payment of her marriage-contract [M. Ket. 8:8]. What should [the levir] do? He should consummate the marriage, then divorce her, and she gives him a quittance for her marriage-contract. [If] his brother left ready cash [M. Ket 8:7A], or the deceased childless brother's widow owed her husband money, he should not say, "Since I am going to inherit it anyhow, I take possession of it." But they seize it from him, and land is purchased for it, and he has the usufruct.

M. 9:1 He who writes for his wife, "I have no right nor claim to your property," lo, this one [nonetheless] has the usufruct during her lifetime. And if she dies, he inherits her estate. If so, why did he write to her, "I have no right nor claim to your property"? For if she sold or gave away [her property], her act is valid. [If] he wrote for her, "I have no right nor claim to your property or to its usufruct [consequent profits]," lo, this one does not have the usufruct in her lifetime. But if she dies, he inherits her estate, [If] he wrote for her, "I have no right nor claim to your property, to its usufruct, to the usufruct of its usufruct, during your lifetime and after your death," he neither has the usufruct in her lifetime, nor, if she dies, does he inherit her.

## IV. Cessation of the Marriage: The Collection of the Marriage-Contract

### A. *Imposing an Oath in Connection with Collecting the Marriage-Settlement*

M. 9:2 He who died and left a wife, a creditor, and heirs, and who had goods on deposit or a loan in the domain of others – they should be given over to the heirs. For all of them have to confirm their claim by an oath. But the heirs do not have to confirm their claim by an oath.

M. 9:3 [If] he left produce harvested from the ground, whoever gets them first has effected acquisition of them. [If] the wife made acquisition of an amount greater than the value of her marriage contract, or a creditor greater than the value of the debt owing to him – as to the excess [of the claims of these respective parties] – it should be given over to the heirs. For all of them have to confirm their claim by an oath. But the heirs do not have to confirm their claim by an oath.

M. 9:4 He who sets up his wife as a storekeeper, or appointed her guardian, lo, this one may impose upon her an oath [that she has not misappropriated any of his property], at any time he wants.

M. 9:5 If he wrote to her, "Neither vow nor oath may I impose upon you," then he cannot impose an oath on her. But he imposes an oath upon her heirs and upon those who are her lawful successors. [If he said], "Neither vow nor oath may I impose upon you, upon your heirs, or upon your legal successors," he cannot impose an oath upon her or upon her heirs or legal successors. But his heirs do impose an oath upon her, upon her heirs, or upon her legal successors. [If he said,] "Neither vow nor oath may I or my heirs or my legal successors impose upon you, upon your heirs, or upon your legal successors," neither he nor his heirs or legal successors can impose an oath upon her, her heirs, or her legal successors.

M. 9:6 [If] she went from her husband's grave to her father's house, or if she went back to her father-in-law's house and was not appointed guardian, the heirs do not impose an oath on her [that she has not misappropriated any property of the estate]. And if she was appointed guardian [of the estate], the heirs do impose an oath on her concerning time to come. But they do not impose an oath on her concerning past time.

T. 9:3 He who died and left movable property, and the marriage-contract of his wife and a creditor laid claim against whoever seizes it first has effected acquisition [of whatever he left] [M. Ket. 9:2-3].

And [there being nothing left for burial costs], he is buried by the philanthropic fund. Who are the heirs who are her legal successors [M. Ket. 9:5C]? Any to whom she sold [her property] or to whom she gave [her property] as a gift. [If] he wrote to her, "I have no claim to impose either a vow or an oath upon you" [M. Ket. 9:5A], the heirs [also] cannot impose an oath on her [that she has not misappropriated] items of which she made use after the death of her husband. Under what circumstances? When she went along from the grave of her husband to her father's house [M. Ket. 9:6A]. But if she went from the grave of her husband to her father-in-law's house, even if he wrote to her, "I have no claims to impose either a vow or an oath upon you," the heirs can impose an oath on her concerning items of which she made use after the death of her husband [M. Ket. 9:6D-E]. A husband cannot impose an oath on his wife unless he sets her up as a storekeeper or appoints her guardian [of his property] [M. Ket. 9:4A-C]. A sharecropper – so long as he is a sharecropper, [he is subject to an oath]. When he has gone forth from his position as sharecropper, lo, he is equivalent to any other person. A partner – so long as he is a partner, [he is subject to an oath]. When he has gone forth from his partnership, lo, he is equivalent to any other person. A guardian – so long as he is a guardian, [he is subject to an oath]. When he has gone forth from his guardianship, lo, he is equivalent to any other person. A member of the household of whom they spoke [at M. Sheb.. 7:8] – it is not this one who [merely] walks in and out, but the one who brings in produce and takes out produce, hires workers and dismisses workers. [If] one borrows from him on the eve of the Seventh Year and in the Seventh Year, and, in the year after the Seventh Year, he is made a partner of his, or a sharecropper, he is exempt [from the requirement of an oath]. But if he is made a partner or a sharecropper on the eve of the Seventh Year and in the Seventh Year, and in the year after the Seventh Year he went and borrowed from him, they obligate him for [an oath covering] all.

**M. 9:7 She who impairs her marriage contract collects it only through an oath. [If] one witness testified against her that it had been collected, she collects it only through an oath. From (1) the property of the heirs [orphans], or from (2) property subject to a lien, or (3) in his [the husband's] absence should she collect [her marriage contract] only through an oath.**

T. 9:4 She who claims less than the full value of her marriage-contract collects it without an oath. How so? [If] her marriage-contract had a value of a thousand zuz, and he said to her, "You have collected your marriage-contract," and she says, "I have not collected it, but it is of a value of only a maneh," she collects that amount without an oath [M. Ket. 9:7A, 9:8A – C]. As to [collecting what is owed to her by seizing] mortgaged property [M. Ket. 9:7C2], it is not necessary to say after her husband's death, but even while her husband is yet alive [does she collect only through an oath]. As to the property belonging to the orphans, it is not necessary to say, that of the adults [minors], but even that of the minors [adults] [does she collect only through an oath].

M. 9:8 "She who impairs her marriage contract" [M. 9:7A]: How so? [If] her marriage contract was worth a thousand zuz, and he said to her, "You have collected your marriage contract," but she says, "I have received only a maneh [a hundred zuz]," she collects [the remainder] only through an oath. [If] one witness testified against her that it had been collected: How so? [If] her marriage contract was worth a thousand zuz, and he [the witness] said to her, "You have collected the value of your marriage contract," and she says, "I have not collected it," and one witness testified against her that it had been collected, she should collect the marriage contract only through an oath. "From property subject to a lien" [M. 9:7C2]: How so? [If the husband] sold off his property to others, and she comes to collect from the purchasers, she should collect from them only through an oath. From the property of the heirs [orphans] [M. 9:7Cl]: How so? [If the husband] died and left his property to the orphans, and she comes to collect [her marriage contract] from the orphans, she should collect from them only by an oath. "In his absence" [M. 9:7C3]: How so? [If the husband] went overseas, and she comes to collect [her marriage contract] in his absence, she collects [what is due her] only by an oath.

M. 9:9 [If] she produced a writ of divorce, and a marriage contract is not attached to it, she collects her marriage contract. [But if she produced] a marriage contract, and a writ of divorce is not attached to it, [and if] she claims, "My writ of divorce is lost," [while the husband] claims, "My quittance is lost" – and so, too, a creditor who produced a bill of indebtedness and a prosbol [securing the loan in the year of release] is not attached to it – lo, these [parties] may not collect [what they claim]. [If she produces] two writs of divorce and two marriage contracts – she collects [the value of] two marriage contracts. [If she produces] (1) two marriage contracts but only one writ of divorce, or (2) one marriage contract and two writs of divorce, or (3) a marriage contract and a writ of divorce and a death [certificate], she collects only one marriage contract. For he who divorces his wife and then remarries her – on the strength of the first marriage contract does he remarry her. And a minor boy whose father married him off – her [his wife's] marriage contract is confirmed [as valid after he reaches maturity]. For on the strength of that document he confirmed [the marriage when he came of age]. A proselyte who converted, and his wife alongside [did the same] – her [original] marriage contract is valid. For on the strength of that document he [the husband] confirmed [the marriage].

T. 9:5 [If] she produced a writ of divorce, and a marriage-contract is not attached to it [M. Ket. 9:9A] – a virgin collects two hundred zuz, and a widow, a maneh. [If she produced] a marriage-contract, and a writ of divorce is not attached to it [M. Ket. 9:9B], she collects nothing, because if she says, "My writ of divorce got lost," then he counters, "My quittance got lost" [M. Ket. 9:9C-D].

T. 9:7 [If] she gave him a quittance while she is subject to his authority, then he divorced her and remarried her and died, (and) she collects a maneh as her marriage-contract. But if he made a new document, she collects what he has made afresh. A minor-boy whose father married him off – the [wife's] marriage-contract is confirmed [as valid after he reaches maturity]. For on the strength of that document he confirmed the marriage [M. Ket. 9:9Q-R]. And if he made a new document, she collects what he has made afresh. And so: A proselyte who converted, and his wife alongside [did the same] – her [original] marriage-contract is valid. For on the strength of that document he [the husband] confirmed the marriage [after conversion] [M. Ket. 9:9S-U]. And if he made a new document, she collects what he made afresh.

B.   *Multiple Claims on an Estate, Including the Wives' for their Marriage-Settlement*

**M. 10:1 He who was married to two wives and died – the first [wife] takes precedence over the second, and the heirs of the first take precedence over the heirs of the second. [If] he married the first and she died, then he married the second, and he died, the second and her heirs take precedence over the heirs of the first.**

T. 10:1 He who was married to two wives and died – the first [wife] takes precedence over the second, and the heirs of the first take precedence over the heirs of the second [M. Ket. 10:1A-C]. [If] he divorced the first and remarried her, and made a new marriage-contract for her, the first marriage-contract of the first wife takes precedence over the second and her heirs, then the second [wife] and her heirs take precedence over the second marriage-contract of the first wife. Under what circumstances? In the case of [the collection of] the marriage-contract. But as to maintenance, both of them are equal [and neither claims priority]. The wife and daughters – both of them enjoy equal claim. [If] he married the first and she died, then he married the second and he died [M. Ket. 10:1D], and there was there [the value of both marriage-contracts], plus one denar, then these collect the marriage-contract of their mother, and those collect the marriage-contract of their mother. And the rest do they divide [as an estate]. But if there is not there [the value of both marriage-contracts], plus one denar, the second wife or her heirs collect the marriage-contract of their mother, and the rest divide equally [the residuary estate].

Y. 10:1 I:3 *[The Mishnah has] spoken [thus far] only of [the wife's] dying [at M. 10:1D]. [That is to say, the husband marries and the first wife dies. He therefore inherits her estate. Then he remarries. Then he dies. The second wife takes precedence over the heirs of the first. Why? Because in this case the property of the first wife has entered the husband's estate before he encumbered his estate with the debt constituted by the marriage contract of the second wife. The creditor takes precedence over the heir. So the second wife or her heirs take the value of the marriage contract, and then the estate is divided equally among the heirs.] Lo, if the wife was divorced, she is in the status of a creditor.*

**M. 10:2 He who was married to two wives and they died, and afterward he died, and the orphans claim the marriage contract of their mother – and there are there [funds to pay] only two**

marriage contracts – they divide equally. [If] there was there an excess of a denar [over the necessary funds], these collect the marriage contract of their mother, and those collect the marriage contract of their mother. [If] the orphans said, "We reckon the value of the estate of our father at one denar more," so that they may collect the marriage contract of their mother, they do not listen to them. But they make an estimate of the value of the property in court.

M. 10:3 [If] there was property which was going [to accrue to the estate], it is not deemed equivalent to that which is in [the estate's] possession.

B. 10:2-3 I:1/91A IF THE MARRIAGE CONTRACT OF ONE WIFE WAS FOR A THOUSAND ZUZ AND THE OTHER FIVE HUNDRED, IF THERE IS A SURPLUS OF A DENAR, THESE COLLECT THE MARRIAGE SETTLEMENT OWING TO THEIR MOTHER, AND THOSE COLLECT THE MARRIAGE SETTLEMENT OWING TO THEIR MOTHER. BUT IF NOT, THEY DIVIDE EQUALLY.

M. 10:4 He who was married to three wives and died, the marriage contract of this one was a maneh, and that of the next two hundred zuz, and that of the last three hundred – and there is there only a maneh – they divide it equally. [If] there are two hundred, the one who is owed a maneh takes fifty, and the ones who are owed two hundred and three hundred each take three golden denars [seventy-five zuz each]. [If] there were three hundred zuz there, the one who claims a maneh takes fifty zuz, and the one who claims two hundred takes a maneh, and the one who claims three hundred zuz takes six gold denars [one hundred fifty zuz]. And so [three who put their money into] a single purse – if the capital in the end was too little or too much [they made a loss or a profit], so would they divide up what was available.

M. 10:5 He who was married to four wives and who died – the first takes precedence over the second, and the second over the third, and the third over the fourth. The first is subjected to an oath by the second [that she has not yet collected her marriage contract], and the second to the third, and the third to the fourth, and the fourth collects without an oath. Ben Nannos says, "And is it on account of the fact that she is last that she is rewarded? "She, too, should collect only by means of an oath." [If] all of them [the marriage contracts] were issued on one day, whoever came before her fellow, by even a single hour, has acquired [the right of collection first]. And that is why, in Jerusalem, they write the hours of the day [in a marriage contract]. [If] all of them were issued at the same hour and there is only a maneh there, they divide it up equally.

M. 10:6 He who was married to two women, and who sold off his field and the first woman wrote to the purchaser, "I have no case or claim with you" – the second [wife] nonetheless seizes the field from the purchaser, and the first wife from the second, and the purchaser from the first, and they go around in a circle, until they make a compromise among them. And so in the case of a creditor, and so in the case of a woman who is a creditor.

T. 10:4 Three who put their money into one purse, which was stolen from them bring what is left to the middle [=divided equally] and divide it up. Two who put their money into one purse – this one puts in a maneh and this one put in two hundred zuz, and they did business – the profits are in the middle [divided equally]. [If] this one then took part of his, and that one took part of his, and they entered into partnership, this one then takes in accord with what he has put in. [If] three bills of debt went forth against him simultaneously, the first takes an oath to the second, and the second takes an oath to the third. [If] the second did not want to impose an oath on the first, the third can prevent him from [refraining from doing so]. [If] one borrowed from one person and sold his field to two others, and the creditor wrote to the second, "I have no case or claim against you," he [the creditor] cannot collect what is owing to him, because he has left himself no place from which to make a collection. A proselyte who died and whose property Israelites took over, and the wife's marriage-contract and a debt were brought for collection to his property – they collect from the last who had taken over his property. [If] that one does not have enough, they collect from the one before him, and so they continue.

C.    *Support for the Widow*

M. 11:1 A widow is supported by the property of the orphans. Her wages [the work of her hands] belong to them. But they are not liable to bury her. Her heirs who inherit her marriage contract are liable to bury her.

Y. 11:1 II:2: *And they add extras to the food they supply to her. In the case of a married woman, she has no claim on wine. In the case of a widow, [if she used to have wine,] she has a claim on wine. In the case of a married woman, if she said, "Let the work of my hands be exchanged for my food," they do not listen to her [and allow her such a trade-off]. In the case of a widow who said, "Let the work of my hands be exchanged for my food," they do listen to her [and allow the trade-off].*

B. 11:1 I:8/97A THE WOMAN MAY CONTINUE TO SELL OFF THE PROPERTY UNTIL WHAT IS LEFT IS WHAT IS OWING FOR HER MARRIAGE SETTLEMENT, AND THIS THEN IS A SUPPORT FOR HER SO THAT SHE MAY COLLECT HER MARRIAGE SETTLEMENT FROM WHAT IS THEN LEFT.

M. 11:2 A widow, whether [her husband died when she was] at the stage of betrothal or at the stage of marriage, sells [her husband's estate's property that was security for her marriage contract to realize her marriage contract or to purchase food] without court [permission].

M. 11:3 [If] she sold off her marriage contract or part of it, [or] pledged her marriage contract or part of it, [or] gave away her marriage contract to someone else, or part of it – she sells it even four or five times. And [in the meantime, before collecting her marriage contract] she sells [it] for support without court [permission], and writes, "I sold it for support.'" But a divorcée should sell only with court [permission].

T. 11:1 A widow who lays claim on her marriage-contract, and the heirs say to her, "You have received your marriage-contract" – [if]

this is before she was married, they have to bring proof that her marriage-contract has been received [paid off]. [If] this is after she was married, she has to bring proof that her marriage-contract has not been received. [If] she sold off her marriage-contract, [or] pledged her marriage-contract, [or] set up her marriage-contract as a mortgage, she has lost her claim for support [from the estate of her husband]. One need not say that this is the rule [if she did so] after the death of her husband. But it is even the rule [if she did so] while her husband is yet alive.

M. 11:4 **A widow whose marriage contract was two hundred, and who sold [land of her husband's estate] worth a maneh for two hundred zuz, or worth two hundred zuz for a maneh – her marriage contract has been received thereby. [If] her marriage contract was worth a maneh and she sold [land] worth a maneh and a denar for a maneh, her sale is void. Even if she says, "I shall return the denar to the heirs," her sale is void. [If] her marriage contract was worth four hundred zuz, and she sold [land] to this one for a maneh, and to that one for a maneh, [etc.,] and to the last [fourth] one, what was worth a maneh and a denar for a maneh, the sale to the last one is void. But all the others – their purchase is valid.**

M. 11:5 **[If] the estimate of the value made by judges was a sixth too little or a sixth too much, their sale is void. But if they drew up a deed of inspection, even if they sold what was worth a maneh for two hundred, or what was worth two hundred for a maneh, their sale is confirmed.**

T. 11:2 Three who went down to estimate the value of a field – one says, "It is worth a maneh," and two say, "It is worth two hundred zuz" – one says, "It is worth two hundred," and two say, "It is worth a maneh" – the minority view is null. [If] one says, "It is worth a maneh [100 zuz]," and one says, "It is worth twenty [selas, 80 zuz]," and one says, "It is worth thirty [selas, 120 zuz]," they estimate its value at a maneh.

T. 11:3 What is a deed of inspection [M. Ket. 11:5D]? The time allotted for the estimate of the value of property accruing to orphans is thirty days. And the time allotted for the estimate of the value of property accruing to the sanctuary is sixty days. [If] they sold something worth a maneh for two hundred zuz, or something worth two hundred zuz for a maneh, the sale is confirmed. She who sold what was worth a maneh and a denar for a maneh, even if she says, "I shall return the denar to the purchaser's heirs" – her sale is null.

D. *Rights to, And Collection of, a Marriage Contract: Special Cases*

M. 11:6 **(1) A girl who exercised the right of the refusal, (2) a woman in a secondary remove of prohibited relationship [M. Yeb. 2:4], and (3) a sterile woman do not have a claim on a marriage contract, nor on the increase [on plucking property], nor on maintenance, nor on indemnity [for wear of clothing]. But if to begin with he married her as a sterile woman, she has a claim on a marriage contract. A widow married to a high priest, a divorced** woman or one who has performed the rite of removing the shoe married to an ordinary priest, a mamzer girl and a netin girl married to an Israelite, an Israelite girl married to a netin or to a mamzer do have a marriage contract.

M. 12:1 He who marries a woman, and she stipulated with him that he support her daughter for five years – he is liable to support her for five years. [If] she [the wife, having been divorced] married someone else, and she stipulated with him [the second husband] that he support her daughter for five years, he is liable to support her for five years. The first may not say, "When she will come to my house, I shall support her." But he sends her food to the place where her mother is located. And so the two of them do not say, "Lo, we shall support her together [in partnership]." But one supports her and the other gives her the cost of her support [in addition].

T. 10:2 [If] he promised in writing to support the daughter of his wife and the son of his wife, lo, they are deemed equivalent to creditors and take precedence over all claimants. He may not say to them, "Go and do work, and I will support you." But they remain at home, and he provides food for them. [If] he promised in writing to support the daughter of his wife, and she [the wife] gave him a quittance – she has not the power to do so. For they provide an advantage to a minor, but they do not impose a disadvantage upon him [or her].

T. 10:3 A woman who said, "My husband has died," either derives maintenance or collects her marriage contract. [If she said], "My husband has divorced me," she is supported to the extent of her marriage-contract. What is the difference between [the severance of the marriage through] death and [the severance of the marriage through] divorce? In the case of death, she cannot deny [the facts]. But in the case of divorce, she can deny the facts of the matter. And she indeed may say right to his face, "You did divorce me" [M. Ket. 2:5].

*Y. 12:1 I:2 As to the first five years [to which the husband referred] he supports her whether the cost of the food is high or low. If [he failed to provide food during that period] and the cost was high, but [at the end, when claim was laid against him], the cost had gone down, if he was the cause [of the nonpayment of support] he [now] pays at the highest price [prevailing during that period of years]. But if she was the cause [of the delinquency], he pays at the lowest cost [prevailing during that period of years]. [If, during the five years] the prices had been low but [at the point, at the end, at which claim was laid against the husband], the price had gone up, whether he was at fault or she was at fault, he pays the cost at the low prices [prevailing during the period for which he was obligated].*

M. 12:2 [If the daughter, whom the two husbands have agreed to support] is married, the husband provides support. And they [the mother's successive husbands] pay her the cost of her support. [If] they died, their daughters are supported from unencumbered property, for she is in the status of a creditor. The smart ones would write, "...on condition that I support your daughter for five years, so long as you are [living] with me."

M. 12:3 A widow who said, "I don't want to move from my husband's house" – the heirs cannot say to her, "Go to your father's house and we'll take care of you [there]." But they provide for her in her husband's house, giving her a dwelling in accord with her station in life. [If] she said, "I don't want to move from my father's house," the heirs can say to her, "If you are with us, you will have support. But you are not with us, you will not have support." If she claimed that it is because she is a girl and they are boys, they do provide for her while she is in her father's house.

T. 11:5 She may make use of the old home just as she used it when her husband was alive, so, too, the boy slaves and girl slaves just as she did when her husband was alive, so, too, the pillows and blankets, silver and gold utensils, just as she did when her husband was alive, for thus does he write for her in her marriage contract, "You will dwell in my house and enjoy support from my property so long as you spend your widowhood in my house."

T. 12:3 If there is available only real property of the best quality, all of them [who are owed damages, debts, or marriage-contracts] collect what is due them from property of the best quality. [If there is available only] property of middling quality, all of them collect what is due them from property of middling quality. [If there is available only] property of poor quality, all of them collect what is due them from property of poor quality. [If there is] property of the best and of middling quality, then compensation for damages is collected from property of the best quality, and compensation for a debt and for the marriage-contract is collected from property of middling quality. [If there is] property of the best and of the poorest quality, then compensation for damages is collected from property of the best quality, and compensation for a debt and for the marriage-contract is collected from property of the poorest quality. [If there is available only] property of middling and of poorest quality, then compensation for damages and for debts is collected from property of middling quality, and compensation for the marriage-contract is collected from property of poor quality. [If the party who owes these monies] sold them [his properties] off to one person, or simultaneously three together, and they took over the property in place of the owner – then compensation for damages is collected from property of the best quality, for a creditor from property of middling quality, and for payment of the wife's marriage-contract from property of the poorest quality. [If he sold them off to three people, one after the other in sequence, even compensation for damages, from property of the poorest quality, or payment for the wife's marriage-contract, from property of the finest quality, do they collect from the [land bought by] the last – f the three purchasers. [If] he does not have [enough], they collect from the one before him. [If] he does not have enough, they collect from the one before him. A widow who said, "I don't want to move from my husband's house" [M. Ket. 12:3A] – the heirs cannot stop her. For this is honor paid to her [deceased] husband. [If] she said, "I don't want to move from my father's house," the heirs can stop her. For the blessing of a house [is proportionate to its] size [the larger the household, the lower the individual's cost of living]. Just as she calls attention to her uncollected marriage-contract for a period of twenty-five years, so her heirs and her legal successors call attention to her uncollected marriage-contract for a period of twenty-five years [M. Ket. 12:4G]. But a creditor collects at any time [without limit], even though he has not [before] called attention [to the uncollected debt].

**M. 12:4 So long as she is in her husband's house, she collects her marriage contract at any time. So long as she is in her father's house, she collects her marriage contract within twenty-five years. [If] she died, her heirs call attention [to her uncollected] marriage contract for twenty-five years.**

T. 11:5 A woman whose husband has died dwells in her house just as she did when her husband was alive. She makes use of the man-slaves and women-slaves, silver utensils and golden utensils, just as she made use of them when her husband was alive. For thus does he write for her, "You will dwell in my house and enjoy support from my property so long as you spend your widowhood in my house."

T. 11:6 He who says, "Give over a house of widowhood to my daughter," "Give a house to So-and-so for a dwelling," and the house fell down – the heirs are liable to [pay to] rebuild it. He who says, "This house is a house for the widowhood of my daughter," "This house is for So-and-so for a dwelling" – then the heirs are not liable to rebuild it [if it fell down].

T. 11:7 He who says, "Give a house of widowhood for my daughter" – they give it over to her only if she took upon herself to live in it. The heirs can prevent her should she rent it to someone else. Therefore when she dies, they inherit the house.

T. 11:8 He who lends money to his fellow relying on a pledge, and the pledge is lost, collects the debt from other property [belonging to the debtor]. If he [the borrower] said to him, "On condition that you may make your collection only from this object," then he does not collect the debt from any other property belonging to the debtor. He who sets up his field as a mortgage for the marriage-contract of his wife, and the river washed it out – she collects from other property belonging to him. If he said to her, "On condition that you may make your collection only from this field," then she does not collect the debt from any other property belonging to her husband.

E. *Two Case-Books*

**M. 13:1 He who went overseas, and his wife [left at home] claims maintenance – let her take an oath at the end, but let her not take an oath at the outset [that is, she takes an oath when she claims her marriage contract after her husband's death, or after he returns, that she has not held back any property of her husband].**

T. 12:4 He who went overseas and came back, and his wife claims support – if he said, "Pay out her wages in exchange for her support," he has the right to do so. But if a court had directed that support be provided for her, what [the court] has directed, it has directed [and he has no such claim]. He who makes an agreement to provide funds for his minor daughter and then showed the leg [defaulted] – they force him to provide [what he has promised]. For they impute an advantage to a minor, but they do not put him at a disadvantage.

**M. 13:2 He who went overseas, and someone went and supported his wife – he [who did so] has lost his money.**

**M. 13:3 He who died and left sons and daughters, when the property is ample or negligible, the sons inherit, and the daughters receive support [from the estate].**

T. 6:1 He who died and left sons and daughters – when the property is abundant, the sons inherit and the daughters are fed and maintained [from his estate] [M. Ket. 13:3]. How [do we interpret the statement,] "The sons inherit"? We do not say, "If their father were alive, he would have given such-and-so to them." But we regard one as if he were the father present [for this purpose], and they give to them.

T. 6:2 How [do we interpret the statement], "The daughters are fed and maintained"? We do not say, "If their father were alive, he would have given such-and-so to them." But we regard how [women] who are equivalent to them in status are maintained, and we provide for them accordingly.

**M. 13:4 He who claims that his fellow [owes him] jugs of oil, and the other party admitted that he owes him [empty] jugs – since he has conceded part of the claim, let him take an oath.**

**M. 13:5 He who agrees to give money to his son-in-law but then stretched out the leg [defaulted] – she can claim, "If I had made such an agreement in my own behalf, well might I sit until my head grows white. Now that father has made an agreement concerning me, what can I do? Either marry me or let me go!"**

**M. 13:6 He who contests [another's] ownership of a field, but he himself is a signatory on it [the documents of ownership] as a witness – he has lost every right." [If] he made his field a boundary mark for another person, he has lost every right.**

**M. 13:7 He who went overseas, and the right-of-way to his field was lost – let him purchase a right-of-way with a hundred manehs [if need be], or let him fly through the air.**

**M. 13:8 He who produces a bond of indebtedness against someone else, and the other brought forth [a deed of sale to show] that the other had sold him a field – this [first] man was smart in selling him the field, since he can take it as a pledge.**

**M. 13:9 Two who produced bonds of indebtedness against one another – this one collects his bond of indebtedness, and that one collects his bond of indebtedness.**

**M. 13:10 There are three provinces in what concerns marriage: (1) Judah, (2) Transjordan, and (3) Galilee. They do not remove [wives] from town to town or from city to city [in another province]. But in the same province, they do remove [wives] from town to town or from city to city, but not from a town to a city,**

and not from a city to a town. They remove [wives] from a bad dwelling to a good one but not from a good one to a bad one.

T. 12:5 There are three provinces in what concerns marriage: [I] Judah, [2] Transjordan, and [3] Galilee [M. Ket. 13:10A]: Under what circumstances [does M's rule apply that women may be removed from one town to another, [M. 13:10C]? When the groom was from Judah and betrothed a girl from Judah, or was from Galilee and betrothed a girl from Galilee. But if he was from Judah and betrothed a girl from Galilee, or from Galilee and betrothed a girl from Judah, they force her to go away [M. Ket. 13: 10B], for it was on this assumption that she married him. If, however, he said, "I, So-and-so from Judah, have married a girl from Galilee," they do not force her to go away. But [if he writes, "I married a girl] in Galilee," they force her to go away. They remove a wife from a town which has a gentile majority to a town which has an Israelite majority, but they do not remove a wife from a town which has an Israelite majority to a town which has a gentile majority. [If] he wants to come to the Land of Israel, and she does not want to come, they force her to come. [If] she wants to come, and he does not want to come, they force him to come. [If] he wants to leave the Land of Israel, and she does not want to leave, they do not force her to leave. [If] she wants to leave, and he does not want to leave, they force her not to leave.

M. 13:11 All have the right to bring up [his or her family] to the Land of Israel, but none has the right to remove [his or her family] therefrom. All have the right to bring up to Jerusalem, but none has the right to bring down – all the same are men and women. [If] one married a woman in the Land of Israel and divorced her in the Land of Israel, he pays her off with the coinage of the Land of Israel. [If] he married a woman in the Land of Israel and divorced her in Cappadocia, he pays her off in the coinage of the Land of Israel. [If ] he married a woman in Cappadocia and divorced her in the Land of Israel, he pays her off in the coinage of the Land of Israel. If he married a woman in Cappadocia and divorced her in Cappadocia, he pays her off in the coinage of Cappadocia.

T. 12:6 He who produces a writ [of indebtedness] in Babylonia collects on the strength of it in Babylonian coinage. [If he does so] in the Land of Israel, he collects on the strength of it in the coinage of the Land of Israel. [If] it was written without specification – [if] he produces it in Babylonia, he collects on the strength of it in Babylonian coinage. [If he produces it] in the Land of Israel, he collects on the strength of it in the coinage of the Land of Israel. [If] it was written on coinage without specification, lo, this one collects [in the coinage of] any place which he wants, which is not the case for the marriage-contract of a woman [paid only in Palestinian coinage under this circumstance]. [If he married a girl in the Land of Israel and divorced her in the Land of Israel, he pays her off in the coinage of the Land of Israel [M. Ket. 13:11 D]. [If he married her] in the Land of Israel and divorced her in Babylonia, he pays her off in the coinage of the Land of Israel. [If he married her] in

Babylonia and divorced her in the Land of Israel, he pays her off in the coinage of the Land of Israel. The five selas for redemption of the first born, the thirty for a slave, the fifty paid by the one who rapes or seduces a girl, the hundred paid by one who spreads malicious rumors about a girl – all of them, even though they are in Babylonia, collect on their account in the coinage of the Land of Israel. The coinage concerning which the Torah speaks at every point, this is the coinage of Tyre. Tyrian coinage – this is the coinage of Jerusalem.

## II. Analysis: The Problematics of the Topic, Ketubot

The halakhah takes as its problem the balancing of the rights and obligations of the two household-families that are united, the girl's and her father's, the boy's and his family's. The one contributes a dowry, to be utilized by the groom but subject to restoration to the household of the bride under specified conditions or, more commonly, handed on to the male children of the bride (in a polygamous society, an important consideration indeed). The other undertakes to support the bride and to treat her honorably. How that fair exchange of persons and property plays itself out in the details of the document and the relationships it represents then forms the burden of the halakhah. The point of liberation then is clear: the reciprocity of obligation, not only of family to family, but of husband to wife and wife to husband.

In the formation of the marriage three parties, wife and husband and wife's father, enjoy material rights, the father to certain fees and fines under conditions specified by Scripture, and, more to the point, the wife to protection and support in the event of divorce or widowhood, the husband to the dowry. Scripture's component of the halakhah, suitably honored and expounded, proves not entirely symmetrical to the main body of the halakhah, with its interest in the document and what rests upon it. There we find the focus of the halakhah, and, as we shall note in the next section, that is with good reason.

The Ketubah, the husband's undertaking of obligations to the wife, forms the principal components of the transaction outlined in the halakhah at hand. We begin with the basic sum of money represented by the document, that is, minimum alimony in the case of a divorce or death. The distinction between the widow and the virgin makes a difference because of the greater alimony paid to the virgin should the husband die or divorce her. The virgin gets about a year of maintenance, two hundred zuz, the widow, about six months, a maneh or one hundred zuz. That leads to the adjudication of conflicting claims and the rules of evidence adduced in support of said claims. The father is accorded the ownership of the woman's bride-price and hence has an interest in her virginity, which accounts for the halakhah concerning the fine that is paid to the father for rape or seduction. The father further owns the marriage-settlement in cases in which he will continue to support the woman should she be divorced or widowed, e.g., in the case of betrothal. When the girl is under-age, that is, younger than twelve and a half, the father retains control as well, and for the same reason. She will return to his household. Throughout the issue is, who is liable to maintain, ransom, and bury the woman. It is the father until consummation of the marriage, the husband thereafter, and the woman herself if in her mature years she is divorced or widowed. That will then account for the disposition of the marriage-settlement. The Ketubah further assigns to the husband a considerable stake in the success of the marriage; he alone can issue a writ of divorce, but, if he does so, he pays a meaningful indemnity in the form of alimony. All of this is the minimum commitment that he makes to the marriage; the dowry and further add-ons, the provision of luxuries for the wife – these represent further provisions by which the husband responds to the dowry handed over as the bride's inheritance from her father's estate.

Clearly, the Ketubah represents a transaction that vastly transcends the document itself, and, while the writing out of the document and its proclamation under the marriage-canopy form part of the rite of marriage, the legal relationship that the Ketubah establishes does not depend upon the jot and tittle of the document; in this regard the divorce-document, the *Get,* differs radically. If that document is improperly prepared, there is no divorce. Here, by contrast, the document symbolizes a set of conditions that pertain whether articulated or not. How explain the difference? The sanctification of the wife and the consummation of the marriage involve several procedures, as we know from Qiddushin, while the divorce rests only on the document. The Ketubah finds its confirmation in the relationship it inaugurates; the couple lives together in accord with its conditions. So by deed the couple embodies the contract. The Get, by contrast, has on its own to validate the right of the woman to return to her father's house for good, until she chooses to remarry; everything depends upon the effect of the writing, and the cessation of her previous condition as a married woman, now radically changed, finds its confirmation and legitimation only in the correctly-prepared writing. The upshot is, the writ of divorce stands on its own, the Ketubah forms only one component of a composite of transactions that accomplish a single coherent goal.

That explains why, unlike the writ of divorce, the marriage-settlement or Ketubah is effective even if the document is not written out; it is an unstated condition "imposed by the court," meaning, valid even when not documented. The protections of the settlement extend to all details normally written in the contract itself. The mutual obligations that apply through the course of the marriage present no surprises. The wife is obligated to work for the upkeep of the household, though if she brought in her dowry slave-girls able to do the work, she is relieved of these obligations. The household work carried out by the wife involves provision of food, clothing, and child-care. The husband's obligations are spelled out in the marriage-settlement; he must provide food, clothing, shelter, and the like. The one important obligation over and above the practical ones concerns sexual relationships; the husband must have sexual relations on a weekly basis, no matter how many wives he may have. The dowry represents the woman's share in her father's estate, collected at the point at which ownership of the woman is transferred to the husband. If the marriage is dissolved, the dowry reverts to the household of the father and his male heirs. The husband may not use the power of the vow to disrupt the wife's normal conduct of her life. Such a vow is treated as a form of abuse of the wife. For her part the wife may not violate her unstipulated obligations, e.g., she must feed him proper food and conduct herself with piety and modesty. During the course of the marriage the husband controls the wife's property, enjoying the usufruct; but the property reverts to the wife, that is, to her family's household, when the marriage has run its course, or it is inherited by her male children. As to collecting the marriage-settlement, e.g., in the event of divorce or widowhood, the matter is complicated by the existence of other claims, besides the widow's or divorcee's, to the husband's property. The widow is supported by the husband's estate, but then her wages belong to the estate ("the orphans").

### III. Interpretation: Religious Principles of Ketubot

The nature of the halakhah at hand and its exposition of the topic before us make it easy to lose sight of the religious context in which the Ketubah finds its place, hence to miss the very particular statement of a religious character to which the Ketubah contributes a formidable component. The halakhah, its exposition and generative problematic, scarcely allude to the change in relationships embodied in the Ketubah, which takes its place in a process to which the language of sanctification is applied. Nonetheless, even the details of the law contribute to the main point: through this piece of writing, a woman becomes sacred to a particular man; without the document (at least in implicit form), the relationship is not legitimated. That is, the Ketubah is integral to the transaction by which there takes place the sanctification of the woman to a particular man, in the analogy of the sanctification of an animal to the altar. The language of Qiddushin, the rules and conceptions of the marital bond in general – these require that we ask, what has the marriage-document to do with the process of sanctification of the relationship of the wife to the husband, how is the woman transformed, in part, through this document and the procedures to which the contract is critical?

Through the language of Qiddushin and of Ketubot a woman formerly free to mate with any Israelite is restricted, for the duration, to a particular man. And that restriction is recognized by God ("Heaven") and deemed sacred by him. So we deal with other than an ordinary legal document, e.g., a bill of sale of a piece of property or a will. Not all formulaic writings effect sanctification; this one does. And at specific points the halakhah itself confirms the transformative power of the language and writing at hand. How come language exercises such power, and what analogies or models define the context in which to interpret the religious meaning of the halakhah of Ketubot?

To answer that question, we recall the power of language to effect sanctification in the two other critical contexts of the halakhah, the separation of heave-offering from the crop and the designation of an animal for the offering. The involves the rations for the priesthood to be separated out of the crop. These rations constituted God's share and are holy; the rest of the crop, once the rations have been taken out, is deemed available for ordinary use. When the farmer evinced the desire to utilize the produce, then God responded by imposing the requirement of separating his share; at that point, the crop became liable to tithing and the separation of other offerings. Then a portion of the crop shared by the farmer and God grown on land ownership of which is invested in the farmer and God was to be removed, leaving the rest free for the farmer's use. And the act of separation took the form of a statement, a formulaic act of transformation. To accomplish that end, the farmer recited a formula that serves to designate as holy to the priesthood a portion of the grain at the threshing floor. That part of the whole crop, called variously "heave-offering" or "the priestly ration" enters into the status of sanctity – is sanctified – when the farmer says something along the lines of, "The heave-offering of this heap [of produce] is in its northern portion" [M. Ter. 3:5C]. At that point, the designation portion of the grain enters the status of sanctity, with the result that a non-priest who eats that grain incurs severe punishment.

Second comes the consecration of an animal for the altar. The householder who wishes to make an offering has first to designate an animal for the purpose of that offering, and that designation, the act of consecration, involves stating something along the lines of, "This lamb is a sin-offering for such-and-such an inadvertent sin that I have committed." So too, if someone says, "This beast is instead of that beast, a sin-offering," the beast to which he makes reference is consecrated, even while the one to which he made reference remains consecrated. And that language effects even parts of the beast, so M. Tem. 1:3: "he who says, 'The foot of this is a burnt offering' – the whole beast is a burnt offering."

And, it goes without saying, we recall full well from the halakhah of Qiddushin, if a woman agrees when one who says, "Lo, you are sanctified to me on the strength of this coin," the formula, along with the woman's agreement, constitutes the act of consecration. She then is transformed, and if she violates the rules governing her status of sanctity, God expects the holy community to inflict appropriate punishment.

It is in that context that the Ketubah, too, finds its place. Even though the halakhah frames the topic in other than mythic language and terms, the Ketubah forms an integral component in the process by which, through the evocation of certain language, a woman's status as to all men in the world radically shifts. Before the recitation of the correct formula, including (as in the case at hand) a written record, the woman was free to marry any appropriate Israelite (excluding male relatives); afterward she is not. The upshot is, the Ketubah represents the formula of sanctification.

That the document bears its own significance, beyond the language that is used in it, is shown by a simple, much-explored fact. The Ketubah's power is fully present even when the requisite language is not written and properly articulated, just as much as the formula of Qiddushin commences the process of sanctification, the formula of designating priestly rations changes the status of both the portion of the crop so designated and the remainder of the crop, no longer containing inherent sanctification, and the formula of designating an animal for the altar. The upshot is, in the transaction represented by, as much as in the language used in, the Ketubah inheres the power of sanctification, such that the status of the woman is redefined and transformed. That explains why clauses take effect even when not written out. Before us is language that evokes conditions and establishes facts not through what is said, but through the transformative power of what is evoked.

So when the Ketubah evokes the transformation of the status of the woman, it takes its place in those formularies – whether documentary or not, whether fully articulated or not – that bear the power to change facts on earth. That is because Heaven responds to and confirms that same language. Say the right words and Heaven hears. Then what happens upon earth is affected – in that order. And, it goes without saying, Heaven takes seriously the language of human transactions, in oaths and vows as other formularies in which Heaven has a special interest, so that if man violates his commitment to man, God intervenes. What is important is, when we ask where, in the entire corpus of the halakhah, we find the greatest weight placed upon the language of human transactions in which Heaven involves itself, the answer is, in transactions of the Israelite household. The entire relationship of betrothal and marriage, fidelity in marriage on the part of the woman, and the dissolution of marriage – all of these transactions are effected through Heavenly-supervised formularies, and all are deemed consecrated in a way in which transactions involved in Israel's social order are not. That is to say, when the language of consecration occurs, it finds its location in two of the three dimensions of Israel's existence, in relationships with God in Heaven and within the Israelite household on earth – but rarely in the Israelite social order. And, when it comes to relationships with God in Heaven, where the language of consecration proves effective, it is ordinarily in the context of the household, e.g., providing God with his share of the household's product.

In that context of divine supervision falls the formulary of betrothal, the Ketubah, and the Get. But what defines Heaven's interest, and why should the use of the specified language attract Heaven's attention? Must the relationship of man to woman invariably involve documents that embody the sanctity of the relationship and effect sanctification? To understand the answer, we have to ask, is there a transformation that takes place in a woman's status as to sanctification to a given man? Can a woman's status in relationship to all men but one change without the provision of a particular document, meaning, without the recitation of a specified formula, properly witnessed? Of course there is, and of course it can. A particular man may be singled out as the sole man in the world to whom a given woman is available for marriage and procreation, and no documentary media for the transaction of transformation are required. I refer to the transaction covered by the levirate connection (Deut. 15:1-5), when a man dies and his childless widow forthwith becomes consecrated to a surviving brother. Before the man died, she was forbidden to the brother, and had the man had children, she would have remained forbidden to him. But now, by reason of the decedent's childlessness, she is automatically deemed to have entered into a consecrated relationship with her brother-in-law. On what basis? Heaven has imposed that relationship; then no document by man is required. And to respond to that relationship, one of two things must happen. Either the surviving brother states in advance his intention of entering into levirate marriage with the sister-in-law and then has sexual relations with her – the counterpart to the act of betrothal and the consummation of the marriage, respectively – or he goes through a rite of "removing the shoe," prescribed by Scripture to sever the levirate connection. In neither case is a document essential to the transaction.

What is the difference, and why is a document required, then, in the case of a betrothal and marriage and divorce in other-than-levirate circumstances but not in the levirate one? We have come far enough into this inquiry to identify the answer without difficulty. What God does requires no documentary confirmation effected by man, what man does requires transformative language, whether or not in written form; and – more to the point – the actions of God find their counterpart in the documents of man. Specifically, God has established the levirate connection, and man merely proceeds through the rites that will either realize or sever that connection. The connection comes about because of the death of the childless husband. No document is called for. The woman is automatically restricted to the decedent's brother. God does it all, having created the conditions that transfer the woman from one man to another. In an ordinary act of betrothal and marriage by contrast, man – the offer of the man, the acceptance by the woman – effects that other connection, the ordinary one between the man and the woman where no intervention on Heaven's part, e.g., in the form of childlessness and death, has taken place.

The upshot is that when Heaven intervenes, documents representing the enactment of formulary language of transformation play no role. When man acts on his on account and enters into a relationship of sanctity through an act of sanctification, then man must speak the words that articulate and realize – make real – his intention in that circumstance, for the object of his intentionality, whether grain, whether beast, whether woman. God acts by speaking, as in creation. Man speaks but then confirms in writing the announced intention: let there be…. Then the document lends palpability to the intention, not so much confirming it as realizing it in an exact sense of the word, just as much as the statement in connection with a specific animal accomplishes the same goal. Sanctity overtakes the animal of which man has spoken; no further documentation in the context of the cult is necessary. Sanctity overtakes the woman in the agreed-upon transaction of betrothal and marriage, but, in the context of the household, documents do play their part. In that context the Ketubah or the Get forms a statement, in material form, of the intentionality of the man, to consecrate the woman or to suspend and annul the status of consecration, as the case may be. The documents form concrete representations of intentionality. To those representations, to that intentionality, the conditions and clauses of the contract of marriage form mere details; they state the consequences of the realization of the intentionality to consecrate the woman to that particular man, or to release the woman to all men.

What, finally, defines the religious meaning of the Ketubah in particular, and what statement did sages choose to make through the halakhah of Ketubot and only there? The answer is, sages wished to define the actualities of the condition of the consecrated woman not in mythic terms but in those pertinent to the household, and it was only through the halakhah, with its preoccupation with the small and the intimate, that they could make their comment. To understand the entire implicit statement made by sages through the halakhah, we have to revert to the liturgical statement of the aggadic view of Man and Woman in consecrated union. Only having scaled the heights of the aggadah will we grasp the proportionate response: the humility of sages' framing of the ordinary and the everyday context of sanctification.

To identify the aggadic-liturgical statement on the same topic, we turn from the halakhic contexts and readings of the matter to the language of sanctification applying to the woman and man under the huppah or marriage-canopy. The reason is that, self-evidently, the rite of the marriage-canopy demands consideration in any religious commentary to the halakhah of Ketubot, since the Ketubah is integral to that rite – it is read, start to finish, within the transaction under the marriage-canopy. That that is the fact is shown by the inclusion of the very un-liturgical language of the Ketubah in the very rite under the marriage-canopy. First the Ketubah is read. Then comes the liturgical moment. The operative language, defining the transaction, is contained in the blessings that are said over the cup of wine of sanctification, which are as follows:

> Praised are You, O Lord our God, King of the universe, Creator of the fruit of the vine.
> Praised are You, O Lord our God, King of the universe, who created all things for Your glory.
> Praised are You, O Lord our God, King of the universe, Creator of Adam.
> Praised are You, O Lord our God, King of the universe, who created man and woman in his image, fashioning woman from man as his mate, that together they might perpetuate life. Praised are You, O Lord, Creator of man.
> May Zion rejoice as her children are restored to her in joy. Praised are You, O Lord, who causes Zion to rejoice at her children's return.
> Grant perfect joy to these loving companions, as You did to the first man and woman in the Garden of Eden. Praised are You, O Lord, who grants the joy of bride and groom.
> Praised are You, O Lord our God, King of the universe, who created joy and gladness, bridge and groom, mirth, song, delight and rejoicing, love and harmony, peace and companionship. O Lord our God, may there ever be heard in the cities of Judah and in the streets of Jerusalem voices of joy and gladness, voices of bridge

and groom, the jubilant voices of those joined in marriage under the bridal canopy, the voices of young people feasting and signing. Praised are You, O Lord, who causes the groom to rejoice with his bride.[1]

From the reading of the mundane, detailed, and this-worldly marriage-contract, with its talk of dowry and of the groom's selling the shirt off his back to maintain his wife, then, we rise upward, surveying Israel's life with God. Now, at the new beginning represented by the household, we recall Eden. Israel's history begins with creation – first, the creation of the vine, symbol of the natural world. Creation is for God's glory. All things speak to nature, to the physical as much as the spiritual, for all things were made by God. In Hebrew, the blessings end, "who formed the *Adam*." All things glorify God; above all creation is Adam. The theme of ancient paradise is introduced by the simple choice of the word *Adam*, so heavy with meaning. The myth of man's creation is rehearsed: man and woman are in God's image, together complete and whole, creators of life, "like God." Woman was fashioned from man together with him to perpetuate life. And again, "blessed is the creator of Adam." We have moved, therefore, from the natural world to the archetypal realm of paradise, backward to the mythic beginnings of Man, Woman, Eden, the household now transformed into something much beyond the young groom and his bride and the household they found. Before us we see not merely a man and a woman, but Adam and Eve.

In no detail does the halakhah of Ketubot demand interpretation in the mythic context evoked at the very point at which the Ketubah is proclaimed in public and takes effect. Unlike the halakhah of Qiddushin, when we consider the halakhah of Ketubot, none of the points of amplification, sources of problems requiring analysis, or issues of protracted consideration, requires us to ask questions of a religious character. The language of sanctification does not enter in, and considerations of God's stake in the transaction never arise. And yet the power of language to sanctify remains at the heart of matters. The language at hand has that power. Ketubot flows from Qiddushin, the requirement of the (verbal) documentation of the marital bond from the (verbal) act of sanctification of the woman to the man. It is the simple fact that without completion in documentation, including a Ketubah, the act of Qiddushin is incomplete, the marital union premature. The act of sanctification takes place through the exchange of a token of betrothal, or a writ, or sexual intercourse, we recall, and the next step is the provision

---

[1] *A Rabbi's Manual*, ed. by Jules Harlow (New York: The Rabbinical Assembly, 1965), p. 45. The "seven blessings" said at a wedding are printed in traditional Jewish prayer books.

of the Ketubah, at which point the relationship of sanctity is established. So what connection can we identify between the act of sanctification and the provision of a document specifying the conditions of the relationship – between religion and law, in gross categories?

Let me now answer the question in a simple way: what connection does the halakhah identify between the status of sanctification and the use of language, whether oral or written, to declare and establish said status? Why of the three media of sanctification of a woman, the exchange of a token, the provision of a writ, and the act of sexual relations – all of which, after all, effect the marital bond and bring about the sanctification of the woman to the man – does the provision of the Ketubah take priority? The reason, in the context now established, is self-evident. The Ketubah takes over the rite of the marriage-canopy and defines its this-worldly venue. The marriage-rite invokes the creation of the world, Adam and the creation of Eve in God's image, after God's likeness." The rite compares bride and groom to the loving companions of Eden, invoking too the ultimate return of Israel to Zion, the eschatological restoration of Adam and Eve to Eden. So much for large and public matters. Why should the Ketubah know nothing of all this? That is precisely the wrong question, for everyone knows that the Ketubah is read just moments before we evoke Adam and Eve in Eden and Israel's future return to the Land, its Eden.

So what has taken place in the legal-liturgical transaction at hand? The Ketubah at that very moment of the marital union under the marriage-canopy serves to define the interior dimensions of Eden, explains what makes the groom into Adam and the bride into Eve, specifies the worldly meanings of paradise – so completing the public realm of the aggadah with the private preserve of the halakhah. Israel in the household realizes Eden through the relationships defined as norms by the halakhah, portrayed as ideals by the aggadah. The one makes its full and complete statement only in dialogue with the other. Under the huppah, therefore, the halakhah turns exalted matters upside down and draws them down to earth. The halakhah in that unique setting makes its statement, and it is only through halakhah on this particular subject – the topic before us – that our sages can have delivered their message. For the halakhah declares, if you want to know Eden, come to the Israelite household, where the woman is fairly and considerately provided for, and where the man's obligation to found a household in Israel is diligently carried out by the wife. Of that Eden consists. To more than that let no man aspire, therein is the consecrated relationship realized. How in this context to pay a higher tribute to woman I cannot imagine.

In the heightened reality of high mythic being embodied in the powerful imagery of the marriage-canopy, Eden in the here and now, the Ketubah does more than bring matters down to earth. It declares, here on earth, in the household in particular, is where the sanctified relationship governs. So from the exalted re-embodiment of Adam and Eve in Eden, the Ketubah reminds all parties to the transaction of what really is at stake in the holy union of man and wife, the woman consecrated to this particular man. The most humble and hidden activities register. He who takes a vow not to have sexual relations with his wife may allow this situation to continue for one week. She who rebels against her husband declining to perform wifely services – they deduct from her marriage contract seven denars a week. And those women go forth without the payment of the marriage contract at all: She who transgresses against the law of Moses and Jewish law. How better define Eden than the marital relationship where obligations such as these are honored. The halakhah for the interiority of Israel's being, with its attention to the workaday details of documents, turns the Ketubah into not only a transformative formulary, but also a powerful, wry commentary to what is truly at stake. Most formularies turn the secular into the sacred. The Ketubah turns the sacred on high into the sacred here on earth, identifying the dimensions of consecration that take the measure of the marriage. And with what result? Adam and Eve, husband and wife – each owes much to the other, the one is responsible to the other. In the context of the Written Torah's presentation of matters, that represents a liberating fact.

# South Florida Studies in the History of Judaism

| | | |
|---|---|---|
| 240001 | Lectures on Judaism in the Academy and in the Humanities | Neusner |
| 240002 | Lectures on Judaism in the History of Religion | Neusner |
| 240003 | Self-Fulfilling Prophecy: Exile and Return in the History of Judaism | Neusner |
| 240004 | The Canonical History of Ideas: The Place of the So-called Tannaite Midrashim, Mekhilta  Attributed to R. Ishmael, Sifra, Sifré to Numbers, and Sifré to Deuteronomy | Neusner |
| 240005 | Ancient Judaism: Debates and Disputes, Second Series | Neusner |
| 240006 | The Hasmoneans and Their Supporters: From Mattathias to the Death  of John Hyrcanus I | Sievers |
| 240007 | Approaches to Ancient Judaism: New Series, Volume One | Neusner |
| 240008 | Judaism in the Matrix of Christianity | Neusner |
| 240009 | Tradition as Selectivity: Scripture, Mishnah, Tosefta, and Midrash in  the Talmud of Babylonia | Neusner |
| 240010 | The Tosefta: Translated from the Hebrew: Sixth Division Tohorot | Neusner |
| 240011 | In the Margins of the Midrash: Sifre Ha'azinu Texts, Commentaries and Reflections | Basser |
| 240012 | Language as Taxonomy: The Rules for Using Hebrew and Aramaic in the Babylonia Talmud | Neusner |
| 240013 | The Rules of Composition of the Talmud of Babylonia: The Cogency of the Bavli's Composite | Neusner |
| 240014 | Understanding the Rabbinic Mind: Essays on the Hermeneutic of Max Kadushin | Ochs |
| 240015 | Essays in Jewish Historiography | Rapoport-Albert |
| 240016 | The Golden Calf and the Origins of the Jewish Controversy | Bori/Ward |
| 240017 | Approaches to Ancient Judaism: New Series, Volume Two | Neusner |
| 240018 | The Bavli That Might Have Been: The Tosefta's Theory of Mishnah  Commentary Compared With the Bavli's | Neusner |
| 240019 | The Formation of Judaism: In Retrospect and Prospect | Neusner |
| 240020 | Judaism in Society: The Evidence of the Yerushalmi,Toward the Natural History of a Religion | Neusner |
| 240021 | The Enchantments of Judaism: Rites of Transformation from Birth Through Death | Neusner |
| 240022 | Åbo Addresses | Neusner |
| 240023 | The City of God in Judaism and Other Comparative and Methodological Studies | Neusner |
| 240024 | The Bavli's One Voice: Types and Forms of Analytical Discourse and their Fixed Order of Appearance | Neusner |
| 240025 | The Dura-Europos Synagogue: A Re-evaluation  (1932-1992) | Gutmann |
| 240026 | Precedent and Judicial Discretion: The Case of Joseph ibn Lev | Morell |
| 240027 | Max Weinreich Geschichte der jiddischen Sprachforschung | Frakes |
| 240028 | Israel: Its Life and Culture, Volume I | Pedersen |
| 240029 | Israel: Its Life and Culture, Volume II | Pedersen |
| 240030 | The Bavli's One Statement: The Metapropositional Program of Babylonian Talmud Tractate Zebahim Chapters One and Five | Neusner |

| 240187 | Jewish Law from Moses to the Mishnah | Neusner |
| 240188 | The Language and the Law of God | Calabi |
| 240189 | Pseudo-Rabad: Commentary to Sifre Numbers | Basser |
| 240190 | How Adin Steinstalz Misrepresents the Talmud | Neusner |
| 240191 | How the Rabbis Liberated Women | Neusner |
| 240192 | From Scripture to 70 | Neusner |

# South Florida Academic Commentary Series

| 243001 | The Talmud of Babylonia, An Academic Commentary, Volume XI, Bavli Tractate Moed Qatan | Neusner |
| 243002 | The Talmud of Babylonia, An Academic Commentary, Volume XXXIV, Bavli Tractate Keritot | Neusner |
| 243003 | The Talmud of Babylonia, An Academic Commentary, Volume XVII, Bavli Tractate Sotah | Neusner |
| 243004 | The Talmud of Babylonia, An Academic Commentary, Volume XXIV, Bavli Tractate Makkot | Neusner |
| 243005 | The Talmud of Babylonia, An Academic Commentary, Volume XXXII, Bavli Tractate Arakhin | Neusner |
| 243006 | The Talmud of Babylonia, An Academic Commentary, Volume VI, Bavli Tractate Sukkah | Neusner |
| 243007 | The Talmud of Babylonia, An Academic Commentary, Volume XII, Bavli Tractate Hagigah | Neusner |
| 243008 | The Talmud of Babylonia, An Academic Commentary, Volume XXVI, Bavli Tractate Horayot | Neusner |
| 243009 | The Talmud of Babylonia, An Academic Commentary, Volume XXVII, Bavli Tractate Shebuot | Neusner |
| 243010 | The Talmud of Babylonia, An Academic Commentary, Volume XXXIII, Bavli Tractate Temurah | Neusner |
| 243011 | The Talmud of Babylonia, An Academic Commentary, Volume XXXV, Bavli Tractates Meilah and Tamid | Neusner |
| 243012 | The Talmud of Babylonia, An Academic Commentary, Volume VIII, Bavli Tractate Rosh Hashanah | Neusner |
| 243013 | The Talmud of Babylonia, An Academic Commentary, Volume V, Bavli Tractate Yoma | Neusner |
| 243014 | The Talmud of Babylonia, An Academic Commentary, Volume XXXVI, Bavli Tractate Niddah | Neusner |
| 243015 | The Talmud of Babylonia, An Academic Commentary, Volume XX, Bavli Tractate Baba Qamma | Neusner |
| 243016 | The Talmud of Babylonia, An Academic Commentary, Volume XXXI, Bavli Tractate Bekhorot | Neusner |
| 243017 | The Talmud of Babylonia, An Academic Commentary, Volume XXX, Bavli Tractate Hullin | Neusner |
| 243018 | The Talmud of Babylonia, An Academic Commentary, Volume VII, Bavli Tractate Besah | Neusner |
| 243019 | The Talmud of Babylonia, An Academic Commentary, Volume X, Bavli Tractate Megillah | Neusner |

| 243110 | The Talmud of the Land of Israel: An Academic Commentary of the Second, Third, and Fourth Divisions, II. Yerushalmi Tractate Shabbat. B. Chapters Eleven through Twenty-Four and The Structure of Yerushalmi Shabbat | Neusner |
| 243111 | The Talmud of the Land of Israel: An Academic Commentary of the Second, Third, and Fourth Divisions, ÎII. Yerushalmi Tractate Erubin | Neusner |
| 243112 | The Talmud of the Land of Israel: An Academic Commentary of the Second, Third, and Fourth Divisions, IV. Yerushalmi Tractate Yoma | Neusner |
| 243113 | The Talmud of the Land of Israel: An Academic Commentary of the Second, Third, and Fourth Divisions, V. Yerushalmi Tractate Pesahim A. Chapters One through Six, Based on the English Translation of Baruch M. Bokser with Lawrence Schiffman | Neusner |
| 243114 | The Talmud of the Land of Israel: An Academic Commentary of the Second, Third, and Fourth Divisions, V. Yerushalmi Tractate Pesahim B. Chapters Seven through Ten and The Structure of Yerushalmi Pesahim, Based on the English Translation of Baruch M. Bokser with Lawrence Schiffman | Neusner |
| 243115 | The Talmud of the Land of Israel: An Academic Commentary of the Second, Third, and Fourth Divisions, VI. Yerushalmi Tractate Sukkah | Neusner |
| 243116 | The Talmud of the Land of Israel: An Academic Commentary of the Second, Third, and Fourth Divisions, VII. Yerushalmi Tractate Besah | Neusner |
| 243117 | The Talmud of the Land of Israel: An Academic Commentary of the Second, Third, and Fourth Divisions, VIII. Yerushalmi Tractate Taanit | Neusner |
| 243118 | The Talmud of the Land of Israel: An Academic Commentary of the Second, Third, and Fourth Divisions, IX. Yerushalmi Tractate Megillah | Neusner |
| 243119 | The Talmud of the Land of Israel: An Academic Commentary of the Second, Third, and Fourth Divisions, X. Yerushalmi Tractate Rosh Hashanah | Neusner |
| 243120 | The Talmud of the Land of Israel: An Academic Commentary of the Second, Third, and Fourth Divisions, XI. Yerushalmi Tractate Hagigah | Neusner |

# South Florida-Rochester-Saint Louis
# Studies on Religion and the Social Order

| 245001 | Faith and Context, Volume 1 | Ong |
| 245002 | Faith and Context, Volume 2 | Ong |
| 245003 | Judaism and Civil Religion | Breslauer |
| 245004 | The Sociology of Andrew M. Greeley | Greeley |
| 245005 | Faith and Context, Volume 3 | Ong |
| 245006 | The Christ of Michelangelo | Dixon |

## South Florida International Studies in Formative Christianity and Judaism